INSIDERS' GUIDE®

OFF THE BEATEN PA

D0877940

Off the

EIGHTH EDITION

Beaten Path®

A GUIDE TO UNIQUE PLACES

alabama

GAY N. MARTIN

DISCARD

INSIDERS' GUIDE®

GUILFORD, CONNECTICUT
AN IMPRINT OF THE GLOBE PEQUOT PRESS

The prices, rates, and hours listed in this guidebook
were confirmed at press time. We recommend,
however, that you call establishments to obtain
current information before traveling.

To buy books in quantity for corporate use
or incentives, call **(800) 962–0973, ext. 4551,**
or e-mail **premiums@GlobePequot.com.**

INSIDERS' GUIDE ®

Text design by Linda Loiewski
Maps created by Equator Graphics © Morris Book Publishing, LLC
Illustrations by Carole Drong
Spot photography throughout © Byron Jorjorian/Alamy

ISSN 1535-8291
ISBN-13: 978-0-7627-4194-6
ISBN-10: 0-7627-4194-5

Manufactured in the United States of America
Eighth Edition/First Printing

This one's for my mother,
Edith Sorrells Newsom, who's a great traveler
and who accompanied me on many of the excursions described in this book.

Contents

Acknowledgments

As I crisscrossed Alabama while researching this book, many people offered suggestions and provided information. I want to thank everyone who helped me with the birthing of the previous seven editions. To that original list, I'd like to add the following people, in random order, who assisted in the most recent delivery: Lee Sentell, Ami Simpson, Brian S. Jones, Peggy Collins, John Wild, Robyn L. Bridges, Carolyn and Dan Waterman, Wendy and Bill James and Koa, Marge Shaw, Bill Charles, Sharon Quinn, Lisa O. Socha, Susann Hamlin, Debbie Wilson, Alison Stanfield, Lindsey Holt, Alex and Jim Cox, Pam Swanner, Patty Tucker, Chrissy Byrd, Susan Robertson, Leigh Ann Rains, Julia B. Brown, Robert E. Lee, Linda and Earl Fisher, Jan and Joe Wood, James W. Parker, Mayor Al Kelley, Jeanne Hall Ashley, Robert Ratliff, Maria Traylor, Tom Barker, Al Mathis, Lin Graham, Rich Lopez, Stephanie Behrens, Bebe Gauntt, Jane McClanahan, Bob Doyle, Tom Walker, Kelly Durban, Myrna Hertenstein, Georgia Turner, Doug Purcell, Deborah Gray, Marynell Ford, Janet S. Shelby, Cherie M. Wynn, Dilcy Windham Hilley, Vickie Ashford, Lauri Cothran, Sandy Smith, Kathy Johnson, Becky Jones, Deborah Stone, Danky and Al Blanton, Linda Vice, Kathy Danielson Williams, and Suzanne Pittinos. Also, my gratitude extends to Miss Lola Grimes, Wanda Braun, Jim Long, Maj. Tommy Hart, Gayle Etheridge, Louis Finlay, Carmella and Obbie Coleman, Geiger and Associates, Bill Lang, David Clark, Philip D'Amico, Bruce Skidmore, the White-Spunner hard-hat crew, Harriet Shade, Landon Howard, Margo Gilbert, Gordon Tatum Jr., Vicki Morese, Karen Beasley, Judy Manning, Judy Ryals, Beth Goodwin, and Elwanda Olander. And a champagne toast (make that Dom Perignon, please) to Lori Boatfield for her superb research assistance.

Others who contributed to this project include Robin Cooper, Alex Mastin, and Carolyn Mason. I'm also grateful to writers Mary Eloise Leake, Alice Duckett, Barbara Eubanks, Kathryn Tucker Windham, Jesse Culp, Mary Kay Remich, Shirley Mitchell, Joan and Neal Broerman, and the two Lynns.

Marshmallow hugs and chocolate kisses go to my family and especially to Carlton Martin—my husband, best friend, navigator, and photographer.

Introduction

"Hurricanes hardly ever happen."

Well, Eliza, maybe not in *My Fair Lady,* but in Alabama and neighboring states, it's a different story. Lately, hurricanes have been happening with some unfortunate degree of regularity.

As for Alabama, coastal rebuilding efforts in the wake of Ivan's visitation in 2004 were underway with some return to normalcy when Katrina wreaked her vengeance in 2005. But the happy message boils down to this: Alabama's Gulf Coast is back in business with beautiful new replenished beaches awaiting your visit.

Mobile rebounded quickly. The Museum of Mobile flooded, and the USS *Alabama* floated—for the first time in decades. The storm's outgoing surge, bigger than the incoming one, settled the battleship back down with a list—now corrected to two degrees and still being addressed. Both popular sites reopened to the public as soon as possible. The downtown Battle House Hotel renewal project took a hit, but the construction goes on with plans for a late 2006 completion.

Even though Katrina produced a tsunami at Point Clear, you'll find the Grand Hotel Marriott Resort, Golf Club & Spa once again dispensing its legendary hospitality. Dauphin Island (still a bird-watching paradise) and Bayou Le Batre took a battering, but the Blessing of the Shrimp Fleet and its attendant festivities will go on as usual. And speaking for our beloved Southeast, we hope that Eliza Doolittle's quote about hurricanes hardly ever happening will ring more true than it has the past two seasons as we go forward with resilience and cautious optimism. So come on down.

As a vacation destination, Alabama surprises most first-time visitors. With its varied and splendid geography, moderate climate, and Southern hospitality, the state makes an ideal year-round getaway. From its craggy Appalachian bluffs to sugar-sand beaches on the Gulf of Mexico, Alabama's wealth of natural beauty offers a happy (and uncrowded) vacation choice for everyone.

Alabama's link with sports is legend—think Bear Bryant, Joe Namath, Bo Jackson, Pat Sullivan, John Hannah, Hank Aaron, Joe Louis, Willie Mays, Jesse Owens, LeRoy "Satchel" Paige, Bobby Allison—and the list goes on. Although racing fans throng Talladega's speedway and Birmingham's Alabama Sports Hall of Fame represents diversity, visitors soon discover that football reigns supreme here. The first Alabama–Auburn clash dates to February 22, 1893, and loyalty lines continue to divide families, friends, and lovers. The stirring words "Roll Tide" and "War Eagle" enter the typical childhood vocabulary early on.

Designed by Robert Trent Jones, the largest golf course construction project ever attempted winds its way through Alabama. The world-famous golf architect, who died in 2000, called this project the greatest achievement of his career; the *New York Times* calls it "some of the best public golf on Earth." Conceived by David G. Bronner and funded by the Retirement Systems of Alabama (RSA), the Robert Trent Jones Trail has transformed the state into a golfing mecca, even making *Money* magazine's group of the eight best vacation spots in the world.

Unless you agree with Mark Twain that golf is a good walk ruined, you can't pass up the RTJ Trail, which will test the skills of all golfers from scratch handicappers to hopeless duffers. Beginning in the mountains and lakes of the Appalachian foothills and continuing southward to the white sands and wetlands of the Gulf Coast, this group of ten PGA tour–quality courses, ranging from thirty-six and fifty-four holes each, provides superb golfing and splendid scenery. From Huntsville's Hampton Cove, Gadsden's Silver Lakes, Birmingham's Oxmoor Valley, and Prattville's Capitol Hill to Grand National in the Auburn–Opelika area, Highland Oaks at Dothan, Cambrian Ridge at Greenville, and Magnolia Grove near Mobile, travelers can enjoy the exclusive country club experience at affordable prices. *Golf Magazine* called the RTJ Trail number one in the world for value. Capitol Hill, the trail's flagship addition, allows you to pick your pleasure from among three challenging courses: the Judge, the Legislator, and the Senator.

The Montgomery Marriott Prattville Hotel and Conference Center at Capitol Hill and the Auburn Marriott Opelika Hotel and Conference Center at Grand National continue to make great places to stay and play. And now, golfers and traveling families can enjoy the trail's two newest resort hotels, the Marriott Shoals Hotel and Spa in Florence and the Renaissance Ross Bridge Golf Resort and Spa (with a hotel reminiscent of a Scottish castle) in the Birmingham area.

Golf Magazine calls the Fighting Joe, which opened at the Shoals in 2005, one of the top-ten new courses. Named for Gen. Joe Wheeler, the course regularly attracts near overflow crowds and has also earned top honors from publications like *Travel and Leisure Golf*. To play any or all of these public courses, call (800) 949–4444. With either a phone call or online visit to www.rtjgolf.com, you can make arrangements for tee times at any of the trail's sites and/or lodging reservations.

Speaking of trails, anglers will want to follow their bliss on the new Alabama Bass Trail. Developed by the state Department of Conservation and Natural Resources and the first of its kind in the country, this trail consists of five sites showcasing major lakes across the state with plenty of outstanding bass tournaments on the agenda. And that's not all. *Audubon* magazine named the Alabama Coastal Birding Trail, which stretches through Baldwin and Mobile counties, one of the country's best viewing sites. Birders will find directional and interpretive signs all along the way.

Stars still fall on Alabama, and visitors can dip into a rich musical heritage throughout the state. Depending on your own particular penchant, you may catch a classical music concert at the Birmingham Civic Center or a swinging jazz session during Florence's yearly tribute to the "Father of the Blues," W. C. Handy. The Alabama Music Hall of Fame, near Tuscumbia, features memorabilia of Nat King Cole, Hank Williams, Sonny James, Lionel Richie, the Commodores, Emmylou Harris, Dinah Washington, the Temptations, and many other musicians with Alabama connections.

This guide book spotlights some of the state's special places—not only major sites such as the United States Space & Rocket Center in Huntsville but also small towns frozen in time and tucked-away treasures occasionally overlooked by the natives. In the state's northern section, Huntsville makes a handy launching pad from which travelers can easily loop both east and west to take in north Alabama's unique attractions. Heading south, the Birmingham area serves as a convenient base from which to branch out into the state's central section. From there you can sweep farther south to Montgomery to see the state capital area and southeastern section, which includes the historic Chattahoochee Trace. This account concludes with the beaches of Gulf Shores and one of the state's most beautiful cities, Mobile. In his book *A Walk Across America,* Peter Jenkins describes being captivated by Mobile, calling it a fantasy city. "Even more than by the psychedelic azaleas," he said, "I was moved by the great-grandfather live-oak trees."

Alabama's surprises start as soon as you cross the border, and the following sneak preview will give you an idea of what to expect. Huntsville, while playing a strategic role in the nation's space program, also preserves its past at EarlyWorks and at Alabama Constitution Village, a living-history museum. Delegates drafted Alabama's first constitution here in 1819, and when you open the gate and walk through the picket fence, you may smell bread baking and see aproned guides dipping beeswax candles or carding cotton—quite a contrast to the future-focused Space & Rocket Center. By the way, if you've harbored a secret yen to taste the astronaut's life but always thought Space Camp was just for kids, you're in for another surprise: The Space & Rocket Center offers programs for all who dare to delve into space technology, from fourth graders to grandparents. You might even participate in a simulated space-shuttle mission. If you're not ready for such a challenge, you can still stop by the gift shop and sample some freeze-dried astronaut ice cream.

Heading east gets you to Scottsboro, home of the "First Monday" market, one of the South's oldest and largest "trade days." Also known for its many caves, this area attracts spelunkers from around the world. Russell Cave, located at Jackson County's northeastern tip, could be called Alabama's first welcome center. Some 9,000 years ago bands of Native Americans began occupying the large cave; archaeologists, using carbon dating, have determined it to be the oldest known site of human occupancy in the southeastern United States.

At DeSoto State Park, also in the northeast region, visitors can view Little River Canyon National Preserve, the largest and one of the deepest gorges east of the Mississippi River. Near the charming mountain hamlet of Mentone, Cloudmont Resort features a dude ranch and ski slopes (albeit with Mother Nature getting some assistance from snow machines).

Lakes Guntersville, Wheeler, and Wilson make northern Alabama a haven for water sports enthusiasts. Lake Guntersville State Park hosts an Eagle Weekend in January, a good time of the year to spot bald eagles. Many visitors report being surprised by Alabama's state parks, which offer a sampling of some of the state's most spectacular vistas, such as the awe-inspiring Cathedral Caverns, plus a host of recreation options—and at bargain prices.

At Cullman, visitors can take a Lilliputian world tour at Ave Maria Grotto, a unique garden filled with more than 125 miniature reproductions of famous buildings. The reproductions were made by a gifted Benedictine monk named Brother Joseph Zoettl. And nearby Hanceville has become a mecca for pilgrims who want to visit the Shrine of the Most Blessed Sacrament of Our Lady of the Angels Monastery.

In Blount County you can see three of the state's covered bridges. Master-and-slave team John Godwin and Horace King built a number of Alabama's early bridges. After gaining his freedom, King joined Godwin as a business partner, later erecting a monument in "lasting remembrance of the love and gratitude he felt for his lost friend and former master." The monument can be seen at a Phenix City cemetery.

Each summer visitors can witness the reenactment of a miracle in northwest Alabama at Ivy Green, home of America's courageous Helen Keller.

As Alabama's major metropolis, Birmingham's paths are well trampled. Still, the Magic City offers some not-to-be-missed treats, such as the historic Five Points South area with its boutiques and outdoor eateries and the 740-acre Barber Motorsports Park near Irondale. On the somber side, the Birmingham Civil Rights Institute and nearby complex re-creates a journey through the darkness of segregation.

Farther south you'll find Montgomery, a backdrop for sweeping drama since Jefferson Davis telegraphed his "Fire on Fort Sumter" order from here and the Civil War proceeded to rip the country apart. Less than a century later, the Civil Rights Movement gained momentum in this town, paving the way for overdue national reform. The interpretative Rosa Parks Library and Museum offers an in-depth look at the Montgomery bus boycott and pays tribute to the "Mother of the Civil Rights Movement." Also located here, the Alabama Shakespeare Festival provides top dramatic entertainment.

Don't miss Selma, a quintessential Southern city, but one that preserves its drama-filled past—from Civil War to civil rights. Spring Pilgrimage events include home tours, a reenactment of the Battle of Selma, and a grand ball on Sturdivant Hall's lovely lawn. Selma also stages an annual Tale Tellin' Festival featuring Alabama's first lady of folk legends and ghost stories, Kathryn Tucker Windham (whose intriguing tales you may have heard on National Public Radio broadcasts).

Traveling down to Monroeville, the Literary Capital of Alabama, you'll see the courthouse and surrounding square where Truman Capote and Harper Lee, author of *To Kill a Mockingbird,* roamed as childhood friends.

Still farther south, the Gulf Shores and Orange Beach area, with glistening white beaches, sea oats, and sand dunes, lures many visitors. The coastal area also offers historic forts, grand mansions, a multirooted (French, British, and Spanish) heritage, and superb cuisine.

On Mobile Bay's eastern shore, a strange spectacle known as "Jubilee" sometimes surprises visitors. Spurred by unknown forces, shrimp, flounder, crab, and other marine creatures suddenly crowd the shoreline, usually several times a summer. When the cry of "Jubilee!" rings along the beach, people rush to the water's edge to fill containers with fresh seafood.

Alabama's colorful celebrations run the gamut from Mobile's Mardi Gras (which preceded New Orleans's extravaganza), and Gulf Shores's National Shrimp Festival to Opp's Rattlesnake Rodeo, Dothan's National Peanut Festival, and Decatur's hot-air balloon gala called the "Alabama Jubilee."

When making travel plans, call ahead because dates, rates, and hours of operation change from time to time. Unless otherwise stated in this guide, all museums and attractions with admission prices of $5.00 or less per adult are labeled modest. A restaurant meal (entree without beverage) classified as economical costs less than $8.00; moderate prices range between $8.00 and $20.00; and entrees $20.00 and above are designated expensive. As for accommodations, those that cost less than $80 per day are described as standard; an overnight price between $80 and $150 is called moderate; and lodging costing more than $150 is designated deluxe.

Director of tourism Lee Sentell and the Alabama Bureau of Tourism & Travel encouraged everyone to eat their way around the state by designating 2005 the "Year of Alabama Food." If you're lucky, you may still be able to get hold of the coveted brochure, *100 Dishes to Eat in Alabama Before You Die.* With 2006 came the Year of Alabama Outdoors and opportunities to work off some of those earlier calories. In 2007 we celebrate the Year of Alabama Arts.

Back to food though, many of us agree with a quote by Linda Vice, who represents Alabama's Black Belt in the state's southwestern section: "We can cook like Grandma did, or we can cook fancy. We draw from a number of food traditions. Food is one of our religions, and we worship at every shrine we pass!"

For travel information, maps, and brochures, stop by one of the eight Alabama Welcome Centers; call (800) ALABAMA; write to Alabama Tourism and Travel, P.O. Box 4927, Montgomery 36103–4927; or visit www.touralabama .org. To preview the state parks, log onto www.alapark.com. You can make reservations at any Alabama state park by dialing (800) ALA–PARK. So pack your bags, head for the unforgettable Heart of Dixie, anticipate some surprises, and watch out for falling stars.

Fast Facts about Alabama

CLIMATE OVERVIEW

Alabama's climate falls in the temperate range, becoming mostly subtropical near the Gulf Coast. Spring's first flowers appear early, often in February. By April, average statewide temperatures reach the 60s. Summer days often fall in the hot and humid category. Fall brings changing foliage and refreshing cooler weather. Snow is such a rarity in most parts of the state that when the weather person predicts it, everyone gets excited and makes a mad dash to the grocery stores for bread and milk.

FAMOUS ALABAMIANS

Some famous Alabamians include Condoleezza Rice, Helen Keller, Harper Lee, Winston Groom, Fannie Flagg, the country music group Alabama, Hank Williams Sr. and Jr., Rosa Parks, Kenny Stabler, Hank Aaron, Willie Mays, and Tallulah Bankhead.

NEWSPAPERS

The state's major newspapers include the *Huntsville Times,* the *Birmingham News,* the *Montgomery Advertiser,* and the *Mobile Press Register.* Since printed papers started in the state around 1806, according to Bill Keller, former executive director of the Alabama Press Association, Alabamians have demonstrated a long-standing appreciation for newspapers. Every county in Alabama produces a newspaper.

General Alabama Trivia

- In 1540 Hernando de Soto traveled through much of what is now Alabama.
- On December 14, 1819, Alabama became the twenty-second state in the Union.
- Alabama seceded from the Union on January 11, 1861, and rejoined on June 25, 1868.
- Montgomery has served as the state capital since 1846. Former capitals included St. Stephens, Huntsville, Cahaba, and Tuscaloosa.
- In 1959 the camellia became Alabama's state flower, replacing the goldenrod, which held that honor from 1927.
- The tarpon was designated as Alabama's official saltwater fish in 1955.
- Red iron ore, scientifically known as hematite, is the state mineral.
- Distinguished educator and humanitarian Julia Tutwiler wrote the words for "Alabama," the state song.
- Alabama comprises sixty-seven counties.
- Mobile's new RSA Battle House Tower is the state's tallest structure.

Northeast Alabama

Space Capital

Traveling through this area of Alabama, with its wooded glens, rugged mountain vistas, and sparkling lakes, is almost like moving through a calendar of splendid landscapes. Keep your camera handy because you'll discover some spectacular scenery.

Entering at the state's northern border, you'll drive through the rolling Tennessee Valley to reach *Huntsville,* a handy hub whether you're heading east or west to explore north Alabama's numerous attractions.

The birthplace of America's space program, Huntsville also served as an early capital of Alabama and later grew into a cotton mill town. After Dr. Wernher von Braun and his crew of German scientists arrived in the 1950s to pioneer the space program at Redstone Arsenal, Huntsville traded its title as World Watercress Capital for World Space Capital. The decade from 1950 to 1960 saw the population in Rocket City, U.S.A., mushroom from 15,000 to 72,000. Even today, ongoing road construction cannot keep pace with the burgeoning population and traffic.

A good place to start a local tour is the ***Huntsville Depot Transportation Museum*** (256–564–8100) at 320 Church Street.

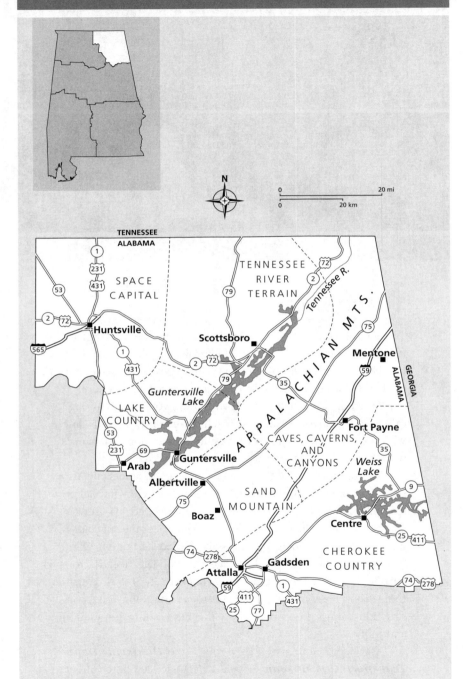

N

0   20 mi
0   20 km

TENNESSEE
ALABAMA

1
231
431
53
SPACE
CAPITAL

TENNESSEE
RIVER
TERRAIN

72
2

Tennessee R.

2 72
565

■Huntsville

79

1

431

2 72
Scottsboro ■

75

Mentone ■

59

APPALACHIAN MTS.

79

35

Guntersville
Lake

LAKE
COUNTRY

ALABAMA
GEORGIA

53

231 69

Fort Payne ■

CAVES, CAVERNS,
AND
CANYONS

35

Weiss
Lake

■ Guntersville

■
Arab

Albertville ■

75

9

Boaz ■

SAND
MOUNTAIN

Centre ■

25 411

74 278

CHEROKEE
COUNTRY

Attalla ■ Gadsden

59

411

1

74 278

25 77

431

Take time to tour the authentically restored depot, a big yellow building where a robotic telegrapher, stationmaster, and engineer welcome visitors and describe railroad life in 1912. During the Civil War the depot served as a prison, and upstairs you'll see some interesting graffiti such as a rather unflattering drawing of Union officer Major Strout and an inscription that reads HAPPY NEW YEARS TO ALL IN THE YEAR OF OUR LORD 1864. The depot's hours are 10:00 A.M. to 4:00 P.M. Wednesday through Saturday, March through December. The museum is closed January and February and on major holidays. Admission is charged.

As you drive around the area, check out the Von Braun Civic Center at 700 Monroe Street. This large multipurpose complex may well be hosting a concert, sporting event, or play you'd like to take in while in town.

Continue your self-driving tour through Huntsville's Historic Twickenham District with more than sixty-five antebellum houses and churches. Architectural

Watercress Capital of the World

Huntsville acquired the title "Watercress Capital of the World" because in earlier days it produced and shipped a large volume of watercress throughout the eastern half of the country. A member of the mustard family, watercress thrives in limestone springwater and once grew prolifically in the Tennessee Valley's many limestone springs.

Huntsville's old Russell Erskine Hotel was noted for its watercress salad, and several local cookbooks feature this specialty, sometimes known simply as "cress." The *Huntsville Heritage Cookbook* contains a section devoted to watercress including the following tasty recipe, once served at a White House state banquet. Long a local favorite, this book is again in print, thanks to the Huntsville Junior League. Look for it at gift shops and bookstores throughout Huntsville, and while browsing, pick up a copy of the Junior League's award-winning *Sweet Home Alabama,* a handsome volume featuring "Food for Family and Friends from the Heart of the South."

Frozen Cheese and Cress Salad

1 teaspoon plain gelatin

⅛ cup cold water

1 cup hot water

½ teaspoon salt

8 ounces cream cheese

1 small jar pimientos, chopped

1 cup heavy cream, whipped

Soak gelatin in cold water. Add hot water and salt. Strain and set aside until barely jelled. Beat until fluffy and fold in cream cheese that has been creamed. Add pimientos and fold in cream. Mold and chill. Serve on bed of watercress.

styles represented include Federal, Greek Revival, Italianate, Palladian, Gothic Revival, and others. For a fine example of Federal architecture, tour the **Weeden House Museum** (256–536–7718) at 300 Gates Avenue. Built in 1819, the home contains period antiques and features the work of Huntsville artist and poet Maria Howard Weeden, who lived here until her death in 1905. Her impressive body of work includes book illustrations, whimsical drawings, fascinating character studies, and portraits. Hours are 11:00 A.M. to 4:00 P.M. Monday through Friday, with group tours available on weekends by appointment. Admission.

On the square in downtown Huntsville, stop by **Harrison Brothers Hardware Store** (256–536–3631), located at 124 South Side Square. The store celebrated one hundred years on the Square in 1997. Here you can purchase marbles by the scoop, old-fashioned stick candy, cast-iron cookware, kerosene lamps, seeds, scrub boards, and other merchandise that speaks of yesteryear. Historic Huntsville Foundation volunteers ring up sales on a 1907 cash register. The interior, with pot-bellied stove, ceiling fans, rolling ladders, barrels, tools, and antique safe, looks much as it did in 1879 when the store opened for business. Hours are 9:00 A.M. to 5:00 P.M. weekdays and 10:00 A.M. to 4:00 P.M. Saturday.

Don't miss **Alabama Constitution Village** (256–564–8100) just around the corner. Entering the picket-fence gate at Franklin Street and Gates Avenue takes

GAY'S TOP PICKS IN NORTHEAST ALABAMA

Alabama Constitution Village,
Huntsville

Buck's Pocket State Park,
Grove Oak

Burritt on the Mountain,
Huntsville

Cathedral Caverns,
Grant

DeSoto State Park,
Fort Payne

EarlyWorks,
Huntsville

Huntsville Museum of Art,
Huntsville

Lake Guntersville State Park,
Guntersville

Little River Canyon National Preserve,
Fort Payne

Noccalula Falls and Park,
Gadsden

Sequoyah Caverns & Ellis Homestead,
Valley Head

Town of Mentone

U.S. Space & Rocket Center,
Huntsville

A Tribute to Everybody's Favorite Aunt

For more than half a century, the late Eunice Merrell served what many considered the best country ham and homemade biscuits in the world. Former governor Fob James declared her biscuits "the best in Alabama," and his proclamation made them the official state biscuit.

Although Eunice (better known to her customers as "Aunt" Eunice) described her diner as "just a little greasy spoon," the fame of her homemade biscuits made the *Congressional Record* in a tribute introduced by U.S. Senator Howell Heflin, who represented Alabama.

At Eunice's Country Kitchen, you often had to wait a bit for a table or share one with someone else. Some people even kept their own favorite brand of jelly or preserves in Eunice's refrigerator, retrieving it when the hot biscuits arrived, but most folks dipped into the honey or Sand Mountain sorghum on every table.

In this small cafe that did a booming business with no advertising, it was customary to warm up your neighbors' coffee if you got up to pour yourself a refill. In fact, when prospective candidates for office visited (this was a popular stop on political campaigns), Aunt Eunice expected them to follow protocol and wait on her customers; otherwise, they did not deserve the office to which they aspired—and she told them so.

Look for an authentically replicated Eunice's Country Kitchen at the Historic Huntsville Depot. You'll see the cafe's famous "Liars' Table," with its suspended wooden sign reserving it for politicians and preachers. (During a meal, Eunice sometimes presented customers with an official "Liar's License," permitting them to prevaricate "at any time or place without notice.") Other memorabilia include favorite quotes and an extensive collection of autographed photos from governors, congressmen, actors, astronauts, sports figures, and even a president.

Aunt Eunice, we miss you.

you back to 1819, when delegates met here to draft Alabama's first constitution. Afterward, on a tour of the complex, you'll see costumed guides going about their seasonal business of preserving summer's fruits or making candles at hog-killing time.

Stop by the gift shop, with such unique items as "ugly jugs," once used as containers for harmful substances. Hours are 10:00 A.M. to 4:00 P.M. Wednesday through Saturday. The village is closed January and February and on major holidays. Admission.

Kids—both young and old—love traveling back in time to the nineteenth century and exploring *EarlyWorks,* a hands-on history museum (256–564–8100) at 404 Madison Street, where new adventures await around every corner.

Special exhibits include an amazing 16-foot-tall tale-telling tree, giant-size musical instruments, and a 46-foot keelboat. Youngsters can dress up in vintage clothing and practice tasks that children in the "olden days" performed, and toddlers can milk a "pretend" cow and gather garden vegetables. Except for major holidays, hours run from 9:00 A.M. to 4:00 P.M. Tuesday through Saturday. Admission. Special prices are available for combination tours of EarlyWorks with the historic Huntsville Depot and Alabama Constitution Village. Parking is available throughout the downtown area with handicapped parking on the Gates Avenue side. Learn more about this hands-on facility on the Internet at www.earlyworks.com.

Afterward, head south on Madison Street until you reach Governor's Drive, then turn left. Don't miss Monte Sano Mountain, which offers sweeping views of Huntsville and the surrounding Tennessee River Valley. ***Burritt on the Mountain,*** a living-history museum (256–536–2882), at 3101 Burritt Drive, just off Monte Sano Boulevard, features 167 wooded acres with walking trails and picnicking facilities. At this living-history site, you'll find a blacksmith shop, smokehouse, church, and some log houses depicting rural life between 1850 and 1900. An X-shaped house, built in 1937 by Dr. William Henry Burritt, serves as the park's focal point. Both a physician and gifted inventor who held twenty patents during his life, Burritt combined Classical and art deco elements when he designed this unusual home.

alabamatrivia

Alabama's Robert Trent Jones Golf Trail is the world's largest golf-course construction project.

Inside you'll see archaeological and restoration exhibits, clothing, toys, and displays on Huntsville's history. One room features the paintings of local artist Maria Howard Weeden. Special events include Spring Farm Days, City Lights concert series (May through August), fall festivals, and Candlelight Christmas. Admission prices are slightly higher for special events. Rand McNally editors recently tapped Burritt on the Mountain for one of its "Best of the Road" picks. The museum is open Tuesday through Saturday from 10:00 A.M. to 4:00 P.M. and Sunday noon to 4:00 P.M. November through March. Summer hours are Tuesday through Saturday 9:00 A.M. to 5:00 P.M. and Sunday noon to 5:00 P.M. The grounds can be visited daily from 7:00 A.M. to 5:00 P.M. Admission.

Dogwood Manor (256–859–3946) at 707 Chase Road makes a lovely base for exploring the Huntsville area. Valerie and Patrick Jones own this restored Federal-style home, set on a sweeping lawn with century-old trees. The home's builder once operated a thriving nursery here and shipped his plants all over the country. Patrick, an attorney, shares history about the home and the Chase community with interested guests.

GAY'S FAVORITE ANNUAL EVENTS IN NORTHEAST ALABAMA

Seige of Bridgeport
Bridgeport, fourth weekend of March
(256) 259–5500 or (800) 259–5508

Art on the Lake
Guntersville, April
(256) 582–3612 or (800) 869–5253

Panoply, Huntsville's Festival of the Arts
Big Spring International Park, Huntsville
last full weekend of April
(256) 519–2787
www.panoply.org

Riverfest
Gadsden, May
(256) 543–3472

Stevenson Depot Days
Stevenson, first full week of June
(256) 437–3012
www.stevensondepotmuseum.com

Taste of Freedom BBQ Cookoff
Albertville, first full weekend of July
(256) 878–5188

World's Longest Yard Sale
Gadsden, Alabama, to Covington
Kentucky, early August
(888) 805–4740

St. William's Seafood Festival
Guntersville, early September (Labor
Day weekend)
(256) 582–4245

Big Spring Jam Music Festival
Big Spring International Park, Huntsville
last full weekend of September
(256) 551–2359
www.bigspringjam.org

Depot Days Festival
Hartselle, September
(256) 773–4370
www.hartsellechamber.com

Harvest Festival
Boaz, early October
(256) 593–8154 or (800) 746–7262

Heritage Festival
Attalla, October
(256) 543–3472

Mentone Fall Colorfest
Mentone, third weekend of October
(256) 845–3957 or (888) 805–4740

Christmas on the Rocks
Noccalula Falls, Gadsden
Thanksgiving through December
(256) 490–7111

Galaxy of Lights
Huntsville/Madison County Botanical
Garden, Thanksgiving through New
Year's Eve
(256) 830–4447

The couple reserves four charming rooms—appropriately named Dogwood, Magnolia, Azalea, and Rose—for overnight visitors and serves afternoon tea on request. Valerie, a school counselor, prepares gourmet breakfasts, complemented by her own homemade breads and muffins. She often makes apple French toast, crumpets, and English scones. Moderate rates. Visit Dogwood Manor's Web site at www.dogwoodmanorhuntsville.com.

Fine Dining at 801 Franklin

While enjoying Huntsville's many attractions, stop by *801 Franklin* (256–519–8019), where the name and address are one and the same. At this upscale restaurant you'll always find an eye-catching art exhibit. The eatery features contemporary American cuisine with one of the finest menus in town plus an award-winning wine selection. Try 801's signature crab cakes with lemon beurre blanc, a flavorful soup (such as the oyster stew; see recipe), or a delectable entree of seafood, beef, lamb, and more.

When *The Valley Planet,* a regional publication, polls its readers on their favorites, 801 regularly takes top awards. In a recent issue the restaurant placed number one in fine dining, best place for a glass of wine, most romantic restaurant, best lunch, and best dessert, and ranked among the top three in nine other categories.

Lunch hours are 11:00 A.M. to 2:00 P.M. Monday through Friday, and dinner is served from 5:00 to10:00 P.M. Monday through Thursday and until 11:00 P.M. Friday and Saturday. The lounge opens at 4:00 P.M. on weekdays and at 5:00 P.M. on Saturday. See www.801franklin.com for more background.

Oyster Stew

1 large yellow onion, medium dice

3 celery stocks, medium dice

6 cloves of garlic, minced

3 large shallots, minced

3–4 Idaho potatoes, medium dice

1 gallon milk

½ gallon fresh oysters with liquor

2 tablespoons Florida Bay seasoning

1 bay leaf

1 tablespoon white pepper

3 tablespoons kosher salt

Roux

¾ pound butter

¾ pound flour

Melt butter. Add vegetables. Cook until clear. Add flour mixture thoroughly, then add milk and potatoes. Bring to a boil; add oysters and seasoning. Makes enough for a party.

Across from Dogwood Manor's driveway stands the **North Alabama Railroad Museum** (256–851–NARM) at 694 Chase Road. The restored green-and-yellow Chase Depot houses a waiting room and agent office filled with exhibits. Home of the Mercury and Chase Railroad and the country's smallest union station, the facility now features a walk-through passenger train and twenty-seven pieces of major railroading stock. Except for major holidays, the museum can be visited from 9:00 A.M. to 4:00 P.M. daily, and a staff member is available each Wednesday and Saturday from 8:30 A.M. to 2:00 P.M. April through October. The facility offers guided tours and excursion train rides. Children enjoy watching for the concrete animals staged along the track. In addition to regular trips, a Goblin Special and Santa Trail Special are also scheduled. Call for more information on schedules, fares, and reservations, or visit the Web site at www.suncompsvc.com/narm/ for current happenings.

Tennessee River Terrain

From Huntsville take U.S. Highway 72 east to *Scottsboro,* home of *First Monday,* one of the South's oldest and largest "trade days." This outdoor market might feature anything from cast-iron skillets, church pews, and collie puppies to butter churns, gingham-checked sunbonnets, and pocketknives—all displayed around the Jackson County Courthouse Square. Lasting from morning till dark, the event dates to the mid-1800s, when people met at the courthouse square on the day Circuit Court opened to visit as well as to trade horses, mules, and other livestock. The merry mix of folks who still come to browse, banter, and barter carry on a Southern tradition, and many have honed their trading techniques to a high level of skill. Although this event takes place on the first Monday of every month (plus the Saturday and Sunday preceding it), the Fourth of July and Labor Day weekends typically prove most popular.

If you miss Scottsboro's First Monday, you can console yourself by dipping into a chocolate milk shake, ice-cream soda, or banana split at *Payne's* (256–574–2140), located at 101 East Laurel on the town square's north side. Owned by Shay and Gene Holder, this eatery occupies the site of a former drugstore dating from 1869. The interior, complete with old-fashioned soda fountain, features a black-and-white color scheme with red accents. You can perch on a bar stool, order a fountain Coke that's mixed

alabamatrivia

During its territorial and statehood days, Alabama has had five capitals.

on the spot and served in a traditional Coca-Cola glass, and munch on a hot dog with red slaw straight from the original drugstore menu. Other options include Payne's popular chicken salad and a variety of sandwiches along with homemade desserts. Hours are 11:00 A.M. to 4:00 P.M. Monday through Saturday (except on Thursday, when closing time is 3:00 P.M.). The eatery is also open

11:00 A.M. to 4:00 P.M. on the Sunday before First Monday unless the weather is unusually rainy or cold thus deterring customers.

To learn about the area's history, visit the **Scottsboro-Jackson Heritage Center** (256–259–2122), located at 208 South Houston Street. This Neoclassical–style structure, built in 1881, houses some interesting exhibits, including Native American artifacts found on land later flooded by the Tennessee Valley Authority (TVA) and rare photographic displays depicting the early days of Skyline, a unique community north of Scottsboro.

Behind the big house stands the small 1868 Jackson County Courthouse. Nearby, a pioneer village called Sage Town features a collection of authentic log structures that includes a cabin, schoolhouse, barn, and blacksmith shop, all filled with vintage items.

The museum offers a wealth of genealogical materials, says Judi Weaver, who promotes archaeological awareness in her role as director. The facility focuses on the area's history from the Paleo-Indian era through the 1930s. Special events include heritage festivals and art exhibitions. Hours are 11:00 A.M. to 4:00 P.M. Monday through Friday, or by appointment. A modest admission is charged.

If, after a plane trip, you've ever discovered yourself divorced from your bags and wondered about their final destination, it's entirely possible that your lost luggage wound up at Scottsboro's **Unclaimed Baggage Center** (256–259–1525), located at 509 West Willow Street (although your bags may have traveled instead to nearby Unclaimed Baggage in Boaz). At this unique outlet you can find such items as cameras, caviar, clothing, hammocks, hair dryers, jewelry, scuba gear, and ski equipment. The ever-changing merchandise from around the world also features baby strollers, books, briefcases, luggage, personal electronic devices, and high-tech equipment.

"We have to stay on top of technology to know what's coming in here," says a company executive. The diverse inventory of lost, found, and unclaimed items comes from various airlines to be sorted and offered for sale at reduced rates—20 to 80 percent or more off retail prices. In this shopping mecca, which now covers more than a city block, you can enjoy a mug of brewed Starbuck's coffee at the facility's in-house cafe, called Cups.

Business boomed here—even before Oprah spread the word on her TV show. The parking lot gets especially crowded on weekends, and car tags reveal shoppers from many states. Recent visitors also came from Ontario, Bavaria, New Zealand, South America, France, and England. Closed on Sunday, hours are 9:00 A.M. to 6:00 P.M. Monday through Friday and 8:00 A.M. to 6:00 P.M. Saturday. The Web site is www.unclaimedbaggage.com.

After sightseeing in the Scottsboro area, you can easily head south on State Route 79 toward Guntersville to take in some Marshall County attractions, or you can continue your loop northeast to Stevenson. ***Goose Pond Colony*** (256–259–2884 or 800–268–2884), a peninsula surrounded by the Tennessee River, is located 5 miles south of Scottsboro on State Route 79 at 417 Ed Hembree Drive and offers vacation cottages, picnic facilities, camping sites, swimming pool, marina and launching ramp, golf course, and nature/walking trail. Popular with both geese and golfers, the golf course is noted for its beauty and design. Named by *Golf Digest* as one of "The Places to Play," Goose Pond's course also made the top five in a previous PGA opinion poll ranking courses in the Dixie section. For more information visit www.goosepond.org.

The Docks (256–574–3071), a restaurant on the grounds behind the swimming pool, offers a variety of seafood including Cajun fare. You can dine on the deck with a fine view of the water. Some diners arrive by boat and tie up at the property's private pier. The restaurant is open from 5:00 to 9:00 P.M. Tuesday through Thursday and 5:00 to 10:00 P.M. Friday and Saturday. Prices range from moderate to expensive.

Before leaving this area, you may want to call the Scottsboro/Jackson County Chamber of Commerce (256–259–5500 or 800–259–5508) or stop by the headquarters at 407 East Willow Street to pick up brochures on various local and area attractions.

A squirrel's nest with a Web site? It's true. Way off the beaten path near Grant, you may or may not find ***The Squirrel Nest*** (256–571–0324), a restaurant at 2219 Baker Mountain Road. When owner Doris Smith transformed her secluded family home into a restaurant, she chose the name because of the setting. "We are in the woods," she says, "and surrounded by squirrels' nests."

Guests will find a comfortable, homey atmosphere with plenty of whimsical touches both inside and out. A wall-size mural depicts deer in a woodland scene. Doris does the cooking, and her daughter Carmen assists in serving. The most popular breakfast choice here is country ham with homemade biscuits, eggs, gravy, grits, and the works. Dinner entrees come with soup, salad, homemade bread, a triangle of Vidalia onion pie, and dessert. (You may want to request a box for leftovers.) Also, The Squirrel Nest houses a getaway suite complete with hot tub. Call for dinner reservations (required) and specific directions. Breakfast hours run from 6:00 to 11:00 A.M. Tuesday through Saturday. Dinner hours are 5:00 to 9:00 P.M. Friday and Saturday. Also, The Squirrel Nest opens from 11:00 A.M. to 3:00 P.M. for Sunday lunch. Scurry to www.thesquirrelnest.com for more information.

Tucked away in a sylvan setting about halfway between Scottsboro and Guntersville, ***Ivy Creek Inn Bed and Breakfast*** (256–505–0108) awaits the traveler who wants to get in touch with nature but still enjoy creature comforts. To reach the property at 985 Carlton Road, you'll take a turn off State Route 79 North (marked by a sign) that leads down a wooded route and over a couple of single-lane bridges to the bed-and-breakfast inn, fronted by a creek. In fact, the creek's gurgling will probably be the first thing you hear upon arrival because the two resident Lassie-like collies, Lucy and Jack, don't bark—they simply wag their tails in greeting. The inn was opened in 1999 by Kathy and Hess Fridley, who fell in love with this wooded hollow while visiting and soon found themselves the owners—thanks to an auction. In addition to a large house to maintain, their property of twenty acres features an underground lake, a cave, and a waterfall, which make an enchanting backdrop for outdoor dining.

You'll see an incredible arrowhead collection amassed by Hess's father and exhibited in handmade cabinets, plus works by Colorado artist Bev Doolittle. Kathy reserves two rooms called The Country Store to showcase items handcrafted by area artisans. Don't miss the white oak baskets created by Jesse Thomason from Blountsville. Ivy Creek offers five guest rooms plus an apartment, all with private baths. Breakfast arrives on lovely ivy-patterned china and might feature Kathy's delicious version of eggs Benedict or stuffed French toast with blackberries. Moderate rates. View the property at www.ivycreekn.com.

Although you might find the tiny town of Pisgah on your road map, you won't find ***Gorham's Bluff*** (256–451–VIEW [8439])—yet. This traditional neighborhood community (inspired by Florida's Seaside) offers travelers some stunning scenery, especially from the Overlook Pavilion, and accommodations at The Lodge. The property commands sweeping bluffside views of the Tennessee River. *Travel and Leisure* magazine chose Gorham's Bluff for inclusion in "The 30 Great U.S. Inns," and *Southern Living* magazine voted the property "Most Romantic Spot in Alabama."

Overlook Pavilion at Gorham's Bluff

This lovely site remained undeveloped until Clara and Bill McGriff (a CPA still remembered by locals as a basketball star) started exploring their daughter Dawn's idea of creating a brand-new, arts-oriented Appalachian town—a walking town with a strong sense of community where residents stop for front-porch chats. With each new home and resident, the McGriffs watch the family vision being translated to reality.

"There is a peace that pervades this place," says Clara, a former English teacher. "We feel it, and guests feel it." The Lodge on Gorham's Bluff gives guests ample opportunity to sample this serenity and beauty. Spacious suites, individually decorated by Clara (who also creates the beautiful floral arrangements), double-sided fireplaces, and whirlpool tubs make accommodations even more inviting.

Hiking, biking, birding, rocking, reflecting, reading, and listening to classical music all rank as popular pastimes here. Dawn frequently schedules special events such as concerts, the Alabama Ballet's summer residency, and storytelling and theater festivals.

Sometime during your stay, slip up to the observation deck for a panoramic overview. Many visitors want to linger at Gorham's Bluff forever. A quote from the guest book reads: "Forward our mail. We are not leaving."

Meals (enhanced by the property's own fresh herbs) feature traditional Appalachian food—served with flair. "Breakfasts, included in the rates, are huge Southern-style affairs," notes Dawn. Dinners are served with candlelight and white tablecloths as a pianist plays old and new favorites by request. By reservation only, the lodge's thirty-seat dining room offers dinner for guests and the public nightly at 7:00 P.M. Dress is casual. From Pisgah, located on Jackson County Road 58, signs point the way to Gorham's Bluff. Call for hours and specific directions or write the staff at 101 Gorham Drive/Gorham's Bluff, Pisgah 35765. Lodge rates range from moderate to deluxe. Make reservations for an evening or a weekend. You just may decide to become one of the town's new residents. For more background or a map, visit www.gorhamsbluff.com or e-mail reservations@gorhamsbluff.com.

To reach the *Stevenson Railroad Depot Museum* (256–437–3012), take US 72 and travel northwest. Near Stevenson turn at State Route 117 to go downtown. At 207 West Main Street, you'll see the museum positioned between two railroad tracks. Look carefully before crossing the tracks because the Iron Horse still whizzes by. This railroad junction played a strategic role during the Civil War, and the museum director showed me an assortment of uniform buttons, coins, and other military items brought in by a resident who had dug them up nearby. The Stevenson Depot also contains displays of Native American artifacts, period costumes, early farm tools, and railroading history information.

Stevenson Railroad Depot Museum

Each June the annual Stevenson Depot Days celebration commemorates the city's past with a variety of family activities that might include an ice-cream social, spelling bee, pioneer breakfast, wagon ride to the nearby Civil War fort, square dancing, tour of homes, parade, old-fashioned street dance, and fireworks. The museum is open Monday through Saturday from 8:00 A.M. to 4:00 P.M. April through November. It closes on Saturday December through March. Admission is free.

From Stevenson return to US 72 and continue to **Bridgeport,** in Alabama's northeastern corner.

Caves, Caverns, and Canyons

While exploring this region in June 1540, Spaniard Hernando de Soto and his crew chose this area for their entry into what is now Alabama. You might like to take a driving tour of Bridgeport, once called Jonesville but renamed in the 1850s for the railroad bridge that spans the Tennessee River.

Drive through Kilpatrick Row Residential District and up bluff-based Battery Hill, the site of several Civil War battles, to see the lovely historic homes of Victorian vintage with turrets, fishscale shingles, and wraparound porches.

Russell Cave National Monument (256–495–2672), about 8 miles west of Bridgeport, is located at 3729 Jackson County Road 98. Long before de Soto's visit, the large limestone cave served as an archaic hotel for Native Americans traveling through the area about 9,000 years ago.

Exploring Cathedral Caverns

Both Native Americans and Confederate soldiers used these caverns as a refuge, and Disney used them as a movie setting for *Tom and Huck*. Ensconced in Marshall County's northeastern corner near the town of Grant, Cathedral Caverns (256–728–8193) opened as a state park in August 2000.

You don't have to assume a crouching position to enter because the opening to these caverns measures 125 feet wide by 25 feet high. Meandering along the lighted walkway takes you past Goliath, a massive stalagmite that appears to be a floor-to-ceiling column, and what are believed to be the world's largest stalagmite forest and frozen waterfall. Besides stalagmites and stalactites, other cave features include drapery, soda straws (capillary tubes), all the common types of shields, and "just about any formation you can expect to find in a cave," said a guide.

The deeper you go into the cave's interior, the more wondrous the surroundings. Before the grand finale, you'll enter a magnificent chamber that soars to a height of 120 feet and presumably contains the largest flowstone wall in any commercial cave. Then, to top that off, the Cathedral Room features a staggering number of fanciful, stalagmitic formations. Beyond the portion open to the public lies a magnificent crystal room with stunning calcite configurations (or so they say).

Former owner Jay Gurley, who died in 1996, dedicated much of his life and fortune to making the caverns accessible so others might share their wonder. His active involvement in developing the park spanned the period from 1952 until 1974 when he sold the property. Although the caverns were open from time to time after Gurley's tenure, they closed in 1986, and the state bought the site in 1987. Inside the cave, a plaque acknowledges Gurley's contribution and serves as a monument, as does the Jay Gurley Memorial Bridge that transports visitors across Mystery River.

The river is aptly named. "We can't see where the stream comes from or where it goes," said park manager Danny Lewis. Normally placid, the river can reach a depth of 40 feet during flooding conditions when the swirling water becomes chocolate-colored.

Bring a jacket (the temperature hovers at 57 to 60 degrees Fahrenheit) and jogging shoes. The 1½-mile round-trip takes about an hour and fifteen minutes. Future plans for this 461-acre park include additional hiking trails and camping facilities. Hours change seasonally. Call or check the schedule at www.alapark.com and follow the link to Cathedral Caverns. Admission.

The visitor center, in addition to housing a museum that displays weapons, tools, pottery, and other artifacts found in the cave, also offers several audio-visual presentations. After browsing through the museum, you can walk about 250 yards to the cave's big opening at the base of craggy bluffs. A ranger-led tour takes you to the cave, where you can learn about how the occupants fed, clothed, and protected themselves.

One of the century's most significant archaeological finds, the relic-filled cave remained pretty much a secret until 1953 when some members of the Tennessee Archaeological Society discovered the history-rich shelter and alerted Smithsonian Institution officials, who collaborated with the National Geographic Society to conduct extensive excavations here. The National Park Service carried out more excavations in 1962. Their joint research revealed Russell Cave to be one of the longest, most complete, and well-preserved archaeological records in the eastern United States. Radioactive carbon from early campfires placed human arrival between 6500 and 6145 B.C. Remains of animal bones, tools, weapons, and pottery all helped archaeologists fit together portions of this ancient jigsaw puzzle. The evidence implies seasonal occupation, suggesting that various groups of early people wintered in Russell Cave, then moved on to hunt and live off the land during warm-weather months.

Be sure to ask a ranger about a living-history demonstration. I found it fascinating to watch a piece of flint fashioned into an arrowhead in about four minutes with the same simple tools early Native Americans used.

Except for Thanksgiving, Christmas, and New Year's Day, you can visit Russell Cave from 8:00 A.M. to 4:30 P.M. seven days a week, and there's no admission charge. For more information, write to park personnel at 3729 County Road 98, Bridgeport 35740. Explore the cave on the Internet by clicking on www.nps.gov/ruca.

A cave adventure of a different sort awaits at **Sequoyah Caverns & Ellis Homestead** (256–635–0024 or 800–843–5098), located at 1438 County Road 731, about 6 miles north of Valley Head. Returning to Stevenson, you can follow State Route 117 South to reach the caverns, well marked by signs. Travelers arriving on Interstate 59 can take either the Hammondville–Valley Head exit or the Sulphur Springs–Ider exit to the caverns, located a few hundred yards off the interstate between these two exits.

The caverns take their name from Sequoyah (also spelled Sequoya or Sequoia), who moved to this part of Alabama as a young man. California's giant trees and Sequoia National Park were also named in honor of this Cherokee chief, who developed an alphabet for his people after being intrigued by the white man's "talking leaf." As a result the Cherokee people learned to read and write in a matter of months and soon started publishing books and newspapers in their native language.

You'll enter the caverns through the Cherokee Cooking Room, so called because of the salt troughs, cooking implements, pottery, and blackened walls found here. Wending your way through this magical world of spectacular stalactites and stalagmites in gorgeous colorations is like traveling through a giant kaleidoscope. The many reflecting pools known as "looking-glass lakes" allow you to study remote features on the multilevel ceiling that rises as high as a twelve-story building in certain portions of the caverns. A guided tour takes about an hour, and the temperature remains a constant sixty degrees Fahrenheit. Admission. From March through November the caverns are open from 8:30 A.M. to 5:00 P.M. and 11:00 A.M. to 5:00 P.M. Sunday; however, they are open only on Saturday and Sunday from December through February. Owner Roy Jones is a descendant of James Ellis, a pioneer from Tennessee, who moved here in 1841 and acquired the vast acreage that is home to Sequoyah Caverns. Visit the site at www.sequoyahcaverns.com.

In *Valley Head,* only a few miles south of the caverns, you'll find *Wood-haven* (256–635–6438), a bed-and-breakfast owned by Judith and Kaare Lollik-Andersen. Located on Lowry Road and fronted by a wooden fence, the 1902 three-story white house features a wraparound porch with an inviting swing and white wicker furniture. A creek runs through the pastures of the forty-acre farm, making it a pleasant place to explore, hike, jog, or bike. Children especially enjoy helping feed the animals.

While living in south Florida, Judith and Kaare started searching out a location for a bed-and-breakfast inn because they enjoyed staying in such facilities in Europe. They wanted mountains, trees, water, and a gentle climate, "but one with seasons." Their search brought them to this part of Alabama, where the geography reminded Kaare of his native Norway, with the nearby Tennessee River a substitute for the sea.

For early risers, Judith serves a pre-breakfast snack of Danish or muffins with coffee and juice. Later comes the

alabamatrivia

In Valley Head's "triangle," you can delve into the mystery of a vanished village at the Ruins of Battelle. For more background on this supposedly haunted site, click on www.tourdekalb.com.

real thing with fresh fruit, croissants or English muffins, oatmeal or cereal, and one of the house specialties: eggs (provided by the farm's own chickens) with bacon or a Norwegian dish of herring and eggs with caviar on toast. You can also expect afternoon tea and evening snacks. Moderate rates. For reservations and specific directions, call or write to Woodhaven, 390 Lowry Road, Valley Head 35989.

One block off State Route 117 in the center of Valley Head stands *Winston Place* (256–635–6381 or 888–494–6786), a white-columned antebellum mansion owned by Leslie and Jim Bunch. Located 2 miles from Mentone, the property features a panoramic view of Lookout Mountain. Two levels of encircling porches with ferns, white wicker rocking chairs, and a nanny swing invite guests to relax and savor the setting. Built by William Overton Winston from

Virginia, the circa-1831 home boasts a rich history. During the Civil War, Union officers occupied the home, and 30,000 soldiers camped on its grounds before leaving to fight at Chickamauga. Leslie, who shares anecdotes about her family home and its fascinating background, has amassed a collection of books and articles detailing Winston Place's role in history.

Previously selected for inclusion in *National Geographic's Small Town Getaways,* Winston Place contains lovely period antiques and lends itself well to entertaining, just as its builder intended. Original outbuildings include servants' quarters, a slanted-wall corncrib, and a smokehouse with hand-painted murals depicting the area's history.

While immersing yourself in the home's ambience, take time to see the tucked-away media room with Jim's football awards—trophies, plaques, and photos. A former Alabama football All-American (whose mastery of the game took him to three Sugar Bowls and a Liberty Bowl), Jim played under legendary coach Bear Bryant.

The couple offers five elegant suites for guests and a continental breakfast, served in the dining room. Rates range from moderate to deluxe. Visit Winston Place's home in cyberspace at www.virtualcities.com/al/winstonplace .htm. "For an easier way to find us," suggests Leslie, "go to google.com and type in 'Winston Place.'"

From Valley Head it's a short but scenic drive up to **Mentone,** a charming hamlet perched on the brow of Lookout Mountain at the intersection of State Route 117 and DeKalb County Route 89. Once a fashionable summer resort town that flourished through the Gay Nineties, Mentone attracted visitors from all over the country with its cool mountain temperatures, especially appealing in the days before air-conditioning.

Shops, rustic and quaint, line the single main street, but the large, rambling **Mentone Springs Hotel** (6114 State Route 117; 256–634–4040) remains the town's focal point. The three-story structure with turrets, dormers, porches, and steep-sloped roof captured my imagination the first time I saw it three decades ago. Open for bed-and-breakfast guests, the building also houses a restaurant called Caldwell's, named for the doctor who built the hotel in 1884. Rates are moderate. Go to www.mentonespringshotel.com for more information.

The name *Mentone* translates into "musical mountain spring," appropriate because the hotel's grounds once boasted two springs—Mineral Springs and Beauty Springs—which were reputed to possess "strengthening and curative properties." The hotel's early guests enjoyed nature walks, croquet, billiards, boating, and other genteel pursuits.

Although you can't join a picnicking party with a basket lunch packed by the hotel and you won't be summoned to meals by a dinner bell, you can explore the town's shops. Some of them close or limit their hours in winter, so it's best to check ahead. Also, you might inquire about the dates of upcoming festivals because Mentone stages special events throughout the year.

The downtown **Log Cabin Restaurant and Deli** (6080 State Route 117; 256–634–4560), originally a Native American trading post, serves sandwiches, salads, plate lunches, and dinner entrees with home-cooked vegetables and desserts. The eatery, where you'll find a cozy fire when temperatures drop, is open Tuesday through Sunday. Call ahead for hours. Prices range from economical to moderate. Nearby **Dessie's Kountry Chef** (5951 State Route 117; 256–634–4232), closed on Tuesday, serves evening fare along with short orders and home-style lunches. Call for hours. Prices range from economical to moderate.

Stop by **The Hitching Post** on the corner of County Road 89 and State Route 117, and take a break at **The Wildflower Café** (256–634–0066), which you'll enter from the porch on the back. The eatery offers espresso, cappuccino, and other specialty coffees and a variety of food choices from soups, sandwiches, and vegetarian dishes to gourmet pizzas and a five-course dinner on weekends. Hours are 9:00 A.M. to 3:00 P.M. Wednesday through Saturday; 5:00 to 9:00 P.M. Friday and Saturday; and 10:00 A.M. to 2:00 P.M. for Sunday brunch. Ask about the musical nights featured on the first and third Thursdays of each month. Standard to moderate.

Take time to browse for antiques and collectibles in the complex, which houses several interesting shops including the Crow's Nest. At the Gourdie Shop you'll see Sharon Barron's unique and whimsical creations made from locally grown gourds, each signed and dated by the artist. Hours vary.

Across the road from the old hotel is St. Joseph's on the Mountain. Be sure to notice the log structure, dating to 1826, that serves as the central portion of this unusual church. North of the church on the mountain's brow, you'll find Eagle's Nest, a massive rock formation overlooking Valley Head.

After exploring the village, take a drive along the area's meandering roads. You'll see strategically placed destination markers nailed to trees and posts at junctions—these are quite helpful because the mountain terrain can prove confusing to newcomers.

Tucked away at 651 County Road 644 stands **Raven Haven** (256–634–4310), a bed-and-breakfast perched atop Lookout Mountain. Owners Eleanor and Tony Teverino welcome travelers to share their ten acres of nature and theme rooms: Queen Anne, Nautical, Casablanca, and Little Room on the Prairie—each with private bath.

"Two things that drew us here were the beauty of the place and the people," said Eleanor, who was born in Northern Ireland. "When I came to Mentone, it was very much like going back home." The Teverinos hosted recent guests from

Ireland, who compared some of Mentone's narrow boulder-flanked curves with "driving on the roads right back at home."

Eleanor whisks warm and wonderful pastries from her oven and prepares a delightful breakfast daily, complete with homemade jams. Served buffet style, the menu always features a main dish, fruit, and vegetable to get your day off to a good healthy start. From Scotch eggs to fried green tomatoes to sticky buns, each morning's choices offer plenty of variety. A copy of *The Raven Haven Cookbook* makes a great souvenir. Afterward, you can trek through the woods and admire the wildflowers along the property's ¼-mile walking trail. Standard rates. For more information on this hideaway, pay a Web visit to www.ravenhavenbandb.info.

While driving through the area, you'll pass a number of summer camps for youngsters. In fact boyhood days spent at one such camp called Cloudmont inspired local landowner Jack Jones to pursue his unlikely dream of creating a ski resort in Alabama. After buying Cloudmont in 1947, he started developing the property as a resort and opened "the southernmost ski resort in the country" in 1970. ***Cloudmont Ski and Golf Resort*** (256–634–4344), about 3 miles from Mentone on DeKalb County Road 89, is marked by a large roadside sign on the left. To reach the information center, take a left onto County Road 614 for a half mile or so. Besides skiing (and yes, Mother Nature does get help from snow machines), this unique family enterprise offers golfing, hiking, fishing, and swimming for guests. Jack's

alabama trivia

Alabama ranks twelfth in the nation for attracting retirees, and eighth in the nation for attracting military retirees.

son Gary and his instructors have taught thousands of people to ski. Winter season at Cloudmont usually begins around mid-December and extends through March 15. It's a good idea to call ahead and check on slope conditions. Better yet, log onto www.cloudmont.com for lodging packages, schedules, rates, and information on current activities, which include golfing, horseback riding, and more at both Cloudmont and ***Shady Grove Dude Ranch.*** You can write the resort at P.O. Box 435, Mentone 35984.

Cragsmere Manna Restaurant (256–634–4677 or 256–845–2209), located about a half mile beyond the resort (at 17871 DeKalb County Road 89) in one of the area's oldest houses, offers a "country gourmet" dinner on Friday and Saturday from 5:00 to 9:00 P.M. Prices are moderate.

While in this area, don't miss the ***Sallie Howard Memorial Chapel,*** on County Road 165 located 6.7 miles from downtown Mentone and adjacent to DeSoto State Park. A 20-foot-tall boulder serves as the rear wall of the small church, and stones from Little River form the pulpit. Visitors often attend worship services held here each Sunday at 10:00 A.M.

To more fully explore this area's magnificent terrain, consider headquartering at **DeSoto State Park** (256–845–5380 or 800–568–8840) on County Road 89, about 7 miles from Mentone. You'll find almost 5,000 acres of breathtaking beauty and glimpses of unspoiled nature at every turn. The gorgeous scenery around here makes it hard to concentrate on driving, but if you don't, you might bash into one of the big weathered boulders that partially jut into the road.

The park extends about 40 miles along Little River, a unique waterway that runs its complete course on top of a mountain. Resort facilities include a stone lodge with large restaurant, chalets, cabins, nature trails, playgrounds, a store, and picnic areas. Miles of hiking trails, bordered by Queen Anne's lace, blackberry vines, honeysuckle, and black-eyed Susans, beckon you to explore the terrain. The park's wheelchair-accessible boardwalk attracts families and features a covered pavilion and waterfall view. Don't miss spectacular **DeSoto Falls** (about 7 miles northeast of the park's Information Center), where water rushes over a dam to crash more than 100 feet before continuing its journey.

About 10 miles away in the park's southern section, you'll find the beginning of **Little River Canyon National Preserve,** the largest and one of the deepest chasms east of the Mississippi River. Stretching about 16 miles, the canyon drops to depths of some 700 feet. Skirting the western rim, a canyon road offers breathtaking views of rugged bluffs, waterfalls, and the rushing river.

Don't miss **Fort Payne,** the stomping ground of award-collecting country music group ALABAMA and home to the redbrick **Fort Payne Opera House** at 510 North Gault Avenue. The building, which dates to 1889, has served as a vaudeville playhouse, a theater for silent movies, and an upholstery shop. The opera house is listed on the National Register of Historic Places and the National Register of Nineteenth-Century Theatres in America. Restored in 1969 the opera house now opens for special events and performances. Tours can be arranged by appointment. Call (256) 845–3957.

The building on the opera house's north side is home to the **DeKalb County Hosiery Museum** and the **Richard C. Hunt Reception Hall.** The hall's interesting mural, entitled *Harvest at Fort Payne,* dates back to the Great Depression when President Franklin D. Roosevelt initiated the Work Projects Administration (WPA) to aid the unemployed. Harwood Steiger, an out-of-work artist from New York, received a commission to paint murals for Southern post offices, and this is one of his creations. Before its placement here, the mural was housed in the old post office building and later the DeKalb County Courthouse. Visitors to the hosiery museum can see early mill machinery and other exhibits as well as a video providing background on the industry that played a major role in the area's history and economy. For more information contact the DeKalb County Tourist Association at (256) 845–3957.

Nearby, the Fort Payne Depot at 105 Fifth Street Northeast houses the *Fort Payne Depot Museum* (256–845–5714). Completed in 1891, the handsome Romanesque depot of pink sandstone served as a passenger station until 1970. The museum's permanent collection includes artwork, early farm equipment, pottery, glassware, and a restored caboose containing railroad memorabilia. You'll also see beaded moccasins, Iroquois baskets made of birch bark trimmed with porcupine quills, and Mayan and pre-Columbian artifacts dating from A.D. 400 to 800. An area resident willed to the museum her Cherokee, Hopi, Pueblo, Apache, and Seminole artifacts. Be sure to notice the collection of dioramas that were once part of a traveling medicine show and an unusual bed that belonged to local resident Granny Dollar, whose lifetime spanned more than a century. The museum is open 10:00 A.M. to 4:00 P.M. on Monday, Wednesday, and Friday. Sunday hours are 2:00 to 4:00 P.M. Admission is free, but donations are welcome.

Before leaving the "Sock Capital of the World," stop by *Big Mill Antique Mall* (256–845–3380) and browse among yesteryear's treasures. Located at 151 Eighth Street Northeast, this 1889 structure, once home to Fort Payne's first hosiery mill, now houses antiques, collectibles, reproductions, and a deli. Mall hours are 10:00 A.M. to 4:00 P.M. Monday through Saturday and 1:00 to 4:00 P.M. on Sunday.

Also housed here, you'll find *The Grill at the Mill* (256–845–3820), a full-service restaurant with loft and outdoor seating. You can choose from a variety of beverages and menu items here. Try the filet tips, the garlic butter shrimp with fried green tomatoes and a remoulade sauce, or another of the restaurant's delectable specialties. Hours are 4:00 P.M. to midnight Monday through Friday and 4:00 P.M. to 2:00 A.M. Saturday. Economical to moderate.

While traveling through *Collinsville,* you might want to consider spending some time at *Trade Day,* an event that draws some 30,000 or so bargain hunters and browsers every Saturday. Spread over sixty-five acres near Collinsville on U.S. Highway 11 South, this weekly occasion has had a country carnival flavor since it first cranked up in 1950. Vendors start setting up their wares at the crack of dawn and stay until early afternoon. "We offer today's collectibles at yesterday's prices," says owner Charles Cook. Sightseers can munch on snacks such as boiled peanuts and corn dogs while surveying displays of wares from antiques and crafts to fresh vegetables and houseplants. Swans, ducks, rabbits, geese, goats, peacocks, hunting dogs, game cocks, and exotic pets often find new owners here. Parking costs 50 cents, but admission is free. For more information call (256) 524–2536 or (888) 524–2536.

Cherokee Country

From Collinsville it's just a short jaunt to **Leesburg** and **the secret Bed & Breakfast Lodge** (256–523–3825). Located at 2356 Highway 68 West on a mountaintop overlooking Weiss Lake, the lodge boasts a view that won't stop. "Last summer our guests saw Fourth-of-July fireworks in three cities from our rooftop pool," says Diann Cruickshank, who with husband, Carl, owns this property perched on the eastern brow of Lookout Mountain.

The view, the sunsets and sunrises, and the deer (which guests can feed) make the secret a special place. Carl cooks a delicious country breakfast, which Diann serves on a 10-foot-wide round table topped by a lazy Susan. You'll see a collection of porcelain dolls made by Diann's mother and a showcase containing Carl's interesting memorabilia. Bring your camera and prepare for surprises galore here because Diann delights in acquiring the unusual. (Not to divulge any secrets, but one surprise may leave you feeling a bit like Goldilocks.) For each guest room, the Sugar Shack, and other theme cottages on the grounds, Diann compiled a booklet of her engaging anecdotes along with recommended local attractions and restaurants. Movie buffs will find a video library containing more than 300 titles. Moderate to deluxe rates. Visit the secret Bed & Breakfast Lodge via the Web at www.bbonline.com/al/thesecret.

Cherokee County, home of **Weiss Lake,** offers beautiful scenery. Add a chunk of Little River Canyon to this 30,200-acre lake bordered by 447 miles of shoreline, and you've got plenty of recreational options. Famous for its fine fishing, the Crappie Capital of the World also offers ample opportunities for catching bass and catfish. The water attracts large populations of wintering birds such as seagulls, wild ducks, and cranes.

While exploring Cherokee County's many scenic spots, don't overlook **Cornwall Furnace Park,** about 3 miles east of Cedar Bluff. To reach the park, take State Route 9 east and turn left onto Cherokee County Route 92. Then make another left onto a gravel road and follow the signs. A flight of steps leads down a steep bank (covered by lilies in spring) to the picturesque stone stack that stands about 5 feet tall—all that remains of a structure built to supply crude iron to be transformed into Confederate arms. General Sherman's forces destroyed the furnace works during the Civil War.

The well-kept grounds offer attractive picnicking facilities and a short nature trail. The park, which opens at daylight and closes at sundown, can be visited year-round. Running water is available, but there are no bathroom facilities. Admission is free.

Afterward take State Route 9 to **Centre,** about 6 miles away. Next to the courthouse stands the **Cherokee County Historical Museum** (256–927–7835), located at 101 East Main Street. This museum, formerly a department store, houses historical objects and memorabilia that characterize the area's past. You'll see a Pennsylvania Amish town buggy. Other exhibits include Bob Hope's first typewriter, Grand Ole Opry memorabilia, wagons, housewares, antique telephones, Civil War relics, early appliances, Native American artifacts, a printing press, a telephone switchboard, a doll collection, and a bale of cotton. The basement contains a blacksmith shop as well as old farm equipment such as plows, mowing machines, cotton planters, and tractors. Modest admission. The museum is open from 9:30 A.M. to 4:00 P.M. on Tuesday and from 8:30 A.M. to 4:00 P.M. Wednesday through Saturday.

Continue toward *Gadsden,* situated in Lookout Mountain's foothills. Turkeytown, named for Chief Little Turkey during the late 1700s, is a tiny community on the Coosa River's banks near Gadsden that once served as the capital of the Cherokee nation.

Although long known as one of the state's leading industrial centers with abundant deposits of iron, manganese, coal, and limestone, Gadsden is gaining recognition for its rich Cherokee legacy The Turkeytown Association of the Cherokee, a nonprofit organization, works to preserve and promote the region's Native American heritage.

Downtown at Gadsden's Broad Street entrance to the Coosa River Bridge stands the statue of Emma Sansom, who, at age sixteen, helped Confederate troops find a place to ford Black Creek after Union forces crossed and burned the local bridge.

While in Gadsden, stop by the *Mary G. Hardin Center for Cultural Arts* (256–543–2787) on the corner of Fifth and Broad Streets. The complex, with a bold gold-and-black exterior in a Mondrian-like design, offers plays, concerts, lectures, classes, and art exhibits. To see the current art shows, take the escalator to the second floor. Before returning downstairs, be sure to notice the model railroad layout depicting Gadsden

alabamatrivia

Alabama ranks among the top ten states with conditions most favorable for starting a small business.

during the 1940s and 1950s with trains traveling past miniature reproductions of more than one hundred historical structures, including the Gulf States Steel complex. The complex also houses the Courtyard Café. Modest admission. Call for information on current exhibits and hours or visit the Web site at www.culturalarts.org.

Adjacent to the Center for Cultural Arts, the historic Kyle Building now houses the *Imagination Place Children's Museum.* Youngsters can play in

Center Pieces

Members of the Cultural Arts League of Gadsden worked diligently on a cookbook called *Center Pieces,* which "tells the story of the Mary G. Hardin Center for Cultural Arts by using each chapter to describe a 'piece' of the whole." The handsome publication contains illustrations of creations by nationally recognized floral designer Benny Campbell, owner of Attalla Florist and Landscape.

For a tantalizing preview, try the following recipe from the appetizer section. Each time I make this treat for my guests, it gets rave reviews. Pick up a souvenir copy of the book for yourself and get some extras for gifts.

Nova Scotia Salmon Mold

1 envelope unflavored gelatin

¼ cup cold water

½ cup whipping cream

1 (8-ounce) package cream cheese, softened

1 cup sour cream

1 teaspoon Worcestershire sauce

Dash of hot sauce

1 teaspoon fresh lemon juice

2 tablespoons green onions, finely chopped

1 tablespoon fresh parsley, finely chopped

1 tablespoon prepared horseradish

8 ounces Nova Scotia salmon, chopped

1 (4-ounce) jar red caviar, drained

Sprinkle gelatin over ¼ cup cold water in a small saucepan; let stand 1 minute. Cook over low heat, stirring constantly, for 2 minutes or until gelatin dissolves. Stir in whipping cream.

Beat gelatin mixture and cream cheese at medium speed with an electric mixer for 5 minutes or until mixture is smooth. Add sour cream, Worcestershire sauce, hot sauce, and lemon juice; beat at low speed 1 minute to blend.

Fold in green onions, parsley, horseradish, and salmon. Gently fold in caviar. Pour into a lightly greased 3-quart plastic or ceramic mold. Chill 3 hours or until firm.

Unmold and serve. Yield: 20 servings.

a life-size tree house or a kid-size city complete with Grandma's House, a bank, grocery store, doctor's office, fire station, and other interesting sites. Hours are 9:00 A.M. to 5:00 P.M. Monday through Friday; 10:00 A.M. to 5:00 P.M. Saturday; and 1:00 to 5:00 P.M. Sunday. Admission is free for kids three and under; a modest fee is charged for others.

At **Noccalula Falls and Park** (256–549–4663), situated on Lookout Mountain Parkway (and easily reached from I–59), the bronze statue of a legendary Cherokee princess stands ready to leap to her destiny in a rushing stream 90 feet below. Legend says Noccalula loved a brave of her own tribe and chose to die rather than marry the wealthier suitor selected by her father.

Explore the park's botanical gardens, especially attractive in spring with masses of azaleas in bloom. You can either walk through the park or take a mini-train ride to see the Pioneer Homestead, a village of authentic log structures including a barn, blacksmith shop, gristmill, school, and cabins moved here from various sites in Appalachia. Also here you'll find the restored Gilliland-Reese Covered Bridge and a miniature golf course.

Nearby are campgrounds, hiking trails, picnic tables, play areas, and a pool. The park closes from November through mid-March. Hours are from 9:00 A.M. to sundown. Admission. The campground number is (256) 543–7412.

If you're in the area on a weekend, you may want to schedule a jaunt to **Mountain Top Flea Market,** which is open every Sunday from 5:00 A.M. to about 3:00 or 4:00 P.M. year-round. You'll find this all-day market with some 1,500 dealers about 6 miles west of Attalla on U.S. Highway 278. For more information call Janie Terrell at (800) 535–2286.

Attalla, home of the world's first hydroelectric generator and birthplace of Alabama Power, lures antiques shoppers. Clustered in the downtown area are more than a dozen shops. At **The Cozy Nest** (256–570–0200), 426 Fourth Street Northwest, Vanessa Durham features full-service decorating along with a selection of antiques, primitives, and accessories for home and garden. Continuing down the street, you'll find more vintage items at **Somewhere in Time** (256–538–1899), 402 Fourth Street Northwest, and **Beulah Land Antique Mall** (256–538–1585), 216 Fourth Street Northwest. Call ahead before traveling because dealers keep their own hours, and these vary from shop to shop.

To reach Boaz, located on Sand Mountain, take U.S. Highway 431 north from Attalla.

Sand Mountain

A foothill of the Appalachians, Sand Mountain covers an area 25 miles wide by 75 miles long. Atop this plateau you'll find **Boaz Shopper's Paradise**—so many stores, so little time. Ranked among America's top outlet centers, **Boaz** attracts people from across the country. Shoppers can browse through dozens of stores and specialty shops in the town's outlet centers. For discount coupons and maps, check out the Official Outlet Information office on Billy Dyar Boulevard, the Vanity Fair courtesy desk, or the Tanger Welcome Center.

Strange as It Sounds

Buck's Pocket State Park (256–659–2000), a secluded expanse of rugged nature that spills into three counties—DeKalb, Jackson, and Marshall—is rich in botanical beauty and local lore. Covering more than 2,000 acres of craggy canyon scenery on the western side of Sand Mountain, the park is located near Grove Oak.

For a magnificent overview of the entire canyon, head first to Point Rock, the park's highest area and a wonderful place for picnicking and hiking. According to local legend, early Native Americans took advantage of the area's geography to help them acquire their food supply by driving deer over the edge at Point Rock right into the "pocket." Both spring, with its plentiful supply of wildflowers, and fall make great times to visit.

To reach the headquarters and campground, you'll descend from Point Rock about 800 feet via a curving road to the canyon's base. The bottom line on the park's wooden sign says: HAVEN FOR DEFEATED POLITICIANS. Buck's Pocket acquired its reputation as a refuge for election losers after "Big Jim" Folsom, a former Alabama governor, lost a senate bid and announced his intention to go to Buck's Pocket, get his thoughts together, and "lick his wounds." He invited other defeated candidates to join him at this favorite retreat.

In addition to trails for hiking and rocks for climbing, recreation options include swimming and fishing at South Sauty Creek. Also, nearby Morgan's Cove offers a fishing pier and boat launching ramps. Rappelers and rock climbers should first stop by headquarters for a permit, good for a year. Write to Buck's Pocket at 393 County Road 174, Grove Oak 35975. For reservations call (800) ALA–PARK.

Approximately 40,000 people descend on Boaz, population 8,000, for the annual Harvest Festival. The weekend celebration features an antique car show, musical entertainment, an Indian powwow, and some 200 booths brimming with handcrafted items ranging from birdhouses, cornshuck dolls, and crazy quilts to paintings, leather items, and furniture. Music runs the gamut from bluegrass, country, and gospel to jazz. For more information on the outlets or the festival, contact the Boaz Chamber of Commerce, P.O. Box 563, Boaz 35957, or call (256) 593–8154 or (800) 746–7262.

During your shopping spree, you might enjoy browsing among items from yesteryear at **Adams' Antiques** (256–593–0406) at 10310 State Route 168. Hours are 10:00 A.M. to 4:30 P.M. Tuesday through Saturday.

A favorite with both locals and visiting shoppers, **The Station House Grille** (256–593–6567), located at 101 East Mann Avenue, takes its name from the adjacent railroad-track location. The brick building originally served as a warehouse for cotton storage during the 1920s and later as a lumber supply house. Interior accents include knotty-pine paneling, framed *Life* magazine covers, old movie posters, BOURBON STREET and FRENCH QUARTER signs, and sports memorabilia.

Boaz natives Stan and Johnna Morris offer mouthwatering cuisine with a Cajun accent. Basically self-taught, Stan started cooking in his family's cafe. Later, while based in Baton Rouge with an oil company, he expanded his repertoire to embrace Cajun cuisine. Many of the menu items—from appetizers, salads, and sandwiches (including that New Orleans favorite—po'boys) to entrees and desserts—reflect that influence.

Near the entrance a blackboard announces daily specials. Lunch might feature shrimp Creole, crawfish étouffée, or Louisiana-style fried catfish strips. For dinner the chef's specials could range from rainbow trout Orleans, mahimahi, or Jamaican jerk pork chops to pepper-encrusted filet mignon with soft-shell crab.

The staff offers a variety of freshly made soups like chicken, sausage, and andouille gumbo. Other specialities include Stan's award-winning jambalaya, and prime rib and steaks, prepared with a secret recipe of Cajun seasonings. The signature bread pudding with rum sauce or a slice of homemade cake

Albertville's Downtown Pleasures

Whether your sweet tooth yearns for a French vanilla cappuccino, Godiva chocolates, or a wedge of cheesecake, you'll find all this and more at *Main Street's Coffee, Cappuccino and Ice Cream* (256–878–1948) in downtown Albertville. What's more, you can sip your espresso or latte at a sidewalk table and watch the world go by. In fact, when I last did this, I overheard a woman at the next table say to her companion, "Kinda reminds you of Paris, doesn't it?"

Well, maybe that's a bit of a stretch, but Albertville does have a sister city by the same name in France, a fact that got some attention during the 1992 Winter Olympics when the local chamber of commerce received requests for tickets to certain events.

When Alabama's temperatures crank up to the 90s (as they are prone to do during summer), you can sip your frosty, frothy drink in the cool shop, surrounded by all manner of tempting handmade pastries, attractive gift displays, and possibly two or three tables of bridge players.

A woman who dashed in for a couple of take-away desserts wound up in a thirty-minute conversation, and that often happens here where owners Carrie and Donald Conley have created the inviting atmosphere of a neighborhood coffee house. The Conleys frequently host performing musicians, art exhibits, and special interest groups.

Located at 118 East Main Street, the business also houses a candy and gift shop. Hours run from 8:00 A.M. to 5:00 P.M. Monday through Friday and 9:00 A.M. to 3:00 P.M. Saturday.

make delectable dessert options. So take a shopping break and enjoy some Cajun cookery. Lunch hours run 11:00 A.M. until 2:00 P.M. Monday through Friday, and dinner hours start at 5:00 P.M. on Friday and 4:00 P.M. Saturday with a closing time of 9:00 P.M. Economical to moderate.

Afterward continue about 5 miles north to **Albertville,** the "Heart of Sand Mountain." Albertville's former Freedom Festival, chosen many times by the Southeast Tourism Society as one of July's Top Twenty Events, has evolved into an event called **Taste of Freedom BBQ Cookoff,** which draws a large Independence Day crowd.

alabamatrivia

Boaz, population 8,000, was named for a biblical character in the Book of Ruth.

For a look at some of the city's lovely historic homes, drive along East Main Street off US 431. At the street's end stands the 1891 Albertville Depot, which is listed on the National Register of Historic Places. The depot now houses a senior citizens center.

Albertville acquired its title as "Fire Hydrant Capital of the World" because the local Mueller Company turns liquefied steel into dome-topped fire hydrants and ships them to countries near and far. In front of the chamber of commerce building, you'll see a special nickel-plated version that marks Mueller's one-millionth locally manufactured fire hydrant.

For a sampling of some of the town's interesting stores, head to the **Little Village Shop** (256–878–6400). Located at 123 Sand Mountain Drive NW, the shop offers unique gifts, housewares, china, and Waterford crystal. Hours are 10:00 A.M. to 5:00 P.M. Monday through Friday and 9:00 A.M. to 3:00 P.M Saturday.

At 113 Sand Mountain Drive, you'll find **Whitten's** (256–878–3901), a clothing store that features upscale town and country fashions for women and men. Hours are 9:00 A.M. to 5:00 P.M. Monday through Saturday. The shop closes on Thursday afternoon.

When visiting a new place, some travelers like to search out a restaurant where the locals eat. Here it's **The Food Basket** (256–878–1261), located just off US 431 at 715 Sampson Circle. The Daniel family has been feeding folks in Albertville since 1959.

Noted for its country ham and homemade biscuits, the restaurant draws a big breakfast crowd. Lunch specialties include Sand Mountain fried chicken and home-style fresh vegetables. Dinners feature steaks and seafood. The restaurant's original salad dressing and sweet rolls, served at dinner, prove perennial favorites. Economical to moderate. Hours are 5:00 A.M. to 3:00 P.M. Sunday through Wednesday and 5:00 A.M. to 9:00 P.M. Thursday through Saturday.

To learn more about Alabama's rural heritage, stop by the Albertville Public Library, at 200 Jackson Street, and buy a copy of *The Good Ole Days* by Jesse Culp—broadcaster, author, speaker, syndicated columnist, and former newspaper editor. In his living-history book, Mr. Culp discusses such topics as blue

The Old Meeting House in Douglas

While whipping up a big pot of her tasty chicken and dumplings at **The Old Meeting House Restaurant,** Deborah Powell sometimes reflects on her Sunday mornings spent attending First Baptist Church here as a child. The congregation grew and moved to larger quarters, and the building served other religious groups and also as a residence and an auction house. When the property in Douglas, a hamlet southwest of Albertville, came on the market several years ago, Deborah toyed with the idea of transforming the one-hundred-plus-year-old structure into a restaurant.

"If I buy it, will you help me with the restaurant?" Deborah asked her sister, Belinda Arrington, who agreed on the condition she would not have to cook.

"Our mother was a wonderful cook, and so is Deborah," said Belinda. "And our dad has been mayor of Douglas." The family spent about five months renovating the building and found it basically sound. They retained the original floors and knotty-pine walls and added some church pews, a pulpit, and an upright piano along with other antiques. An armoire holds Deborah's mother's wedding dress and vintage hats, and old family photos are displayed along with other memorabilia.

Daily house specialties might include chicken casserole, meatloaf, beef tips with rice, chicken and dressing, or made-from-scratch chicken and dumplings. The dumplings recipe has never been written down or measured, or else Deborah would have shared it with you. Instead, she provided her recipe for another favorite here—strawberry cobbler, which I just made for a church supper—there was hardly enough left over to bring home.

To dip into some down home cooking, visit **The Old Meeting House Restaurant** at the intersection of State Routes 75 and 168. Hours are 6:00 A.M. to 2:00 P.M. Monday through Friday; 5:00 to 8:00 P.M. Friday and Saturday; and 11:00 A.M. to 2:00 P.M. on Sunday. Economical.

Strawberry Cobbler

2 sticks of butter or margarine

2 cups sugar (reserve two tablespoons of sugar to sprinkle on top)

2 cups all-purpose flour

2 cups buttermilk

1 heaping pint strawberries, hulled and sliced

Melt butter and pour into baking dish or pan. Mix sugar, flour, and buttermilk, and pour on top of butter. Add strawberries. Sprinkle sugar on top. Preheat oven and cook at 350 degrees about 35 minutes or until crust turns golden brown. Yields 10 to 12 servings.

back spellers, log rollings, settin' hens, funeral home fans, and cow pasture baseball, and his gift for reminiscing brings back a bit of yesteryear.

Take time to drive along some of Marshall County's rural roads. Along the way you'll notice fertile rolling farmland and chicken houses. Broilers, eggs, and turkeys produced on the state's individual farms add up to a billion-dollar poultry industry. In broiler production, Alabama ranks second in the nation.

When your taste buds crave Cajun cuisine and you can't make it to Louisiana, then stop by *Papa Dubi's Cajun Kitchen* (256–894–7878) on the Albertville-Guntersville line. Located at 3931 Brasher's Chapel Road (next to Lowe's), the eatery offers seafood gumbo, jambalaya, red beans and rice with sausage, Creole dishes, po'boys, and more.

While living in Germantown, Tennessee, Dan and Lisa Younghouse hit the road to celebrate their twenty-fifth wedding anniversary. After visiting the Shrine of the Most Blessed Sacrament of Our Lady of the Angels Monastery near Hanceville, they toured the surrounding area—never dreaming they would soon become Alabama residents. But that's exactly what happened when they fell in love with the area's beauty while staying at Lake Guntersville State Park Lodge.

Their restaurant takes its name from Lisa's grandfather, a Cajun descendant, who lived in Gulfport, Mississippi, and the recipes—including the one for tasty gumbo—came from her grandmother, Nanny Dubi. Parents of seven, the couple and various family members have some restaurant experience, but starting their own eatery represented a leap of faith. However, the locals kept them so busy they had to expand soon after opening. The kids pitch in to help with this family venture. In fact their son, who previously worked for a restaurant on the Mississippi Gulf Coast, contributes Creole dishes and his steak-cooking skills. Hours are 11:00 A.M. to 8:00 P.M. daily. Economical to moderate.

Lake Country

While in the area, consider headquartering at *Lake Guntersville State Park* (256–571–5440 or 800–548–4553), located just off State Route 227 at 1155 Lodge Drive. Perched on Appalachian bluffs about 6 miles northeast of Guntersville, the park lodge offers panoramic views and 35 miles of hiking trails. You can roam almost 6,600 acres of woodland—much of it undisturbed—and follow paths once used by the Cherokee.

The park naturalist gives guided hiking tours on request, pointing out local flora and fauna. Deer often dash across the road in front of cars and roam the lodge's grounds. In addition to hiking, park activities include camping, canoeing, fishing, and boating. An Eagle Festival takes place in January.

Resort facilities include a restaurant, a lounge, motel rooms, chalets, and campsites ranging from primitive to fully equipped and modern (that is, complete with utility hookups, tables, grills, bathhouses, hot showers, play areas, and a camp store). You'll also find tennis courts, a championship eighteen-hole golf course, a helipad, canoe and boat rentals, and 7 miles of scenic drives. Except for the lodge and restaurant, the park facilities will remain open to the public during its upcoming renovation, scheduled for completion by late 2006.

Continue to nearby Guntersville Lake, a Tennessee Valley Authority (TVA) creation, where sailboats and fishing vessels dot shining expanses of open water. "The most striking thing about Guntersville," says local newspaper editor Sam Harvey, "is that it's a country town with a lake all around it. Of the five approaches to Guntersville, four take you across water." With 69,100 acres of water, *Guntersville* bills itself as a vacationer's paradise. Truly a haven for water-sports enthusiasts, the area offers boating, swimming, skiing, and fishing. The Bass Anglers Sportsman Society calls Lake Guntersville "one of the finest sport fishing lakes in America," and the Alabama Bassmasters stage invitational tournaments here.

Drive through the downtown area and stop by Lake Guntersville Chamber of Commerce and Welcome Center (256–582–3612), which is in a house with a beckoning front porch at 200 Gunter Avenue near the big river bridge. Here you can pick up brochures on area attractions and inquire about current happenings. For instance, the local theater group The Whole Backstage mounts a mix of productions throughout the year, so check on possible performances during your visit.

Atop a hill, *Lake Guntersville Bed and Breakfast* (256–505–0133) at 2204 Scott Street offers suites with private entrances and more lovely water views from its two levels of wraparound porches. While living in Fairfield, Connecticut, former Guntersville resident Carol Dravis dreamed of returning. She got to do just that when an unexpected opportunity came along to purchase the handsome circa-1910 white brick home.

Carol picks up guests who arrive by boat and serves a bountiful breakfast—on the veranda when weather permits. A full gourmet-style breakfast might feature her special European pancakes, beautiful and puffy with various toppings, or a sausage-and-cheese strata. Accompaniments include breakfast breads and a special mixture of fruit juices called morning sunshine. Ask about Carol's cookbook, which contains some of her guests' favorite recipes. Based on individual interests, Carol recommends local activities and provides directions to nearby walking trails and other scenic spots. In the foyer you'll see a small gift shop with works by local artists and writers.

Carol offers several special-occasion packages such as birding, pamper yourself (with one-hour massages), Valentine, anniversary, birthday, theater, etc.

Angels in Arab

One spring day, a friend and I drove to Guntersville for an art exhibit and lunch. Walking into a local restaurant, we saw two angels, dressed in flowing white tunics with gold accessories—which included halos. One of the angel-women wore gold combat boots.

We soon found out the B-Team Angels, Paula Joslin and Kay Jennings, came from nearby Arab. They were "on a quest to earn their wings by spreading happiness." Wafting a wand in our direction, the angels then glided outside, where traffic screeched to a halt.

A year later I met the B-Team Angels and learned their league had grown and their happiness ministry had expanded. Each month, for example, they surprise a local resident with an Earth Angel award, honoring people who bring happiness to others, often without recognition. On Valentine's Day the angelic band entertains at area nursing homes, churches, conferences, and retreats. They charge nothing for their programs of songs, skits, puppet shows, and birthday parties.

"We feel that sharing love with others is what life's all about," writes Kay, in her introduction to *The B-Team Angels' Quest,* a book filled with Paula's whimsical photo-collages featuring 700 Arab residents. (A professional artist, Paula works in all mediums and has won numerous awards in juried shows.) Proceeds from the book sales help defray costs incurred for this ministry—gifts, certificates, photography, costumes, transportation, etc. Also, the group has recently published a cookbook called *Angel Food,* featuring some heavenly recipes.

Arab resident Ralph Hammond (also Alabama Poet Laureate emeritus) describes the angels as a "wonderful group of girls, who have added a luster to Arab." So if you see an angel flitting about Arab, you know why: She's out to brighten someone's day—maybe yours. If you need to speak to a B-Team Angel or order a cookbook, call (256) 586–TIME. Or catch up with this angelic band at www.bteamangels.com.

One guest wrote, "How wonderful to have found such a thoughtful, talented hostess! Your charming B&B has been a true lagniappe [a lower Alabama expression meaning something extra special], and we've discovered again the great delight of porch-sitting. Thank you for a lovely and delicious visit." Visit Lake Guntersville B&B's Web site at www.lakeguntersvillebedandbreakfast.com. Standard to moderate rates.

Don't miss nearby Fant's Department Store at 355 Gunter Avenue. Still locally known as Hammer's, the rambling structure with original wooden floors offers a bargain basement and surprises galore. (You'll enjoy browsing through Hammer's stores in Albertville and Boaz, too.)

Step inside the Guntersville Post Office to see the mural that depicts de Soto's arrival in the area. Located at the north end of the lobby, the large can-

Strange as It Sounds

If a boat outing fits into your travel schedule, try to catch the evening exodus of bats from **Hambrick Cave.** Some 350,000 American gray bats, a protected species, consider this cave home from late April to mid-October (although the females migrate the first of August). You'll probably join a bevy of other boaters, clustered around the water-level cave mouth at the base of a bluff, all waiting for the sunset performance as a cloud of bats swoops overhead on its nocturnal foraging flight. Going downriver toward Guntersville Dam, look for a cave (marked by a small overhead sign) on your right. Flashlights are prohibited. (For more information on this and other area bat caves, call the **Wheeler Wildlife Refuge** at 256–350–6639.)

vas with life-size figures of Native Americans, costumed Spanish, and spirited horses can be seen at any time.

Housed in the historic Glover Hotel at 524 Gunter Avenue, *Restaurant La Strada* (256–505–2250) promises its patrons "a piece of Europe in the heart of Dixie." On the premises you'll see an ongoing art exhibition with items available for purchase.

Owners Beatrice and Markus Bischof, a delightful Swiss couple who gained a loyal following with the fine fare served at their former site on US 431 (now home of the Italian-style restaurant, Sonarpos), welcome guests for lunch and dinner. They offer a varied cuisine and fine wines, both domestic and imported. Dinner selections that include seafood, gourmet pizzas from wood-fired ovens, and more. Dinner is served from 5:00 to 9:30 P.M. Monday through Thursday and until 10:30 P.M. Friday and Saturday. Standard to moderate.

Your sightseeing excursion may take you past the *Guntersville Museum and Cultural Center* (256–571–7597) now at the corner of O'Brig and Debow Streets, but the facility will soon relocate to the old Armory on Ringold Street. This handsome structure of rough limestone and mortar dates to 1936 and will house an art gallery and archives, with collections of documents, photos, and other items relating to the town's early days. You'll find a Tennessee Valley Authority Room, a River Room, and an Indian Room with displays of Native American projectile points and other artifacts. The museum also hosts traveling exhibits. Hours are 10:00 A.M. to 4:00 P.M. Tuesday through Friday and 1:00 to 4:00 P.M. on Saturday and Sunday. Admission is free. See www.guntersvilleal.org/museum.htm.

Other local events include a series of summer evening lakeside concerts on Tuesdays, and the MOVA Arts Festival featuring a songwriter competition. The latter, a fall event presented by the Mountain Valley Arts Council, also features a juried art exhibit, children's activities, and lots of food and drink. For more information or to see a current art exhibit, stop by the Mountain Valley Arts Council (MVAC) office at 300 Gunter Avenue, or call (256) 582–1454. For an updated schedule, see www.mountainvalleyartscouncil.org.

Guntersville's popular two-day *Art on the Lake Show* draws crowds each April.

On the Saturday before Labor Day, *St. William's Seafood Festival* features more than 5,000 pounds of fresh shrimp, oysters, crab, flounder, and other fish imported from coastal waters. Parish members prepare the seafood, which includes making about 400 gallons of gumbo.

For some good old-fashioned fun and a mess of "poke salat," take State Route 69 to *Arab* during the first weekend in May. When the Arab Liars' Club (the self-appointed title for a group of local men who meet daily for coffee at L Rancho Cafe) came up with the idea of the *Poke Salat Festival,* they probably did not expect it to become an annual affair with everything from street dances and craft shows to beauty contests and drama productions.

In downtown Arab, notice the weather-beaten Farmer's Exchange, a local landmark that now houses a garden center. Also, you may wish to explore the city's dozen or so antiques shops.

At the southern edge of town on Arad Thompson Road, you'll find the inviting Arab City Park with the Shoal Creek Trail, ball fields, a pool, and modern, well-equipped playground. The park is also home to several historical structures including the Hunt School, Rice Church, Elvin Light Museum, and Smith's Country Store.

Afterward head toward Huntsville to launch an exploration of Alabama's northwestern region.

Places to Stay in Northeast Alabama

ALBERTVILLE

Jameson Inn
315 Martling Road
(256) 891–2600 or
(800) 526–3766

ATTALLA

Days Inn of Attalla
801 Cleveland Avenue
(256) 538–7861 or
(800) DAYSINN

Econo Lodge
507 Cherry Street
(256) 538–9925 or
(800) 424–4777

BOAZ

Key West Inn
10535 State Route 168
(256) 593–0800 or
(800) 833–0555

FORT PAYNE

DeSoto State Park
265 County Road 951
(256) 845–5380 or
(800) 568–8840

GADSDEN

Gadsden Inn & Suites
200 Albert Rains Boulevard
(256) 543–7240 or
(800) 637–5678

Hampton Inn
129 River Road
(256) 546–2337 or
(800) HAMPTON

GUNTERSVILLE

**Hampton Inn of Lake
Guntersville**
14451 U.S. Highway 431
(256) 582–4176

**Holiday Inn
Lake Guntersville**
2140 Gunter Avenue
(256) 582–2220

**Lake Guntersville Bed
and Breakfast**
2204 Scott Street
(256) 505–0133

**Lake Guntersville
State Park Lodge**
1155 Lodge Drive
(256) 571–5440 or
(800) ALA–PARK

FOR MORE INFORMATION ABOUT NORTHEAST ALABAMA

**Alabama Mountain Lake Tourist
Association**
25062 North Street
P.O. Box 1075
Mooresville 35649
(256) 350–3500 or (800) 648–5381
www.alabamamountainlakes.org
info@alabamamountainlakes.org
This organization covers sixteen north
Alabama counties that are home to
some one hundred attractions
in a 100-mile radius.

DeKalb County Tourist Association
1503 Glenn Boulevard Southwest
P.O. Box 681165
Fort Payne 35968
(256) 845–3957 or (888) 805–4740
www.tourdekalb.com
pattyt@mindspring.com

Gadsden/Etowah Tourism Board, Inc.
105-B Locust Street
P.O. Box 8269
Gadsden 35902-8269
(256) 549–0351 or (888) 565–0411
www.tourism@gadsden-etowahtourism
board.com

**The Greater Jackson County
Chamber of Commerce**
407 East Willow Street
P.O. Box 973
Scottsboro 35768
(256) 259–5500 or (800) 259–5508
www.jacksoncountychamber.com
chamber@scottsboro.org

**Huntsville/Madison County
Convention & Visitors Bureau**
500 Church Street
Huntsville 35801
(256) 551–2230 or (800) SPACE–4–U
www.huntsville.org
info@huntsville.org

**Marshall County
Convention & Visitors Bureau**
200 Gunter Avenue
P.O. Box 711
Guntersville 35976
(256) 582–7015 or (800) 582–6282
www.marshallcountycvb.com
marshallcountycvb@charter
internet.com

HUNTSVILLE

Bevill Conference Center and Hotel
550 Sparkman Drive
(256) 721–9428 or
(888) 721–9428

Courtyard by Marriott
4804 University Drive
(256) 837–1400 or
(800) 321–2211

Dogwood Manor
707 Chase Road
(256) 859–3946

Hampton Inn
4815 University Drive
(256) 830–9400 or
(800) HAMPTON

Holiday Inn Huntsville
401 Williams Avenue
(256) 533–1400 or
(800) 533–1400

Huntsville Marriott
#5 Tranquility Base
(256) 830–2222 or
(888) 299–5174

LEESBURG

the secret Bed & Breakfast Lodge
2356 State Route 68 West
(256) 523–3825

MENTONE

Mentone Springs Hotel
6114 State Route Highway 117
(256) 634–4040

Mountain Laurel Inn
624 Road 948
(256) 634–4673 or
(800) 889–4244

Raven Haven
651 County Road 644
(256) 634–4310

PISGAH

The Lodge at Gorham's Bluff
101 Gorham Drive/
Gorham's Bluff
(256) 451–VIEW

SCOTTSBORO

Goose Pond Colony
417 Ed Hembree Drive
(256) 259–2884 or
(800) 268–2884

Ivy Creek Inn Bed and Breakfast
985 Carlton Road
(256) 505-0108

Jameson Inn
208 Micah Way
U.S. Highway 72
(256) 574–6666 or
(800) 526–3766

VALLEY HEAD

Winston Place
353 Railroad Avenue
(256) 635–6381 or
(888) 4–WINSTON

Woodhaven
390 Lowry Road
(256) 635–6438

Places to Eat in Northeast Alabama

ALBERTVILLE

Asia Garden Restaurant
210 State Route 75 North
(256) 891–1616

Catfish Cabin
8524 U.S. Highway 431 North
(256) 878–8170

The Food Basket
715 Sampson Circle
(256) 878–1261

Giovanni's Pizza Italian Restaurant
711 Miller Street
(256) 878–7881

The Lumpkin House
699 North Carlisle Street
(256) 891–8900

Papa Dubi's Cajun Kitchen
3931 Brasher's Chapel Road
(256) 894–7878

ARAB

Three Guys' Grill
209 Third Avenue
(256) 931–GUYS

BOAZ

Ryan's Family Steak House
568 U.S. Highway 431
(256) 593–1436

The Station House Grille
101 East Mann Avenue
(256) 593–6567

CENTRE

Tony's Steak Barn
804 Alexis Road
(256) 927–2844

DOUGLAS

The Old Meeting House Restaurant
Intersection of State Routes 75 and 168
(256) 840–1571

FORT PAYNE

The Grill at the Mill
151 8th Street Northeast
(256) 845–3820

GADSDEN

The Choice
531 Broad Street
(256) 546–8513

Courtyard Cafe
501 Broad Street
(256) 547–1066

Top O' the River
1606 Rainbow Drive
(256) 547–9817

GRANT

Mi Mi's Café
On Main Street at the corner
of Third Avenue
(256) 728–7483

The Squirrel Nest
2219 Baker Mountain Road
(256) 571–0324

GUNTERSVILLE

El Camino Real
14274 U.S. Highway 431
(256) 571–9089

Neena's Lakeside Grille
Inside the Holiday Inn
2140 Gunter Avenue
(256) 505–0550

Restaurant La Strada
524 Gunter Avenue
(256) 582–2250

Top O' the River
7004 Val Monte Drive
(256) 582–4567

HUNTSVILLE

Cafe Berlin
964 Airport Road
(256) 880–9920

801 Franklin
801 Franklin Street
(256) 519–8019

Green Hills Grille
5100 Sanderson Street
(256) 837–8282

Jazz Factory
109 Northside Square
(256) 539–1919

Landry's Seafood House
5101 Governor's
House Drive
(256) 864–0000

Ol' Heidelberg
6125 University Drive
(256) 922–0556

Surin of Thailand
975 Airport Road
(256) 213–9866

MADISON

Main Street Café
101 Main Street
(256) 461–8096

MENTONE

**Cragsmere Manna
Restaurant**
17871 DeKalb
County Road 89
(256) 634–4677 or
(256) 845–2209

Dessie's Kountry Chef
5951 State Route ⌐17
(256) 634–4232

**Log Cabin
Restaurant and Deli**
6080 State Route 117
(256) 634–4560

**The Wildflower Cafe
(in the Hitching Post)**
County Road 89 and
Alabama Highway 117
(256) 634–0066

PISGAH

**The Lodge at
Gorham's Bluff**
101 Gorham Drive
(256) 451–VIEW

SCOTTSBORO

The Blue Willow
303 East Willow Street
(256) 259–3462

Carlisle's Restaurant
2011 East Willow Street
(256) 574–5629

The Docks
Goose Pond Colony
417 Ed Hembree Drive
(256) 574–3071

Liberty Restaurant
907 East Willow Street
(256) 574–3455

Payne's
101 East Laurel Street
(256) 574–2140

Triple R Bar-B-Q
2940 Veterans Drive
(256) 574–1620

STEVENSON

Friday's
507 Second Street
(256) 437–8201

ALABAMA Fan Club and Museum

101 Glen Boulevard
Fort Payne
(256) 845–1646 or (800) 557–8223
This museum showcases the band's musical achievements, which are many: The group has garnered numerous awards, gold albums, and plaques for such releases as "My Home's in Alabama," "Mountain Music," and "Fallin' Again." Fans can purchase souvenirs ranging from T-shirts and jackets to photographs and mugs—and of course albums. The museum features individual sections on band members Randy Owen, Teddy Gentry, Jeff Cook, and Mark Herndon. For a little background and a Web tour, visit www.thealabamaband.com.

Huntsville Museum of Art

300 Church Street South
Huntsville
(256) 535–4350
Save time for browsing through the new $7.5-million home of the Huntsville Museum of Art. This beautiful building stands in Big Spring International Park, the heart of the city, and offers a wide range of exhibitions, art classes, and educational programs. You'll see an outstanding permanent collection with works by Picasso, Matisse, Toulouse-Lautrec, Goya, and other renowned artists as well as exhibits on loan from major institutions. The museum's plaza level offers the Palette Cafe, Signature Gallery, and other enticing venues. Visit www.hsvmuseum.org.

U.S. Space & Rocket Center

Huntsville
(256) 837–3400
Located at One Tranquility Base on Huntsville's western side, you may feel like a character out of a science fiction movie as you wander through a world of rockets, spaceships, shuttles, nose cones, and lunar landing vehicles. Other interesting exhibits include a moon rock, *Apollo 16*'s command module, the overpowering Saturn V moon rocket, history of the space shuttle with artifacts, and an SR–71 Blackbird reconnaissance plane. Don't miss the featured film presentation at the Spacedome Theater, or, for a unique adventure, sign up for Space Camp. You'll find Space Camp dates, rates, registration information, and everything else you need to know for blasting off at www.spacecamp.com.

Northwest Alabama

Tennessee Valley

Mooresville, just east of Interstate 65 at exit 2 on Interstate 565 between Huntsville and Decatur, makes a good place to start a tour of Alabama's northwest region. For information on local and area attractions, call the North Alabama Tourism Association's office at (800) 648–5381.

To best see Mooresville, a town that dates to 1818 (it's one year older than the state itself), plan to take a walking tour. Not only does everybody know everybody in this community of some twenty families, everybody knows everybody's dog. Don't be surprised if the local canines choose to accompany you on your stroll through town. Listed on the National Register of Historic Places, this charming village occupies an area of one-quarter square mile and can easily be covered in half an hour. Cedar trees and wild hydrangeas make lovely accents as you wend your way through the town. Strolling along streets lined by picket fences and fine old shade trees, you'll see a variety of vintage structures including lovely old Federal-style homes.

On Lauderdale Street you'll pass a brick church that dates to 1839 and contains its original pews. Although regular worship services no longer take place here, the historic structure is

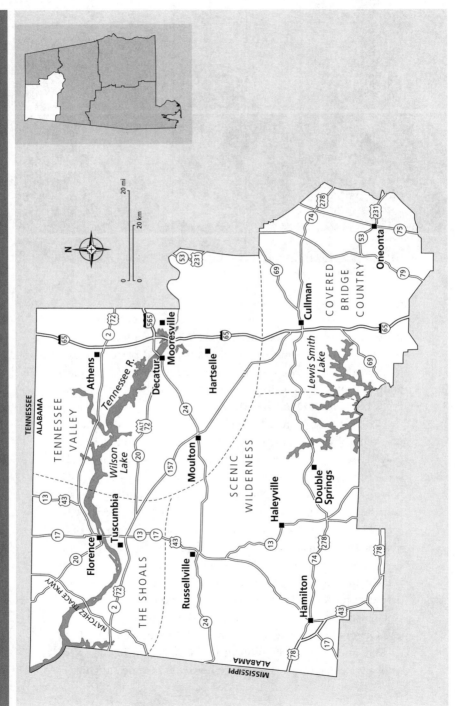

NORTHWEST ALABAMA

sometimes used for weddings and meetings. To book this unique property for a special occassion, call Margaret Anne Crumlish at (256) 351–6043. Notice the herringbone pattern of the brick walkway in front of the church. Mooresville's former postmistress, Barbara Coker, using many of her lunch hours, excavated through grass and layers of dirt to expose the original brickwork.

Be sure to stop by the tiny post office on the corner of Lauderdale and High Streets. Built around 1840, this small weathered poplar building, with tin roof, pegged joints, and square-head nails, contains the town's forty-eight original post boxes (first installed at the nearby Stagecoach Inn and Tavern).

The Stagecoach Inn, built sometime before 1825, once sold "supper for two bits." Across the street from the inn stands a small cottage, an example of Downing Gothic architecture. Dating to about 1890, the home was built and owned by Uncle Zack Simmons, a black carpenter, and his wife, Aunt Mandy. Former Mooresville mayor Kathleen Lovvorn says that Aunt Mandy, famous for her jellies and pickles, often handed out homemade treats to the village youngsters.

The Hurn-Thach-Boozer-McNiell House, built around 1825 and located near the end of Market Street, once housed a tailor shop, where Andrew Johnson, who later became president, studied drafting and construction techniques under the supervision of Joseph Sloss (who specialized in making Prince Albert coats for gentlemen).

After departing Mooresville you may want to travel north to **Athens,** Limestone County's seat. Start your local tour by visiting the downtown courthouse

Turning Back the Clock to Mark Twain's Time

If you saw the Disney production *Tom and Huck,* you visited the well-preserved village of Mooresville via video. Jonathan Taylor Thomas (of TV's *Home Improvement* fame) and Brad Renfro (*The Client*) starred in this remake of a Mark Twain classic.

"The moment I saw Mooresville, I knew this was the perfect setting for Tom Sawyer," said the film's production manager, Ross Fanger, after searching for a town that fit the 1876 era of Mark Twain's novel.

For the movie, Mooresville's paved streets became dirt-covered lanes, and a Hollywood facade of nineteenth-century stores sprang up. Film crews shot some scenes along the Tennessee River and inside **Cathedral Caverns,** a state park in Marshall County. The caverns served as a backdrop for the novel's account of Tom and his girlfriend Becky Thatcher's lost-in-a-cave adventure.

If you missed the movie, don't despair—the film is available as a home video or DVD, and you can still visit Mooresville.

Aunt Mandy and Uncle Zack Simmons Cottage

square with its surrounding stores and stately old churches. Founded in 1818, Athens barely missed being the state's oldest incorporated town. (Nearby Mooresville won the race by only three days.) To see some of the town's antebellum and Victorian homes—many are identified by historic markers—drive along Beaty, Pryor, Jefferson, and Clinton Streets.

You may want to stop by the ***Houston Memorial Library and Museum*** (256–233–8770). Located at 101 North Houston Street, this house dates to 1835 and served as the home of George S. Houston (a former Alabama governor and United States senator) from 1845 to 1879. Exhibits include family portraits, period furniture, Native American artifacts, Civil War relics, and various items relating to local history. Hours are 10:00 A.M. to 5:00 P.M. Monday through Friday and 9:00 A.M. to noon Saturday.

For a toe-tapping good time, plan to take in the ***Tennessee Valley Old Time Fiddlers Convention*** held at Athens State University each October.

Mooresville Walking Tours

Village residents often lead walking tours for groups, large and small. Contact Kathryn Price, who can gear the tour focus to the group's common interest—architectural, gardening, or historical. Tours take from one and one-half to two hours, and the cost is $5.00 per person with a minimum charge of $25.00. All proceeds benefit the Historic Restoration Fund, used for the preservation of Mooresville's town-owned structures and trees. For information e-mail kawprice@bellsouth.net and include "Walking Tour" in the subject line, or call (256) 353–4406.

Traveling the Antebellum Trail

Greater Limestone County boasts a rich legacy of antebellum and late-nineteenth- and early-twentieth-century architecture. Near the neighboring industrial and technological centers of Decatur and Huntsville, you'll find an area of contrasting culture—think past, present, and future tenses if you will. The trail delineates a driving tour with a number of antebellum structures, which translates to the time period between 1812 and 1861. You'll drive past twenty-four homes, three churches, a college, two working cotton plantations, a post office, and stagecoach inn and tavern. Call (256) 232–2600 or (800) 648–5381 for more information.

Visitors converge on campus for two days of outdoor competitions featuring harmonica, banjo, fiddle, mandolin, dulcimer, and guitar playing and buck dancing sessions. For more information on local attractions and events, call (256) 232–2600.

The Greater Limestone County Chamber of Commerce office at 101 South Beaty Street (256–232–2600) stocks brochures the visitor will find helpful. Pick up the *Beaty Historic District Walking Tour* guide to explore this area. Listed on the National Register, this historic district was named for Robert Beaty, cofounder of Athens. Although some of the district's homes date back before the Civil War, most were built during the early 1900s.

Beaty Street takes you to Athens State College, Alabama's oldest institution of higher learning. While on this street, be sure to notice the Beaty-Mason House built in 1826, now the college president's home. Located at 302 North Beaty Street, the lovely 1840s Greek Revival *Founder's Hall* houses school offices, a library, and a chapel. This building's original portion escaped being burned by the Yankees when a letter allegedly written by President Lincoln appeared in the nick of time. On the

alabamatrivia

America's first wave pool was built in 1970 at Point Mallard Park in Decatur.

second floor, the Altar of the New Testament features fine wood carvings in tulip poplar. Founder's Hall may be visited Monday through Friday from 8:00 A.M. to 4:30 P.M. Admission is free. For more information, call (256) 233–8100.

Before leaving Athens, plan to tour the *Donnell House.* Completed in 1851, the T-shaped home contains some period furnishings and is located at 601 South Clinton Street on the Middle School campus. A chinked log cabin kitchen with working fireplace stands nearby. The home is open from 2:00 to 4:00 P.M. on Monday, Wednesday, and Friday, or by appointment. For more information call (256) 232–0743 or (256) 232–7370. Modest admission.

After exploring Athens, head south to **Decatur** for another dose of history along with wildlife. Founded on the banks of the Tennessee River and originally called Rhodes Ferry, Decatur acquired its current name in 1820. At that time Congress and President James Monroe decided to honor Commodore Stephen Decatur by naming a town after him. A daring naval hero who commanded a three-ship squadron during the War of 1812, Decatur once proposed the following toast: "Our country: In her intercourse with foreign nations may she always be in the right; but our country, right or wrong."

You can see mallards along with blue buntings, herons, owls, woodpeckers, bald eagles, and other birds on exhibit at **Cook's Natural Science Museum** (256–350–9347), located at 412 Thirteenth Street Southeast. Hands-on exhibits and changing displays present the world of nature—from insects and seashells to reptiles and rocks. The privately owned museum features displays of iridescent butterflies and a mounted, life-size black bear dripping with honey. Hours are 9:00 A.M. to noon and 1:00 to 5:00 P.M. Monday through Saturday and 2:00 to 5:00 P.M. Sunday. Admission is free.

Nearby at 1715 Sixth Avenue Southeast, the folks who work at **Big Bob Gibson's** (256–350–6969) say they cook "the best barbecue in town." A Decatur tradition since 1925, the restaurant serves real hickory-smoked pit-barbecued pork, beef, and chicken. Barbecued potatoes (baked and topped with meat) also prove popular menu items. You can grab a bite here or get an order to go. Hours are "can to can't" (9:00 A.M. to 8:30 P.M.) seven days a week, excluding Easter, Thanksgiving, Christmas, and New Year's Day. Economical prices.

Stop by Decatur's Visitor Information Center at 719 Sixth Avenue Southeast for a pamphlet called *A Walking Tour of Historic Decatur,* which notes many

GAY'S TOP PICKS IN NORTHWEST ALABAMA

Alabama Music Hall of Fame, Tuscumbia	**Indian Mound and Museum,** Florence
Ave Maria Grotto, Cullman	**Ivy Green,** Tuscumbia
Bankhead National Forest, Double Springs	**Natural Bridge,** Natural Bridge
Blount County Covered Bridges, Oneonta	**The Shrine of the Most Blessed Sacrament of Our Lady of the Angels Monastery,** Hanceville
Dismals Canyon, Phil Campbell	

Simply Delicious

In a recent readers' poll conducted by an area publication, Simply Delicious (256–355–7564) won "Best Bakery" and "Best Desserts" in the Tennessee Valley. Owner Frances Norwood offers a full bakery and serves lunch from 11:00 A.M. until 2:00 P.M., from Monday through Friday, at 2215 Danville Road, Southwest, Suite G. The day's special might feature chicken and dumplings, country-fried steak with gravy, or chicken and dressing. Here, everything is made from scratch—nothing comes from a box.

Famous for her pies, Frances shares the recipe for one of her favorites, Chess Pie. She describes this as "wonderful and very Southern."

Chess Pie

6 eggs

1 cup butter

3 cups sugar

2 tablespoons white vinegar

2 teaspoons vanilla

1 9-inch deep-dish pie shell, unbaked

Preheat oven to 350 degrees. In a mixing bowl, beat eggs. Set aside. In a medium saucepan over low heat, melt butter. Add sugar and vinegar, whisking constantly for 5 minutes, or until sugar dissolves. Then pour sugar mixture over beaten eggs; mix well. Add vanilla and stir. Pour into pie shell. Bake for 1 hour or until center is set.

of the city's late-nineteenth-century homes that can be seen in the Old Decatur and New Albany historic districts. Call (256) 350–2028 or (800) 524–6181 for more information on local attractions.

Head to the city's northern section to tour the handsome *Old State Bank* (256–350–5060), established during Andrew Jackson's presidency. Located at 925 Bank Street Northeast, Alabama's oldest surviving bank building now serves as a museum. Upstairs you'll see the head cashier's spacious living quarters, furnished in the 1830s style.

During the Civil War this classic-style structure served as a hospital for both Union and Confederate soldiers. The bank's thick vault possibly became a shielded surgery chamber during the heat of battle. Outside, the large limestone columns, still retain traces of Civil War graffiti along with battle scars from musket fire. The bank was among Decatur's few buildings to survive the Civil War. Bank tours are free, and the building is open Monday through Friday from 9:30 A.M. to noon and 1:30 to 4:30 P.M., or by appointment. To sample a good mix of shops featuring antiques, clothing, toys, and gifts, take a stroll down Bank Street.

Nearby, at 207 Church Street Northeast, you can view some great traveling exhibits and work by regional artists at **Carnegie Visual Arts Center** (256–341–0562). One of millionaire philanthropist Andrew Carnegie's projects, the building dates to 1904 and served as Decatur's library until 1973. Hours run from 10:00 A.M. to 5:00 P.M. Tuesday through Saturday. Check out www.carnegiearts.org for current offerings and exhibits.

When hunger pangs hit, head to **Simp McGhee's** (256–353–6284), at 725 Bank Street Northeast. Named for a colorful early-twentieth-century riverboat captain, this pub-style eatery offers Simp's stuffed Gulf flounder as well as many pasta, poultry, and beef entrees. Chef Dean Moore directs culinary activities and offers seafood specialties. The upstairs section, Miss Kate's Place, takes its name from a famous former madam, who ran a turn-of-the-century bordello nearby. Dinner hours are Monday through Thursday from 5:30 to 9:00 P.M. and Friday and Saturday from 5:30 to 9:30 P.M.

Standing in Decatur's New Albany downtown area at 115 Johnston Street Southeast, you'll see the **Old Cotaco Opera House.** Often called the Old Masonic Building, the big brick structure dates to 1890. Although you won't see a touring vaudeville act here today, you'll find the complex offers other enticing treats. For instance, hungry travelers can visit **Curry's on Johnston Street** (256–350–6715), located on the building's lower level, for lunch or pick-up items. The eatery serves homemade soups, sandwiches, casseroles, fresh bread, and desserts. Moderate rates. Hours are 8:00 A.M. to 5:00 P.M. Monday through Friday and 11:00 A.M. to 2:00 P.M. Saturday.

To visit one of *The 100 Best Small Towns in America* (selected by Norman Crampton for his nationwide guide), head south for **Hartselle,** now a mecca for antiques shoppers. (For a list of the other ninety-nine towns, you'll have to buy the book.) In the meantime, you can check out *The 50 Best Small Southern Towns* by Gerald W. Sweitzer and Rand McNally's *Best of the Road* to read more about the charm of small-town living and Southern hospitality. Hartselle boasts the largest number of contiguous buildings on the Historic Register in Alabama.

Make your first stop the historic **Depot Building,** which houses the Hartselle Area Chamber of Commerce (256–773–4370 or 800–294–0692). On one wall you'll see a Works Progress Administration (WPA) mural painted in 1937 that illustrates the major role cotton played in the area's early economy. While here collect a map and guide to local shops. Open by 10:00 A.M., most shops close on Wednesday and Sunday. Also, some shops close on Monday.

Afterward stroll to **Giovanni's Italian Grill** (256–773–9669), located at 200 Railroad Street. This former freight building now houses Morgan County's only fine-dining Italian restaurant, and you can enjoy the ambience with walls of wood paneling and old brick and occasionally hear a passing train. Try the lasagna Giovanni or a salad with the house-made soup of the day. Or choose from a variety of pasta dishes, pizzas, and more. Standard to moderate.

Browsing along Main Street, you'll see Spinning Wheel Antiques, Ragtime Antiques, Country Classic Antiques, and other specialty shops, with an array of everything from bric-a-brac and potpourri to primitive antiques and quilts. At Slate Gallery, you'll find work by local artists.

After leaving Hartselle, follow State Route 36 west, watching for the *Oakville* turn and signs directing you to *Jesse Owens Memorial Park* (256–974–3636) at 7019 County Road 203. The park's focal point is an 8-foot, one-ton bronze statue of Owens, who won four gold medals in the 1936 Olympics. Branko Medenica, a native of Germany who now lives in Birmingham, sculpted the piece, which depicts Owens running and incorporates the familiar Olympic rings. Mounted on a 6-foot granite base, the statue was unveiled in a 1996 ceremony attended by members of the athlete's family when the Olympic torch passed through Oakville en route to Atlanta's games.

The park also offers a visitor center, museum, Olympic-size track, softball field, basketball court, walking trail, picnic pavilions, and replicas of the 1936 Olympic torch and Owens's modest home. Owens, who was born in Oakville and spent his early life here, once said, "It behooves a man with God-given ability to stand 10 feet tall. You never know how many youngsters may be watching." The park is open during daylight hours, and admission is

alabamatrivia

Alabama symbols include: the yellowhammer, the state bird; the camellia, the state flower; and the Southern pine, the state tree.

free. The museum is open from 11:00 A.M. to 4:00 P.M. Tuesday through Saturday and from 1:00 to 4:00 P.M. Sunday. Admission for museum. Check out www.jesseowensmuseum.org.

Before leaving the vicinity, take time to visit the *Oakville Indian Mounds,* a park and museum (256–905–2494) at 1219 County Road 187. Located 8 miles southeast of Moulton just off State Route 157, the complex features a massive 2,000-year-old Woodland Indian Mound, a Copena Indian burial mound, and a museum modeled after a seven-sided Cherokee Council House. The museum contains a 12-foot wooden statue of Sequoyah plus thousands of artifacts—some dating back to 10,000 B.C. Generally, hours are 8:00 A.M. to 4:00 P.M. Monday through Friday and 1:00 to 4:00 P.M. Saturday and Sunday April through September. The facility closes on weekends from October through March. Admission is free.

Afterward continue your journey toward *Moulton.* Try to hit Moulton at mealtime so you can sample the terrific lemon-pepper grilled catfish fillet at *Western Sirloin Steak House* (256–974–7191), with a huge grain-bin entrance

GAY'S FAVORITE ANNUAL EVENTS IN NORTHWEST ALABAMA

Bloomin' Festival at St. Bernard
Cullman, early April
(256) 734–0454

Alabama Chicken & Egg Festival
Moulton, April
(256) 974–1658

North Alabama Birding Festival
Wheeler Wildlife Refuge
Highway 67 East
Decatur, May
(256) 350–2028 or (800) 524–6181

**Alabama Jubilee Hot-Air
Balloon Classic**
Point Mallard Park, Decatur
Memorial Day weekend
(256) 350–2028 or (800) 524–6181

Waterloo Heritage Days
Waterloo, Memorial Day weekend
(256) 740–4141

Helen Keller Festival
Tuscumbia, late June
(256) 383–4066 or (888) 329–2124

The Spirit of America Festival
Point Mallard Park, Decatur, July 3–4
(256) 350–2028 or (800) 524–6181

W. C. Handy Festival
Florence, late July to early August
(256) 766–9719

September Skirmish
Point Mallard Park, Decatur
Labor Day weekend
(256) 350–2028 or (800) 524–6181

Oktoberfest
Cullman, early October
(256) 739–1258

Southern Wildlife Festival
Decatur, October
(255) 350–2028 or (800) 524–6181

Alabama Renaissance Faire
Florence, fourth weekend of October
(256) 740–4141 or (888) 356–8687

Covered Bridge Festival
Oneonta, fourth weekend of October
(205) 274–2153

and tin walls. Located at 11383 State Route 157 (behind Winn Dixie), the restaurant also features charbroiled chicken breast and rib-eye steak at economical to moderate rates. The restaurant, which is owned by Ann and Larry Littrell and Barbara and Ray Chenault, is open daily from 11:00 A.M. to 9:00 P.M.

At *Animal House Zoological Park* (256–974–8634), you'll find an unusual place where Dr. Doolittle would feel at home. Take State Route 24 west from Moulton and turn right on Lawrence County Road 101 toward Hatton. Watch for the sign to the facility, located at 2056 Lawrence County Road 161. Owner Carolyn Atchison has been raising exotic and endangered animals for about three decades and now cares for some 400 pets. She works with the federal government to curtail the illegal trafficking of exotic animals and reports of her investigations have appeared on ABC's news magazine *20/20*, the investigative news magazine *Hard Copy,* and in various publications across the country.

At this facility you will see Persian leopards, clouded leopards, black jaguars, African lions, Bengal and Siberian tigers, ligers, panthers, cougars, servals, bears, camels, llamas, Barbados sheep, antelope, capybaras, and a giraffe, plus a varied collection of primates (who dine on fruit medleys that might rival a restaurant's salad creations).

You can visit the park on Saturday from 11:00 A.M. to 3:00 P.M. between June 1 and November 15. The facility closes for repairs from November 15 to March 15 and is reserved for school tours from March through June 1. Click on www.animalhouse.org for more background. Admission.

After talking to the animals, continue west on State Route 20 to **Courtland,** named to the National Register of Historic Places for its 1818 development of the early town plan. Local architectural styles span almost two centuries. For a brochure on Courtland, which details a driving tour of the historical district, stop by Town Hall.

After exploring Courtland, continue to **Doublehead Resort & Lodge** (800–685–9267) for some relaxation and outdoor recreation. Located at 145 County Road 314 near Town Creek, the complex underscores a Native American theme from its name to its design and furnishings. A split-rail fence defines pastures, and wooden poles frame the metal entrance gate with its "Welcome Friends" greeting in Cherokee characters.

The property takes its name from Doublehead, a Cherokee chief who once lived on this land. The management wants to sustain a Native American awareness as it continues to develop this distinctive resort. The main lodge features a 5,000-square-foot deck overlooking Wilson Lake. Hammered metal designs of free-floating feathers and an upward-pointing arrowhead frame the double hand-carved front doors. A locally found Cherokee medallion inspired the lodge's unique chandelier.

Guests occupy cedar log cabins, each with three bedrooms, two baths, and a completely equipped kitchen. (After all, Doublehead's appreciation for creature comforts is well documented.) Beds are constructed from rustic cedar posts, and Indian wall hangings echo the motif. Each cabin comes with a beckoning hammock, grill, picnic table, and private pier. Recreational activities range from fishing, boating, and hunting to horseback riding. Golfers will want to inquire about special packages with land and water shuttles to the nearby Robert Trent Jones championship golf courses, Fighting Joe and the Schoolmaster, at the Shoals. Other amenities include two tennis courts, a basketball court, and a 2½-mile walking/nature trail. The facility offers rentals for jet-skis, pontoons, canoes, and other watercraft, a sporting clays course (shooting range), and a private 1,100-acre hunting preserve. Deluxe rates. Check out www.thecoveatdoublehead.com.

Afterward head west toward Tuscumbia.

The Shoals

You will be transported back in time when you arrive in **Tuscumbia.** At 300 South Dickson Street stands The Log Cabin Stagecoach Stop at Cold Water, an authentic structure from the pioneer period. Continue to Commercial Row, located on the north side of West Fifth Street between Water and Main Streets. This block of seven bordering brick buildings, dating to the 1830s, represents local antebellum commercial architecture. During the 1880s, Capt. Arthur Keller (Helen Keller's father) published his newspaper, *The North Alabamian,* here in the corner building.

While exploring downtown, step inside the restored Palace Drugstore for a bit of nostalgia and maybe a milk shake at the 1950s soda fountain. Also, you'll want to see Spring Park's fifty-one-jet fountain with water surging to heights of more than 150 feet. On weekend evenings, you can take in a special show, choreographed to lights and music. The large fountain serves as a memorial to Princess Im-Mi-Ah-Key, wife of Chickasaw Chief Tuscumbia, for whom the town is named.

Nearby at 300 West North Commons stands **Ivy Green,** the birthplace of Helen Keller. After her graduation from Radcliffe College, Miss Keller worked tirelessly on behalf of the handicapped by lecturing, writing articles and books (some of which have been translated into more than fifty languages), and appealing to legislative bodies to improve conditions for those with impaired sight and hearing. Because she conquered her own handicaps and gained an international reputation for inspiring other handicapped persons to live richer lives, she became known as America's "First Lady of Courage."

Water pump at Ivy Green

Of Ivy Green Miss Keller wrote, "The Keller homestead . . . was called 'Ivy Green' because the house and surrounding trees and fences were covered with beautiful English Ivy." On the grounds you'll also see English boxwood, magnolia, mimosa, roses, and honeysuckle. The family home contains many original furnishings, photographs, letters, awards, books, and Miss Keller's braille typewriter.

Summer visitors can watch a miracle reenacted at a performance of William Gibson's drama *The Miracle Worker* staged on Ivy Green's grounds and directed by Darren Butler. The play culminates with a vivid portrayal of the poignant incident at the water pump when teacher Anne Sullivan helped the blind and deaf child break through her black void into "a wonderful world with all its sunlight and beauty."

Except for major holidays, Ivy Green is open year-round. The home can be toured Monday through Saturday from 8:30 A.M. to 4:00 P.M. and on Sunday from 1:00 to 4:00 P.M. Admission. For more information on Ivy Green, the play, or the annual **Helen Keller Festival** (scheduled for a weekend in late June each year), call (256) 383–4066 or (888) 329–2124. Visit www.helenkellerbirthplace.org for more background information.

About 3½ miles south of Tuscumbia, you'll find another interesting home, **Belle Mont** (256–381–5052, 256–637–8513, or 800–344–0783) on Cook's Lane. Constructed between 1828 and 1832, the U-shaped brick structure suggests the influence of Thomas Jefferson. Dr. Alexander William Mitchell, who moved here from Virginia, built this home now considered the state's finest example of Jefferson Palladian architecture. Partially furnished, most of the home's pieces date to the period between 1840 and 1860. Owned by the Alabama Historical Commission, Belle Mont is open by appointment only. Admission. Check out this property and other historic sites at www.preserveala.org.

At some point during your visit, you may want to learn more about this area, called **the Shoals.** Looping through north Alabama, the Tennessee River comes into its own here in the state's northwest corner. At one time navigators found the Muscle Shoals rapids too formidable to negotiate, but the Tennessee Valley Authority (TVA) solved this problem with a series of strategically placed dams. The jagged rocks that created perilous swirling currents and wrecked boats now lie "buried" far below the water's surface.

To get a good idea of the river's impact on the region, you can visit the TVA Reservation at Muscle Shoals to see **Wilson Dam.** With its north end in Lauderdale County and its south end in Lawrence County, the dam stretches almost a mile and serves as a bridge for State Route 101. Named for President Woodrow Wilson, the dam was initiated during World War I to supply power for making munitions.

Afterward follow Veteran's Drive to downtown **Florence,** which features a number of interesting attractions such as the **Indian Mound and Museum** at 1028 South Court Street near the river. The ancient mound looms to a height of 42 feet, the largest of several in the Tennessee Valley. Near the mound, called *Wawmanona* by Native Americans, stands a museum containing displays of tools, ornaments, pottery, fluted points, and other artifacts along with exhibits on the Mississippian culture's mysterious mound builders. Modest admission. Except for major holidays, the site is open Tuesday through Saturday from 10:00 A.M. to 4:00 P.M. For more information call (256) 760–6427.

Nearby, at 601 Riverview Drive, you ll find the **Frank Lloyd Wright's Rosenbaum Museum** (256–740–8899). Conceived by Wright in 1939 and completed in 1940, the home so reflected Wright's iconoclastic approach to organic domestic architecture that Stanley and Mildred Rosenbaum could not find a local contractor to take on this project. Along with his final plans, Wright sent an apprentice to supervise the construction of this Usonian house, now on the National Register of Historic Places.

Designed for a two-acre site overlooking the Tennessee River, the house utilizes large areas of glass to take advantage of the view and innovative radiant heating because of the proximity of Tennessee Valley Authority's low-cost electricity. "Mr. Wright wanted to use all natural materials," Mrs. Rosenbaum said, "no paint or plaster—only cypress wood, brick, glass, and concrete." After the couple's four sons arrived, Wright designed an addition—its clean lines flow naturally (and imperceptibly) from the original structure. The home is open for tours Tuesday through Saturday from 10:00 A.M. to 4:00 P.M. Admission is charged. Visit www.wrightinalabama.com for more information.

To see the birthplace of the "Father of the Blues," head for 620 West College Street, where you'll find the **W. C. Handy Home and Museum** (256–760–6434), fronted by a fence of split rails. The hand-hewn log cabin, birthplace of William Christopher Handy, contains furnishings representative of the period around 1873. The adjoining museum features Handy's legendary trumpet and the piano on which he composed "St. Louis Blues." Handy also wrote more than 150 other musical compositions, including such standards as "Memphis Blues" and "Beale Street Blues." You'll see handwritten sheet music, photographs, correspondence, awards, and other items pertaining to Handy's life and legacy. The adjacent library houses Handy's extensive book collection and serves as a resource center for black history and culture. The museum is open Tuesday through Saturday from 10:00 A.M. to 4:00 P.M. Modest admission.

For a week of swinging jazz, plan to visit Florence from late July to early August and take in the **W. C. Handy Music Festival.** Special events include parades, jam sessions, the "DaDooRunRun" for joggers, a picnic-jazz evening

Strange as It Sounds

South of Russellville and west of Phil Campbell (that's the town's name) lies a unique attraction known locally as the Dismals. Located at 901 County Road 8, **Dismals Canyon** once served as a ceremonial ground for Native Americans and a hiding place for outlaws. In addition to caves, waterfalls, craggy rock formations, rainbows, and unusual vegetation, the canyon contains phosphorescent creatures called "dismalites" that glow in the dark. By signing up for a guided night tour, offered Friday and Saturday (the time depends on the degree of darkness), you can actually see the rare dismalites. According to a research scientist from Auburn University, these little glow worms only can be found here in this canyon, New Zealand, or China.

Geologists speculate that a prehistoric earthquake produced the place's chaotic geography with its many natural grottoes and bridges. This eerie but intriguing site also features both a natural arboretum and winding staircase.

After hiking through this place primeval, you may decide to take advantage of other activities—canoeing down Bear Creek, biking a 4-mile mountain trail, or swimming in Dismals Creek. For overnight visitors the site offers lodges (with fireplaces), a country store, and camping facilities. Admission. For more information call (205) 993–4559. Pay a virtual visit via www.dismalscanyon.com.

on the Tennessee River's banks, the colorful "Street Strut" led by the Grand Oobeedoo, and a concert with celebrated jazz musicians.

The Handy Festival evolved from a chance meeting in the Muscle Shoals Airport when two men struck up what turned out to be more than a casual conversation. Local veterinarian David Mussleman happened to ask Willie Ruff, a Yale music professor, about the horn he carried. This led to a discussion about native son W. C. Handy and his tremendous musical contribution—and subsequently to the annual festival held in Handy's honor. For more information call the festival office at (256) 766–7642.

While exploring Florence, you'll pass Wilson Park on the corner of Tuscaloosa Street and Wood Avenue. This setting serves as a backdrop for a number of local festivities, such as the *Alabama Renaissance Faire.* In fact, if you visit the park during this October gala, you can enjoy diversions ranging from derring-do with sword and shield to music, dance, and drama as residents bring to life some of the color, action, and excitement of the Renaissance period.

Beside the park you'll see the Kennedy-Douglass Center for the Arts at 217 East Tuscaloosa Street. This 1918 Georgian-style mansion and adjacent structures serve as a performing arts center. Stop by to view the current art exhibit and visit the gift shop.

At 316 North Court Street, you'll find *Trowbridge's* (256–764–1503), which offers sandwiches, salads, soups, chili, ice cream, and Oh My Gosh—a brownie piled high with vanilla ice cream and topped with hot caramel, whipped cream, and a cherry. The dessert gets its name from what most people say when they see it.

A mirrored soda fountain lists ice-cream flavors and drink choices. Third-generation owner Don Trowbridge credits the eatery's longevity to keeping the menu simple. Don's grandfather built Trowbridge's Creamery in 1918, and local farmers brought their milk and cream in to be processed. The family occupied the second floor over the ice-cream shop, and the dairy stood behind. The founder's original recipe for Orange-Pineapple Ice Cream, now shipped from New Orleans, remains a favorite with today's patrons.

A large painting on the rear wall depicts Trowbridge's interior from previous years—with almost no changes. Posters publicizing past local festivals pay tribute to Helen Keller and W. C. Handy, "Father of the Blues." Framed photos depict early Florence scenes and the construction of Wilson Dam, which originated as a World War I project to supply power for making munitions. Hours run from 9:00 A.M. to 5:30 P.M. Monday through Saturday. Economical rates.

A short distance away at 203 Hermitage Drive stands **Pope's Tavern** (256–760–6439), now a history-filled museum. Originally built as a stagecoach stopover and tavern, the attractive structure of white-painted bricks dates to 1811. Travelers on the Natchez Trace stopped here, and so did Andrew Jackson when he passed through in 1814 on his way to fight the British at the Battle of New Orleans. During the Civil War the inn served as a hospital where wounded Confederate and Union soldiers lay side by side to receive medical treatment from local doctors and the townswomen.

Inside the tavern you'll see period furnishings, kitchen utensils, tools, firearms, Civil War uniforms, photos, letters, and pioneer artifacts. Be sure to notice the worn silk Stars and Bars. This flag, hand-stitched by local ladies, traveled to Virginia with the Lauderdale Volunteers (one of northwestern Alabama's first Confederate military units) when they left to fight in the first Battle of Manassas. Before you leave, notice the Florence Light Running Wagon, made in a local factory that at one time was the world's second-largest wagon-building operation. Modest admission. Except for major holidays, hours are 10:00 A.M. to 4:00 P.M. Tuesday through Saturday.

Nearby, at 658 North Wood Avenue in Florence's historic district, stands the **Wood Avenue Inn** (256–766–8441), a turreted, towered Victorian structure with a wraparound porch. Built in 1889, this Queen Anne–style home offers bed-and-breakfast accommodations with private bath and breakfast served in your room or suite. Standard to moderate rates.

Down the street at **The Limestone House Bed and Breakfast** (256–765–0365), at 601 North Wood Avenue, you'll find more warm hospitality—maybe just-baked cookies on arrival and certainly a delectable breakfast (served at your convenience) in the sunroom. Henry Ford and Thomas Edison once visited this handsome 1915 Georgian Revival home, listed on the National Register of Historic Places, and you can sleep in rooms named for them.

The home makes a fitting backdrop for the extensive art collection of owners Carolyn and Dan Waterman, who have lived all over the globe and, in the process, amassed a treasure trove of artifacts such as striking sculptures and the rare African comb collection in the foyer. Visit www.thelimestonehouse.com. Moderate rates.

Scenic Wilderness

Leaving the Shoals, you might enjoy taking the **Natchez Trace Parkway.** A portion of the historic Trace cuts across this corner of Alabama through Lauderdale and Colbert Counties. Once a pioneer footpath, this route took travelers from Natchez, Mississippi, to Nashville, Tennessee. To intercept the Trace, which offers plenty of scenic stops, picnic spots, and nature trails, head northwest on State Route 20.

On the Coon Dog Trail

One sunny morning in August, my mother and I set out to find the **Coon Dog Memorial Graveyard.** Our approach led up a hill, and before reaching the top, my car developed resistance symptoms. Smoke came pouring out from some private place, and the car whimpered and gave a last gasp. Being an auto illiterate, I knew not what to do. "You don't have AAA?!" my mother said in a slightly accusatory tone.

We were in a wooded area, seemingly isolated, but I saw a house in the distance. A woman answered my knock and let me use her phone. As we waited on the porch for a tow truck, she told us much about the surrounding area and its abundant wildlife, even showing us several sizable snake skins. After the arrival of the tow truck, driven by a history buff, I heard even more anecdotes and collected tips on local sites to check out—thanks to a disaster in disguise and two good samaritans.

Anyway, back to Key Underwood's Coon Dog Memorial Graveyard, which is located south of Cherokee, via Colbert County Route 21. Now a park, the site contains markers and tombstones (some with epitaphs) for more than one hundred coon dogs.

The graveyard's origin dates to the death of Troop, a coonhound owned by Key Underwood. Here on September 4, 1937, Underwood and some friends buried the dog at a favorite hunting spot. An annual Labor Day celebration commemorating the anniversary of the graveyard's founding takes place in the park and features bluegrass music, buck dancing, barbecue, and even a liars contest. Political hopefuls often show up for the festivities. Otherwise, the site projects a sense of serenity, and the surroundings look much as they did during the days when Troop picked up the scent of a coon here. This site is open year-round during daylight hours. No admission. Call (256) 383–0783 for more information.

Meet Jerry Brown,
Ninth-Generation Potter

While exploring this region of scenic wilderness, consider a visit to **Brown's Pottery** (205–921–9483, 205–921–2597, or 800–341–4919), located at 1414 County Road 81, 3 miles south of Hamilton. Here, Jerry Brown carries on a family tradition of pottery making that spans nine generations. In 1992 Jerry and his wife, Sandra, made a trip to Washington, D.C., where he received a National Heritage Fellowship Award, presented by President and Mrs. Bush. Jerry's work is exhibited in galleries across the country as well as the Smithsonian, where he has been invited several times to demonstrate pottery making.

The traditional Southern folk potter has captured numerous awards at shows and festivals, and his work is sought by collectors. "Folk pottery increases in value," said Jerry, who signs and dates his pieces. In a "Quest for America's Best," QVC shopping network featured his work on national television. For this show Jerry filled an order for 1,500 pitchers, which sold out in two minutes.

One of the nation's few practicing traditional potters, Jerry remembers "playing around on the potter's wheel before I was old enough to start school." He performs his magic by combining water with local clay, which "looks almost blue. The South is known for its good clay," he added. Using a backhoe to dig the clay from a 150-year-old-pit, Jerry then turns the process over to his four-legged assistant, Blue, who does the mixing by walking circles around a mule-powered clay grinder. Jerry designed and built the brick oval kiln, in which he fires his work at temperatures that exceed 3,000 degrees Fahrenheit.

The pottery's showroom features blue-speckled pitchers, bowls, churns, candle holders, crocks, mugs, pie plates, bluebird houses, and more. Face jugs, Jerry's specialty, were historically used to hold harmful substances. Sometimes called ugly jugs, the vessels feature faces that don't win beauty contests but do earn awards and are coveted by collectors. The jugs sell for prices ranging from $30 to $200 and vary in size up to the largest, a five-gallon container. Jerry's newest additions include bacon cookers, egg separators (with faces), and mule mugs. (And yes, the mule's tail serves as the handle.)

Before leaving the pottery, I purchased several gifts. The crocks do double duty, Jerry pointed out, demonstrating how to use the container's lip to sharpen a knife. Even now as I write, I am drinking coffee from a thick mug with a blue, feathered design. (Ask Jerry to tell you the story of how a mishap with flying chicken feathers inspired one of his popular patterns.)

To view the pottery-making process as it was done in the olden days or to buy unique gifts (for yourself and others), head to Hamilton, near the Mississippi border. The Pottery's hours run from 9:00 A.M. to 5:00 P.M. Monday through Saturday.

Heading south to *Winfield* takes you to *White Oaks Inn* (205–487–4115 or 800–482–4115), at 300 Regal Street. At the end of a driveway flanked by stone lions, this lovely bed-and-breakfast stands on a knoll in a parklike setting. Owners Linda and Roger Sanders have achieved an open, airy look in their renovation of this 1918 home with a welcoming front porch (plus a bit of whimsy with the English telephone booth just inside the entrance). Accommodations include five rooms, each with private bath, in the main house and five cabins on the grounds. Guests can enjoy such amenities as a hot tub and pool (with robes and shower shoes provided). Standard rates. Call for reservations and specific directions.

In this area you'll find yet another fascinating attraction, *Natural Bridge* (205–486–5330). Located on U.S. Highway 278 about a mile west of the intersection of State Routes 5 and 13, this double-span, 60-foot-high sandstone bridge, thousands of years in the making, looms majestically in its pristine setting. Surrounding this impressive formation, presumably the longest natural bridge east of the Rockies, you'll see massive moss-covered boulders and lush vegetation. Local flora includes ferns, bigleaf magnolias, mountain laurel, and oakleaf hydrangeas. Inviting nature paths and picnic areas make this a pleasant place for an outing. Moulton photographer Charles Jordan's postcards, available in the gift shop, capture some of the site's ambience. Modest admission. Except for Thanksgiving and Christmas days, the facility is open daily year-round from 8:00 A.M. till sunset.

To topple back in time a bit, drop by *Dixie Den* (205–486–8577) in nearby *Haleyville* for an authentic chocolate (or your own preference) mixed-in-a-metal-container milk shake. While slurping or sharing it, you can catch a glimpse of the town's past because black-and-white photos of the old Dixie Hotel and other bygone buildings line the walls, and you may also recognize hometown personality Pat Buttram's photo. Owners Judy and Toby Sherrill offer homemade chicken and tuna salads, soups, and sandwiches, including the Dixie Dog for big appetites (two hot dogs on a bun plus chili, kraut, and trimmings). Starting at 10:30 A.M. Monday through Saturday, hours run until 7:00 P.M. on Monday and Tuesday, 4:00 P.M. Wednesday, and 8:00 P.M. Thursday and Friday. On Saturday the cafe closes at 3:00 P.M. Next door in the same 1948 complex, the Dixie Theater's nostalgic lobby beckons. If the theater is closed, you might prevail upon the Sherrills to let you have a peek.

Continuing east through Winston County, you'll find the town of *Double Springs,* located in the *William B. Bankhead National Forest.* This huge forest (named for the distinguished political family of actress Tallulah Bankhead) spreads over most of Winston County and north into Lawrence County.

In front of the Winston County Courthouse at Double Springs stands *Dual Destiny,* the statue of a Civil War soldier flanked by billowing Confederate and

Union flags. Contrary to common assumption, many Alabamians remained staunch Unionists during the Civil War, and "the Free State of Winston" represented such a contingent. After Alabama's secession (which passed by a narrow vote), these hill-country people, led by local teacher Christopher Sheats, took the position that if a state could secede from the Union, then a county could secede from a state.

While visiting the Free State of Winston, take time to explore some of the surrounding **Sipsey Wilderness.** With 25,938 acres, Sipsey provides plenty of off-the-beaten-path territory, including 20 miles of hiking trails.

Afterward take US 278 east and head toward Cullman.

Covered Bridge Country

To see Alabama's largest covered truss bridge, continue east from Winston County on US 278. Watch for the left turn to **Clarkson Covered Bridge** (sometimes called the Legg Bridge), located a short distance north of the highway on Cullman County Road 11. The bridge, situated in a picturesque park setting, stretches 270 feet across Crooked Creek. Supported by four large stone piers, this "town-truss" structure features latticed timbers, clapboard siding, and a roof of cedar shingles. The bridge, restored in 1975, dates to 1904.

Once the site of a Civil War battle, the surrounding area offers picnic grounds and woodland hiking trails. During our visit my husband and I met a man who showed us a gum tree with a carving—a message left for him by a fellow Cherokee some thirty-five years earlier. The park is open year-round, and there's no admission charge.

Continuing east on US 278 takes you to **Cullman,** a city that dates to 1873 when Col. John G. Cullmann bought a large tract of land and established a colony for German immigrants here. A reproduction of the founder's Bavarian–style home (which burned in 1912) now serves as the **Cullman County Museum** (256–739–1258), located at 211 Second Avenue Northeast. The museum's eight rooms, each with a theme, preserve some of the city's German heritage and the area's history. You'll see a 7-foot wooden sculpture of a Native American warrior, china, jewelry, vintage clothing, fainting couches, early tools, a beer wagon, and other local items. Modest admission. Hours run from 9:00 A.M. to noon, and from 1:00 to 4:00 P.M., Monday through Friday. Sunday hours are 1:30 to 4:30 P.M.

For a good meal, stop by **The All Steak** (256–734–4322), located just a few blocks away on 314 Second Avenue Southwest on the fourth floor of the Cullman Savings Bank. (If it's raining, stop at the third level on the parking deck to stay under cover and take the elevator up one floor.) Contrary to its name, the restaurant serves a wide variety of entrees, including seafood and poultry. In addition to its beef specialties, the eatery is famous for homemade breads and desserts, especially the orange rolls, as well as its vegetable lunches. Prices are moderate. Hours are 7:00 A.M. to 9:00 P.M. Monday through Wednesday and 6:00 A.M. to 10:00 P.M. Thursday through Saturday. Sunday's schedule is 6:30 A.M. to 3:00 P.M.

Sample a bit of Cullman's heritage by stepping into *A Touch of German* (256–739–4592) at 218 First Avenue Southeast. Here, you'll be greeted by owner Peggy Grobe plus a flock of chirping birds popping out of their cuckoo clock homes to remind you that time is passing much too fast to browse through all the city's great shops.

Peggy stocks European and American collectibles such as handcrafted nutcrackers, music boxes, German and European Christmas ornaments, Steiff stuffed bears, table linens, laces, tapestries, Dutch blue delftware, Bavarian steins, scrumptious chocolate, Russian nested dolls, Reuge music boxes, and more. You'll also find costumes—dirndls, aprons, lederhosen, and alpine hats—for Oktoberfest, which Cullman celebrates the first week in October each year. Hours run Monday through Saturday from 9:30 A.M. to 5:30 P.M.

Step next door for more browsing at Craig's Antiques and Gifts. Continue a few steps farther to The Duchess Bakery and pick up some doughnuts. This family-owned business at 222 First Avenue Southeast opened in 1939.

At *Southern Accents* (256–737–0554 or 800–737–0554), you'll find an array of architectural antiques—everything from carved mantels, leaded-glass windows, statuary, and stately columns to chandeliers, hitching posts, molding, staircases, and claw-foot bathtubs. Housed in historic quarters at 308 Second Avenue Southeast, the inventory draws clients from across the United States. Owners Dr. Garlan Gudger and his son, Garlan Jr., search the globe for treasures from the past.

Clarkson Covered Bridge

The Grudgers offer an antique floor salvaging and cutting service plus door and window framing, which makes today's carpenters happy.

A sign near the entrance reads: YOUR HUSBAND CALLED . . . HE SAID TO BUY ANY-THING YOU WANT. (I especially admired a Victorian cherry parlor mantel, wearing a SOLD sign and soon to be shipped to New York.) Hours run Monday through Saturday from 10:00 A.M. to 5:00 P.M. Take a look at www.antiques-architectural.com and order anything you want.

While in town be sure to check on local productions at the **Arts Center Dinner Theatre** (256–739–4321). This facility at 802 Main Avenue Northeast offers entertaining performances along with a full dinner or dessert only. Recent productions include *Steel Magnolias, A Bad Year for Tomatoes,* and a variety of seasonal shows. For schedule and ticket information, visit online at www.theartscentercullman.com.

"We will serve no swine before its time," promise Ron Dunn and Gary Wiggins, first cousins who operate **Johnny's Bar-B-Q** (256–734–8539), a family business at 1404 Fourth Street Southwest that opened in the early 1950s. Here, you can opt for a barbecue sandwich or a plate with all the fixings: coleslaw, beans, and potato salad. Other popular items include smoked chicken with white barbecue sauce, catfish, or barbecue-topped baked potatoes. "Closed on Sunday for church and closed on Monday for rest," the restaurant's hours run Tuesday through Saturday from 10:00 A.M. to 9:00 P.M. Economical rates.

Afterward continue to 1600 Saint Bernard Drive Southeast, off US 278, on the town's east side. At **Ave Maria Grotto** (256–734–4110), on the grounds of a Benedictine monastery, visitors can take a Lilliputian world tour in a unique garden filled with more than 150 miniature reproductions of famous landmarks. Brother Joseph Zoettl, a Bavarian, who arrived at St. Bernard Abbey in 1892, constructed these reduced versions of various buildings. At age eighty the gifted monk completed his final work, the Lourdes Basilica. His architectural miniatures also include the Hanging Gardens of Babylon, ancient Jerusalem, Rome's Pantheon, and St. Peter's Basilica.

alabamatrivia

Cullman, known as the City of Churches, has more than 200 churches within its city limits.

Using ingenuity and an unlikely assortment of materials, from playing marbles and fishing floats to cold-cream jars and even a discarded bird cage (for the dome of St. Peter's), along with the more standard cement, limestone, and marble, Brother Joe fashioned a small world that continues to delight travelers. Check it out at www.avemariagrotto.com. Except for Christmas and New Year's days, the grotto can be visited daily from 8:00 A.M. to 5:00 P.M. October through March, and to 6:00 P.M. April through September. Modest admission.

In south Cullman County near Hanceville, you can make a personal pilgrimage to *The Shrine of the Most Blessed Sacrament of Our Lady of the Angels Monastery.* To reach the shrine, take State Route 91 through Hanceville, watching for signs that lead to County Road 747 and then to County Road 548. A long, white-fenced approach winds through a portion of the site's 380 acres of rolling farmland. More than three years in construction, the shrine opened in December 1999, and has become a major mecca for visitors. Mother Angelica, who founded Eternal Word Television Network (EWTN), serves as Abbess here, and the monastery is home to the Poor Clare Nuns of Perpetual Adoration.

alabamatrivia

Cullman acquired the title "Die Deutsche Kolonie von Nord Alabama" because the town's founder, Col. John G. Cullmann, who came from Frankweiler, Germany, attracted approximately 10,000 German settlers to north Alabama.

The shrine's Romanesque–Gothic style of architecture echoes Franciscan churches and monasteries of thirteenth-century Assisi. To reach the shrine, you'll cross an expansive colonaded piazza. As you approach, notice the T-shaped cross. The original top portion was struck by lightning, leaving the form of a Tau cross, the symbol that St. Francis used in signing his letters.

From inlaid Italian-marble floors and stately columns to vaulted ceiling, the awe-inspiring interior leaves no detail to chance. Made of carved cedar, the main altar is covered in gold leaf. The stained-glass windows were created in Munich, Germany, and the stonework embellishments were crafted by artisans in Spain. Other features include mosaics fashioned by Italian artisans using a four-century-old method of hand-chiseling and fitting.

Castle San Miguel stands below the piazza and houses a great hall, conference facilities, and a gift shop; hours are Monday through Saturday from 8:00 A.M. to 4:45 P.M. The shrine is open to the public from 6:00 A.M. to 6:00 P.M. on Sunday and until 9:30 P.M. Monday through Saturday. The nuns' Conventual Mass takes place at 7:00 A.M. daily. To learn more about the circumstances that led to the erection of this magnificent structure in the hills of Alabama, you can attend one of the brother's commentaries, generally scheduled at 9:00 A.M. daily, depending on the crowd. For more information call (256) 352–6267 or visit www.olamshrine.com, where you will find a map and specific directions.

For a relaxing base on crystal blue waters, head to Crane Hill and *Smith Lake Bed and Breakfast* (256–747–6057). Located at 994 County Road 4230 and situated on the Rock Creek branch of the finger-shaped Lewis Smith Lake (the nation's third cleanest), the property promises all the amenities laced with warm hospitality and gorgeous natural surroundings, plus water recreation.

Owners Alexandra (better known as Alex) and Jim Cox offer two suites: the Loft and the Dock. Both have balconies overlooking the lake—wonderful spots for sipping your morning coffee. Jim's job as a civil engineer took the couple to countries all over the world, including Germany, Israel, Saudi Arabia, and Japan. During the decade they lived in Japan, Alex taught cooking classes and conversational English to Japanese ladies and started thinking about a B&B of her own when she returned to the States. Now, that's a reality, and guests can enjoy this inviting getaway filled with antiques and fine Asian art.

Breakfast here starts with a fresh fruit medley and might feature locally smoked and processed ham or tenderloin, eggs, and biscuits. Alex offers information on area restaurants, but some guests enjoy grilling their own dinner while watching a sunset. Perfect for couples or families, the suites can accommodate four comfortably, and the owners welcome kids. When weather permits, Jim takes guests out on his pontoon boat and also provides a double kayak and bikes for their use. The couple will send you to interesting spots nearby, perhaps to an artist's studio in Crane Hill or a year-round trout fishery in Jasper. Visit www.smithlakebandb.com and check out the views. Moderate rates.

Continue east on US 278 until it intersects U.S. Highway 231, then turn south to see the *Blount County Covered Bridges.* Known as the Covered Bridge Capital of Alabama, this area features three covered bridges, all still in daily use and marked by road signs on nearby highways. If you're on a tight schedule, choose the Horton Mill Covered Bridge, probably the most picturesque of the bunch. Located about 5 miles north of Oneonta on State Route 75, the latticed structure looms some 70 feet above the Warrior River's Calvert Prong—higher above water than any other covered bridge in the United States. Adjacent to the highway there's a parking area with nearby picnic facilities and nature trails, making this a relaxing place to take a driving break.

Continuing your exploration, you'll find the county's shortest covered bridge southeast of Rosa. The 95-foot-long, tin-topped Easley Covered Bridge stands about a half-mile off Blount County Road 33 and spans Dub Branch.

Northwest of Cleveland, 1 mile off State Route 79, Swann Bridge appears rather suddenly as you're rounding a curve. The three-span bridge extends 324 feet over the Locust Fork of the Black Warrior River. You can park in a turn-off lane on the bridge's opposite side to explore the nearby terrain, where Queen Anne's lace, ferns, mountain laurel, wild hydrangeas, and muscadine vines grow. You might hear a mockingbird's serenade in the background.

Each October the *Oneonta* area stages an annual *Covered Bridge Festival* featuring bridge tours, arts and crafts exhibits, and other festivities. For additional information on the festival, award-winning Palisades Park, or other area attractions, call the Blount County/Oneonta Chamber of Commerce at (205) 274–2153.

After seeing the bridges of Blount County, you'll probably be ready for a wonderful meal, and Charlie Bottcher promises you one at **The Landmark** (205–274–2821) in Oneonta. Described by one Birmingham visitor as "a little bit of France in the middle of nowhere," the restaurant is at 601 Second Avenue East. Charlie, who's the owner/chef, creates consistently delicious combinations and demonstrates a winning way with vegetables. Be sure to note the board specials, as these change weekly.

Depending on what's fresh, good, and available, dinner selections might mean spicy Greek snapper, filet mignon in puff pastry, or charred ahi tuna with a sauce of soy, ginger, and lime in an avocado fan garnish. Chicken Landmark, a signature dish, features a charbroiled, marinated chicken breast topped with crabmeat, charbroiled shrimp, and clam sauce. Charlie's clientele comes from a 75-mile radius. Moderate prices. Dinner is served from 4:30 to 9:00 P.M. Friday and Saturday.

Before leaving Blount County, head to **Benedikt's Restaurant** (205–274–0230), located at 4125 Blount County Road 27, about 8 miles southeast of Oneonta on Straight Mountain. Some folks just stumble on the restaurant by accident while taking a scenic drive; others make a deliberate effort, traveling regularly from Birmingham and surrounding areas to eat here. The restaurant's Sunday meal is served "buffeteria" style.

On her menu, Ruth Benedikt writes, "Ladies and Gentlemen, we are 12th generation Charlestonians: Scotch, Irish and German. Our recipes belong to our mother, aunts, grandmother and all who came before them." Ruth and her sister Joice have prepared their recipes for the public for three decades and consider themselves "among the last of the scratch cooks in the restaurant business."

Choices might include German pot roast, golden fried chicken, or ham steak along with side dishes of real mashed potatoes, mixed broccoli-cauliflower with cheese sauce, sweet tomato relish, fresh creamed corn, purple hull peas, and fried green tomatoes. In addition to regular menu items, on Friday night a catfish bar features this specialty prepared seven different ways. A barbecue bar supplements the Saturday night menu.

Closed Monday, the eatery is open Tuesday through Thursday from 9:00 A.M. to 2:00 P.M. and until 8:30 P.M. Friday and Saturday. Call the Benedikts for Sunday reservations; serving hours are 8:30 A.M. to 4:00 P.M. Rates are economical to moderate.

Across the road at **Capps Cove** (205–625–3039 or 800–583–4750), you'll find a country getaway with a mountain on one side and a river on the other. Located at 4126 Blount County Road 27, the complex offers bed and breakfast and much, much more. Owners Sybil and Cason Capps, native Alabamians who have lived in several states over the past fifteen years, moved here from St. Louis when Cason retired from a broadcasting career.

"We think we're unique," Sybil says, "a country village with an antiques store, barn, wedding chapel, and two old-style country cabins." Guests can enjoy a full country breakfast—smoked ham, bacon, a house specialty called "naked cowboys," grits, potatoes, the works—in the couple's lovely two-story Colonial house. Moderate rates. Visit the property at www.cappscove.com.

Continue to the state's central section. Nearby Ashville, easily reached by taking US 231 south, makes an interesting stop.

Places to Stay in Northwest Alabama

ATHENS

Country Hearth Inn
1500 U.S. Highway 72 East
(256) 232–1520 or
(888) 443–2784

CRANE HILL

**Smith Lake
Bed and Breakfast**
994 County Road 4230
(256) 747–6057

CULLMAN

Hampton Inn
6100 State Route 157
(256) 739–4444 or
(800) 426–7866

DECATUR

Comfort Inn & Suites
2212 Danville Road
(256) 355–1999 or
(800) 424–6423

Country Inn & Suites
807 Bank Street Northeast
(256) 355–6800

Courtyard by Marriott
1209 Courtyard Circle
(256) 355–4446 or (800)
321–2211

Hampton Inn
2041 Beltline Road
(256) 355–5888 or
(800) 426–7866

Holiday Inn Hotel & Suites
1101 Sixth Avenue Northeast
(256) 355–3150 or
(800) 553–3150

FLORENCE

**The Limestone House
Bed and Breakfast**
601 North Wood Avenue
(256) 765–0365

**Marriott Shoals
Hotel and Spa**
800 Cox Creek Parkway South
(256) 246–3600

Wood Avenue Inn
658 North Wood Avenue
(256) 766–8441

ONEONTA

Capps Cove
4126 County Road 27
(205) 625–3039 or
(800) 583–4750

ROGERSVILLE

**Joe Wheeler
State Park Lodge**
4401 McLean Drive
(256) 247–5461 or
(800) 544–5639 or
(800) 252–7275

TOWN CREEK

**Doublehead
Resort & Lodge**
145 County Road 314
(800) 685–9267

TUSCUMBIA

Key West Inn
1800 U.S. Highway 72 West
(256) 383–0700 or
(866) 253–9937

WINFIELD

White Oaks Inn
300 Regal Street
(205) 487–4115 or
(800) 482–4115

Places to Eat in Northwest Alabama

CULLMAN

The All Steak
314 Second Avenue
Southwest
(256) 734–4322

Johnny's Bar-B-Q
1404 Fourth Street
Southwest
(256) 734–8539

Rumors Deli
105 First Avenue Northeast
Suite 100
(256) 737–0911

DECATUR

Big Bob Gibson's
1715 Sixth Avenue
Southeast
(256) 350–6969

Café 113
113 Grant Street
(256) 351–1400

Curry's on Johnston Street
115 Johnston Street
Southeast
(256) 350–6715

Simp McGhee's
725 Bank Street Northeast
(256) 353–6284

Simply Delicious
2215 Danville Road, SW
Suite G
(256) 355–7564

DOUBLE SPRINGS

Sapore Grill
26641 Highway 195
(205) 489–1172

FLORENCE

Ricatoni's Italian Grill
107 North Court Street
(256) 718–1002

Trowbridge's
316 North Court Street
(256) 764–1503

The 360 Grill
One Hightower Place
(256) 246–3660

HALEYVILLE

Dixie Den
907 Twentieth Street
(205) 486–8577

HARTSELLE

Giovanni's Italian Grill
200 Railroad Street
(256) 773–9669

Las Vias Mexican Grill
101 Railroad Street
(256) 751–1402

MOULTON

**Western Sirloin
Steak House**
11383 State Route 157
(256) 974–7191

MUSCLE SHOALS

New Orleans Transfer
1682 South Wilson
Dam Road
(256) 386–0656

FOR MORE INFORMATION ABOUT NORTHWEST ALABAMA

**Alabama Mountain Lake
Tourist Association**
25062 North Street
P.O. Box 1075
Mooresville 35649
(256) 350–3500 or (800) 648–5381
www.alabamamountainlakes.org
alabamamountainlakes.org
This organization covers sixteen north
Alabama counties that are home to
some one hundred attractions
in a 100-mile radius.

**Colbert County Tourism
& Convention Bureau**
719 Highway 72 West
P.O. Box 740425
Tuscumbia 35674
(256) 383–0783 or (800) 344–0783
www.colbertcountytourism.org
colberttourism@comcast.net

Cullman Area Chamber of Commerce
301 Second Avenue Southwest
P.O. Box 1104
Cullman 35056
(256) 734–0454 or (800) 313–5114
www.cullmanchamber.org
cullman@corrcomm.net

**Decatur/Morgan County
Convention & Visitors Bureau**
719 Sixth Avenue Southeast
P.O. Box 2349
Decatur 35602
(256) 350–2028 or (800) 524–6181
www.decaturcvb.org
info@decaturcvb.org

Florence/Lauderdale Tourism
One Hightower Place
Florence 35630
(256) 740–4141 or (888) 356–8687
www.flo-tour.org
dwilson@flo-tour.org

ONEONTA

Benedikt's Restaurant
4125 Blount County
County Road 27
(205) 274–0230

The Landmark
601 Second Avenue East
(205) 274–2821

SHEFFIELD

George's Steak Pit
1206 Jackson Highway
(256) 381–1531

TUSCUMBIA

Claunch Cafe
400 South Main Street
(in Spring Park)
(256) 386–0222

WINFIELD

Boar's Butt Restaurant
350 Thorndale Street
(205) 487–6600

MAINSTREAM ATTRACTIONS WORTH SEEING IN NORTHWEST ALABAMA

Alabama Music Hall of Fame
617 U.S. Highway 72 West
Tuscumbia
(256) 381–4417 or (800) 239–2643
You can immerse yourself in the state's musical heritage at this facility, which features exhibits, audiovisual galleries, and memorabilia related to musicians either from Alabama or associated with the state. Artists represented include Hank Williams, Elvis Presley, Emmylou Harris, the Temptations, and many others. For a little music and a Web tour of the museum, click on www.alamhof.org.

Point Mallard Park
1800 Point Mallard Drive Southeast
Decatur
(256) 350–3000
Named for nearby Wheeler National Wildlife Refuge's wintering ducks, this park for all seasons offers aquatic fun in the summer and year-round golfing on a championship course. You may even see Capt. Mike Mallard, a human-size mascot in nautical attire, wandering about. Not only does the 750-acre complex contain a wave pool, an Olympic-size diving pool, water slides, sand beach, and "Squirt Factory," but you'll also find a 173-acre campground, hiking and biking trails, and picnicking facilities here.

Central Alabama

Ridges, Springs, and Valleys

Alabama's midsection presents a pleasing pastoral landscape, a panorama of ridges, springs, and valleys. Heading south, the Birmingham area serves as a convenient base from which to branch out into the state's central region. From here, too, you can easily sweep down into Alabama's southeastern section to explore the historic *Chattahoochee Trace* as well as the state capital area.

Start your area exploration with a trip to downtown *Ashville,* home of one of St. Clair County's two courthouses (the other is in Pell City). This Neoclassical Revival structure, an enlargement of an earlier courthouse, dates from the early 1840s.

Only a block from Ashville's downtown square, you'll find *Ashville House* (205–594–7046) at 35 Third Street. This Queen Anne beauty makes a perfect spot for lunch. Painted yellow and trimmed in plum, teal, and other historically correct colors, the house's exterior features turrets, towers, gingerbread ornamentation, and wraparound porches not to mention nine gables, four arches, and two verandas. Original outbuildings include a barn, smokehouse, and carriage house, which now serves as an antiques shop.

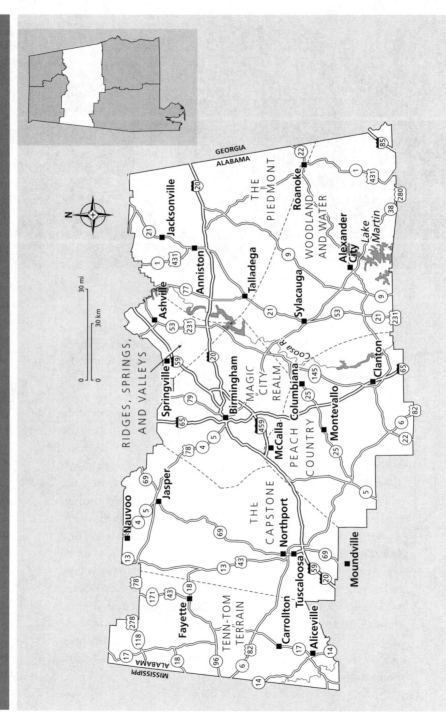

When Pat and Lavon Drake bought the property almost two decades ago, they launched a meticulous restoration of the home, which served as their residence until they converted it to a tearoom. Lunch selections feature salads, soups, quiche, and sandwiches along with daily specials like Pat's seafood delight. Popular desserts include crème brûlée and strawberry Fitzgerald, which consists of cream-cheese filled crepes, fresh berries, and strawberry liqueur.

While here, you can browse through the gift shop with antique glassware and adjacent room filled with specialty children's clothing available for purchase. Hours are 11:00 A.M. until 2:00 P.M. Thursday through Saturday. Because seating is limited to thirty patrons, Pat requests advance reservations. Economical.

Traveling 2 blocks from the courthouse square on U.S. Highway 231 at 20 Rose Lane, you'll see a lovely bed-and-breakfast, *Roses and Lace Country Inn* (205–594–4366). Sometimes called the historic Elisha Robinson House and built for a local judge, the Queen Anne–style home dates to 1890. The inviting porch, complete with hanging Boston ferns, swings, and wicker rocking chairs, may be calling your name.

Innkeepers Suzanne and Jim Haley will welcome you to this charming home. The home offers a honeymoon suite and four bedrooms with four-and-a-half baths. Moderate rates.

Ask the Haleys to make an appointment for you to see the circa-1852 Inzer House next door, a striking, white-brick structure now reincarnated as a Civil

GAY'S TOP PICKS IN CENTRAL ALABAMA

Aliceville Museum,
Aliceville

The American Village,
Montevallo

Anniston Museum of Natural History,
Anniston

Birmingham Civil Rights Institute,
Birmingham

DeSoto Caverns Park,
Childersburg

International Motorsports Hall of Fame,
Talladega

McWane Center,
Birmingham

Moundville Archaeological Park,
Moundville

Paul W. Bryant Museum,
Tuscaloosa

Tannehill Historical State Park,
McCalla

The Westervelt-Warner Museum of American Art,
Tuscaloosa

War museum. A number of black cast-iron Confederate crosses dot the grounds of nearby Ashville Cemetery.

To learn more about local history, drive out to see the *John Looney House,* one of Alabama's oldest two-story log dogtrot structures. (The term "dogtrot" refers to a central hallway connecting two rooms also known as "pens." Although covered, this passage was left open and often proved a popular napping place for the family canines, hence its name.) Located a little over 4 miles southeast of Ashville on St. Clair County Road 24, this rare example of pioneer architecture dating to about 1820 may be visited on weekends. The Haleys at Roses and Lace Country Inn will give you a current status report on this historical site. Current hours are Saturday and Sunday from 1:00 to 4:00 P.M. Modest admission.

From Ashville take State Route 23 south until you reach U.S. Highway 11 leading to **Springville,** a town that takes its name from several area springs. First called Big Springs and settled about 1817, the town became Springville with the post office's establishment in 1834; the entire downtown district is on the National Historic Register.

Take time to explore some of this state historic district's nostalgic shops. Nearby Homestead Hollow, a fifty-five-acre pioneer homestead with a blacksmith shop, log cabin, barn, and gristmill, serves as a quaint backdrop for art-and-craft festivals throughout the year. During such events, visitors may sample sorghum and apple cider made on the premises.

The Piedmont

Located in the Appalachian foothills, Calhoun County occupies a portion of the state's Piedmont region. Start your tour in **Anniston,** an attractive, arts-oriented city that named William Shakespeare its citizen of the year in 1984—before the Alabama Shakespeare Festival left its birthplace here and moved to Montgomery.

"It's your world. Explore it!" urges the staff at the **Anniston Museum of Natural History** (256–237–6766), located a couple of miles from downtown at 800 Museum Drive. Some adventures promised by the museum's slogan include treks through jungles, deserts, and savannahs at this handsome facility surrounded by 187 acres on Anniston's northern outskirts. Entering the museum's Lagarde African Hall, you'll see a rogue elephant keeping vigil beside a towering baobab tree (the world's largest replica of an "upside-down" tree). Preserved specimens of more than a hundred creatures inhabit this African complex, most collected by Annistonian John B. Lagarde, a big-game hunter who donated his award-winning assemblage to the museum.

From antelope to zebras, all animals appear in the most realistic habitats possible. And through it all visitors see the versatility with which nature's creatures adapt to their world. Every effort has been made to achieve the effect

Strange as It Sounds

Deadly beauty and intrigue await at the **Berman Museum** (256–237–6261) in Anniston's LaGarde Park. Here you'll find an arsenal of rare weapons collected from all over the world by a former secret agent. Suits of armor that now stand still once clanked as knights did battle. Beheading axes and swords from ancient China and Japan hang in silence—not divulging their roles in past dastardly deeds.

A stunning royal Persian scimitar set with 1,295 rose-cut diamonds, sixty carats of rubies, and an exquisite forty-carat emerald in a three-pound gold handle mesmerizes sightseers here just as it once did Russian audiences during the reign of Catherine the Great. Other rare items include a Greek helmet dating to 300 B.C., Jefferson Davis's traveling pistols, Adolf Hitler's silver tea service, and Napoleon Bonaparte's ivory comb and brush set. Also displayed is a saber used in the dramatic "Charge of the Light Brigade." The collection contains eighty-eight guns from the American West, Fraser's famous *End of the Trail* sculpture, and bronzes by Frederic Remington, Charles Russell, and Karl Kauba.

Army colonel Farley Lee Berman worked in counterintelligence, and he and his wife, Germaine (a Parisian with a comparable position in French Intelligence), met during World War II. Afterward they traveled the world on a decades-long quest for historical weapons and art.

Personnel from several metropolitan museums approached Berman about acquiring his collection, but he chose to donate it to the city of Anniston, saying he knew "the people of Alabama would enjoy it." Located at 840 Museum Drive next to the Museum of Natural History, the Berman Museum's hours run from 10:00 A.M. to 5:00 P.M. Tuesday through Saturday and 1:00 to 5:00 P.M. on Sunday. The museum opens on Monday from Memorial Day to Labor Day. Modest admission.

of authenticity; for example, light in the bamboo forest filters through a type of Venetian blind to create a network of slanted rays.

Spacious corridors wind from the African depths to the Ornithology Hall with its impressive array of more than 600 specimens of North American birds, many now either extinct or on the endangered species list. Naturalist William Werner assembled this priceless bird collection more than a century ago, and several diorama groupings include nests (some with eggs) built by the birds themselves. The museum boasts one of the world's finest models of a pteranadon, a prehistoric flying reptile with a 30-foot wingspan. In Dynamic Earth Hall, which features a life-size model of an albertosaurus, you can explore an Alabama cave complete with waterfall, stalactites, and stalagmites. The museum's newest hall, "Alabama: Sand to Cedars," features a walk through the state from seashore to mountains. NatureSpace encourages children to explore beyond backyard boundaries with a unique exhibit of natural resources.

Accredited by the American Association of Museums and a Smithsonian affiliate, the Anniston facility has received national recognition for its innovative participatory exhibits. The museum also offers rotating art exhibits, a fine gift shop, picnicking facilities, and several nature trails, including the recently added Bird of Prey Trail. The museum is open Tuesday through Saturday from 10:00 A.M. to 5:00 P.M. (plus Monday during summer) and Sunday from 1:00 to 5:00 P.M. Modest admission.

Don't miss the historic Episcopal ***Church of St. Michael and All Angels*** (256–237–4011) on West Eighteenth Street at Cobb Avenue. With an exterior of Alabama stone, this 1888 Norman-Gothic structure features a magnificent marble altar backed by an alabaster reredos (ornamental screen). Bavarian woodworkers carved the church's entire ceiling by hand, and angels on corbels all face the altar at slightly different angles. Admission is free, and you can visit year-round between 8:00 A.M. and 4:00 P.M.

Take time to drive through the Tyler Hill Historic District and along tree-lined Quintard Avenue, where you'll see grand Victorian homes. At one such mansion, ***The Victoria*** (256–236–0503 or 800–260–8781), you can drop in for a fine meal or an overnight stay. Look for a turreted, three-story structure, painted taupe and trimmed in white with a burgundy awning covering a walkway in front, on a hill at 1600 Quintard. This 1888 home, owned by Betty and Earlon McWhorter, has served as a country inn for two decades. Accommodations include three lovely suites—decorated in period antiques—in the main house, a guest house, and a tasteful addition containing fifty-six rooms (all with private baths) connected to the inn by covered walkways.

alabama**trivia**

Alabama's name comes from a Native American tribe, the Alibamu.

The menu changes seasonally but always includes steak and fresh seafood—and by popular demand, the jumbo lump crab cakes. Appetizers might range from the chef's daily soup creation to fried green tomatoes with lime crème fraîche and tasso ham. The Victoria also offers a wide selection of wines. Prices are moderate to expensive.

The Victoria is open to the public for dinner from 6:00 to 9:00 P.M. Monday through Thursday and to 10:00 P.M. on Friday and Saturday. Guests can enjoy a bountiful breakfast buffet in the main house. Moderate rates. Visit the inn at www.thevictoria.com.

Sometime during your stay stroll down to the old carriage house on the grounds, now home of an art gallery called Wren's Nest, which has original works and limited prints by noted wildlife artist Larry K. Martin.

During your Anniston excursion, take time to explore some of the city's interesting shops such as ***Noble Passage*** (256–237–0266) at 3326 Henry Road. Here, owner/designer Deborah McDaniel offers an array of fine furniture, Persian rugs, and accents for the home plus wine, gourmet food items, and bath and body products. Hours are Monday through Friday from 10:00 A.M. to 5:30 P.M.

While in the area, head to ***Munford*** via State Route 21 for a visit to ***The Cedars Plantation*** (256–761–9090), located at 590 Cheaha Road. Owners Ann and Rick Price traveled widely and called many places home, including South America, before settling on this captivating country estate. "We want to share the house and its history with others," says Ann, whose research has yielded a wealth of information about the home's builder, Joseph Camp. Purchasing the property in 1833 from area Natchez/Creek chieftains, the Reverend Camp completed the main house two years later.

Much Ado in Anniston

For our first anniversary, friends invited my husband and me to visit them in Anniston and take in some plays. At that time summer visitors to Anniston—the birthplace of the Alabama Shakespeare Festival (ASF)—could watch actors "strut and fret their hour upon the stage" in five rotating weekend productions.

Martin L. Platt came from Carnegie Mellon University to direct the community theater and soon started the festival, which attracted throngs each summer. He personally picked the performers, auditioning many of them in New York.

I remember the gorgeous costumes, noted for their quality of workmanship. In a production of *Romeo and Juliet,* for instance, the Capulets were clothed in various shades of bronze and the Montagues in lavender and rose tones, enabling the audience to easily identify members of the feuding families. Gifted ASF Guild members spent countless volunteer hours hand-sewing seed pearls on dress hems or crocheting an army's "chain" mail headgear. Other Guild members found or provided lodging for actors, stuffed envelopes, ushered playgoers, or baked cookies for "meet the cast" parties.

We enjoyed immersing ourselves in the Elizabethan era by attending "Shakespeare Sundays" at the historic Church of St. Michael and All Angels. Filled with pomp and splendor, these services featured the use of a 1559 prayer book and the talents of the festival's company.

We continued to spend each anniversary in Anniston seeing ASF productions until the festival moved to its magnificent home in Montgomery and became a year-round theater. Although we still see occasional plays (Montgomery is much farther from our home), we miss those special summers. And on each wedding anniversary, we propose a toast to Shakespeare and all the wonderful times the curtain went up in Anniston.

GAY'S FAVORITE ANNUAL EVENTS IN CENTRAL ALABAMA

Sakura Festival
Tuscaloosa, March
(800) 538–8696

Dogwood Festival
Aliceville, second weekend of April
(205) 373–2820

Birmingham International Festival (BIF)
Birmingham, April
(205) 252–7652
www.bifsalutes.org

Operation New Birmingham Magic City Art Connection
Linn Park, Birmingham, April
(205) 324–8797
www.magiccityart.com

Indian Dance & Craft Festival
Childersburg, April and September
(800) 933–2283

Heritage Week
Tuscaloosa, third week in April
(800) 538–8696

City Stages
Linn Park, Birmingham, June
(205) 324–6881 or (800) 458–8085

Kentuck Festival of the Arts
Kentuck Park, Northport, mid-October
(205) 758–1257 or (800) 538–8696

Moundville Native American Festival
Moundville Archaeological
Park, October
(205) 371–2234

Nextel Cup Weekend
Talladega Superspeedway
Talladega, October
(256) 362–9064 or (877) 462–3342
www.talladegasuperway.com

Christmas Village Festival
Birmingham-Jefferson Convention
Complex Exhibition Hall, Birmingham
first weekend in November
(205) 836–7178 or (800) 458–8085
www.christmasvillagefestival.com

Sometimes called the "Steamboat House," the raised cottage split-level design features long side porches and double front doors. Period antiques (and perhaps the Reverend Camp's spirit) fill the high-ceilinged rooms. Guests can browse through the Prices' extensive library, which includes the Reverend Camp's interesting 1882 first-person account of history in the making. A post–Civil War skirmish took place at nearby Munford, and the home's east chimney still bears scars from the fire of marching Union soldiers.

Set on a sweeping lawn with stately oak and cedar trees, the home offers a tennis court, large swimming pool, and walking trails. Pleasant pastures surround The Cedars, and Tater Creek runs through the property. Ann recommends outings to Talladega National Forest, Cheaha State Park, and other nearby spots for nature lovers. Guests can enjoy a home-cooked breakfast in the dining room. Rates range from standard to moderate.

After basking in the country's serenity, head to nearby *Talladega* and immerse yourself in history. If you take the Jackson Trace Road, you'll follow a wagon route cut by Gen. Andrew Jackson and his Tennessee Volunteers as they marched southward through the Creek Indian nation. For a self-guided driving map of the town's historical sites, head to the chamber of commerce office just off the courthouse square in the old L&N Depot at 210 East Street. Start with the Silk Stocking District (outlined on your map), a sizable concentration of homes listed on the National Register of Historic Places. Stop by Heritage Hall, a restored 1908 Carnegie Library at 200 South Street East, for a look at its current exhibits. Afterward drive by Talladega College, established in 1867, to see Hale Woodruff's striking *Amistad* murals at Savery Library. Other points of interest include the campus chapel and Swayne Hall, the college's first building.

For a delightful history lesson and a fun-filled family adventure, don't miss nearby **DeSoto Caverns Park** (256–378–7252 or 800–933– CAVE), 5 miles east of Childersburg at 5181 DeSoto Caverns Parkway. A one-hour tour presents highlights of the cave's role in history and features a spellbinding laser light and sound show in the magnificent onyx chamber, taller than a twelve-story building and bigger than a football field.

After the tour children can climb DeSoto's cave wall, wander through a lost trail maze, pan for gemstones, do battle with water balloons, and enjoy a picnic on the grounds. The facility features more than twenty-six attractions, and you can make arrangements to stay overnight in the cave. The park's hours run from 9:00 A.M. to 4:30 P.M. Monday through Saturday, and 1:00 to 4:30 P.M. on Sunday (or to 5:30 P.M. April through October). Admission.

Magic City Realm

Before exploring busy, bustling Birmingham, you can enjoy another back-to-nature experience at **Twin Pines Resort** (205–672–7575) near Sterrett. Although designed as a corporate retreat, travelers on holiday or opting to locate a serene weekend getaway will find a haven at 1200 Twin Pines Road, about 30 miles southeast of Birmingham.

Today's fast-paced world becomes a blur when you turn onto a road lined with nature's greenery. Large log lodges feature porches overlooking a forty-six-acre private lake, and you can opt for a room or a suite with fireplace and kitchen. Standard to moderate rates.

Outdoor recreation opportunities might focus on fishing (no license required on private property), paddleboating, canoeing, swimming, and playing volleyball, softball, tennis, or horseshoes. While exploring the jogging/walking trails, you'll discover a covered bridge and a moonshine still and, in the process, work up a good appetite for the resort's bounteous country-cooked meals. When departure time comes, you may find it hard to tear yourself away.

Another good getaway, **Oak Mountain State Park** (205–620–2524), 15 miles south of Birmingham off Interstate 65, offers canoeing, fishing, swimming, golfing, picnicking, horseback riding, and a demonstration farm. Children especially enjoy seeing the geese, peacocks, rabbits, pigs, calves, donkeys, horses, and other animals. The park, most of it in a natural state, occupies almost 10,000 acres. A drive to the top of Double Oak Mountain affords some sweeping views of the park's steep slopes and rugged terrain.

Other features include some 40 miles of hiking trails and four lakes. Don't miss the Treetop Nature Trail, where the Alabama Wildlife Rescue Service houses injured birds of prey. Climbing a boardwalk through woodsy surroundings takes you past large enclosures containing hawks, great horned owls, and other raptors. Call for park information or reservations at Oak Mountain's lakeside cabins or campground. Modest admission.

After basking in serenity you can pick up the pace with a jaunt to **Birmingham.** Named for the British industrial city, Birmingham acquired its nickname, Magic City, when soon after its 1871 incorporation it burgeoned into Alabama's major metropolis. No longer a fire-breathing, smoke-spewing dragon, the city projects a much-changed image—from gray smog to crisp skyline and green-bordered boulevards. As a leading medical and technological center, the city boasts an economic base broadened far beyond its mineral resources. The financial impact of the University of Alabama at Birmingham (UAB) Medical Center beefs up the local economy enormously.

As the state's biggest city, Birmingham boasts many choice restaurants. For a memorable dinner, add **Highlands Bar & Grill** (205–939–1400) at 2011 Eleventh Avenue South to your itinerary. Classically trained chef Frank Stitt's regional Southern creations have been dubbed "New American" cuisine, and his accolades fill walls and books. *Gourmet* magazine awarded Highlands Bar & Grill its number five slot for the "50 Best American Restaurants" in 2001.

alabamatrivia

Birmingham ranks as the state's largest city.

The James Beard Foundation named Stitt "Best Chef of the Southeast" the same year, and *Bon Appétit* listed him as one of the culinary "Legends of the Decade."

Start with an appetizer of baked grits, and select an entree ranging from beef, venison, duck, and seafood to rabbit and veal. Renowned for its crab cakes, the restaurant also serves such specialties as pan roast quail with corn pudding and grilled leg of lamb with basil aioli and ratatouille. Moderate to expensive. Dinner hours are 5:30 to 10:00 P.M. Tuesday through Thursday and to 10:30 P.M. Friday and Saturday. Visit www.highlandsbarandgrill.com for more background.

All about Art

While in the Birmingham area, stop by **Artists Incorporated** (205–979–8990) at 3365 Morgan Drive in Vestavia Hills. Representing the work of about fifty artists, this cooperative gallery offers a feast for the eyes. Here, you'll find oils by Les Yarbrough and Troy Crisswell, fiber art by Murray Johnston, bronzes by Frank Fleming, and more. Housed in a former dairy barn built in 1928, the gallery boasts the distinction of being Vestavia's oldest commercial building.

"This gallery offers a great variety of art forms in a wide range of prices," says Bill Charles, a fan and former Birmingham resident. "I'm the proud and happy owner of several works including two affordable Frank Fleming pieces, and I'm glad for the chance to have seen any number of [for me] unaffordable pieces, too. The crew here loves art and delights in sharing that love with their customers, be they buyers or browsers."

Hours are Tuesday through Saturday from 10:00 A.M. to 5:00 P.M. except on Friday, when hours extend to 8:00 P.M. A reception, featuring artists, food, wine, and sometimes music, takes place from 5:30 to 9:00 P.M. on the first Friday of every month—and you're invited.

While sightseeing in the Magic City, be sure to visit towering **Vulcan** (205–933–1409), the world's largest cast-iron statue, back in place again after some refurbishing. To reach Vulcan Park atop Red Mountain, take Twentieth Street South and watch for the sign. An observation deck affords a panoramic view of Birmingham and surrounding Jones Valley. Cast from Birmingham iron, *Vulcan* represents the mythological god of metalworking, fire, and forge. Designed for the 1904 St. Louis Exposition by Italian sculptor Giuseppe Moretti, *Vulcan* lifts his torch in tribute to the city's iron industry. At the base of the 55-foot statue, a museum presents *Vulcan's* history along with an overview of steel production. Admission. For a virtual tour, visit www.vulcanpark.org.

Consider stopping by **Birmingham Botanical Gardens** (205–414–3900) at 2612 Lane Park Road, on the lower southern slope of Red Mountain. Stroll through the Japanese garden complete with a fourteenth-century teahouse reproduction. Also on the grounds, *Southern Living* magazine maintains demonstration gardens with plantings that might be duplicated at home. The museum's gift shop offers a fine selection of items, from note cards and prints to unusual plants and garden statuary—great for giving or keeping. Free admission. The gardens are open year-round, from dawn to dusk each day. The gift shop is open 10:00 A.M. to 4:00 P.M. Monday through Saturday.

The Tutwiler (205–322–2100 or 866–850–3053) at 2021 Park Place North makes a comfortable and convenient base for seeing Birmingham's attractions.

The staff at this charming historic hotel will make you glad you came to the Magic City. With its rose-marble foyer, original coffered ceilings, moldings, plasterwork, and brass hardware, the hotel recaptures the elegance of another era. Your room or suite, which might come with a balcony or a marble fireplace, features high ceilings, restored woodwork, marble bathrooms, and custom-designed antique reproductions. You'll also see fresh flowers but few TVs—most are tucked away in armoires.

Built in 1913 as a prestigious apartment/hotel, the redbrick, Italianate Tutwiler recently underwent a renovation. The Tutwiler's meticulous restoration resulted in charter membership in Historic Hotels of America, a select group recognized for preserving historic architectural quality and ambience. The original Tutwiler, the hotel's namesake, made news in 1974 when it became one of the country's first structures to be leveled by "implosion" (also the inspiration for the hotel's specialty drink by the same name).

The first Tutwiler hosted such dignitaries and celebrities as Eleanor Roosevelt, President Warren G. Harding, Charles Lindbergh, Will Rogers, Nelson Eddy, Tallulah Bankhead, Rocky Marciano, and Marilyn Monroe. Carrying on tradition, the current Tutwiler counts former President George Bush, Dan Quayle, Henry Kissinger, Colin Powell, Casper Weinberger, Mick Jagger, Billy Joel, and Henry Mancini among its honored guests. As another honored guest of the Tutwiler you can enjoy such amenities as complimentary shoe shines and newspapers, airport transportation, and valet parking. Rates are moderate to deluxe.

For a glimpse of the city's Iron Age, take First Avenue North over the viaduct to Thirty-second Street toward the towering smokestacks of **Sloss Furnaces** (205–324–1911). Designated a National Historic Landmark, the ironworks that served Birmingham from 1881 to 1971 now serve as a massive walk-through museum portraying the city's industrial past. Near the park gate, a visitor center features exhibits on the various aspects of combining coal, limestone, and ore at high temperatures to produce iron. In its prime, Sloss turned out 400 tons of

Solving Crimes with the Southern Sisters

Before the late Anne George wrote her critically acclaimed novel, *This One and Magic Life,* she penned award-winning poetry and became a Pulitzer Prize finalist. But her legion of mystery fans most miss the zany antics of Patricia Anne and Mary Alice, an unlikely pair of sleuths who live in Birmingham. As the "Southern Sisters" go about their crime solving, the reader gets a light-hearted look at the local landscape and a lot of laughs. Buy a book in this series, pour yourself a tall glass of iced tea and enjoy an easy summer afternoon.

finished pig iron a day. Hours are Tuesday through Saturday from 10:00 A.M. to 4:00 P.M. and Sunday from noon to 4:00 P.M. Admission is free.

For some down-home country cooking, head for *The Irondale Cafe* (205–956–5258)—the inspiration for the Whistle Stop Cafe in the movie *Fried Green Tomatoes*. Located at 1906 First Avenue North in the historic area of Irondale, the cafeteria offers a variety of meats and fresh vegetables including that Southern favorite, fried green tomatoes, that actress/writer Fannie Flagg put in the spotlight. Lunch hours run from 10:45 A.M. to 2:30 P.M. Sunday and 10:45 A.M. to 2:30 P.M. Tuesday through Friday. Supper hours are 4:30 to 7:30 P.M. Tuesday through Friday.

Heading toward the Birmingham International Airport, you'll find the *Southern Museum of Flight* (205–833–8226). Look for the big McDonnell-Douglas F–4N Phantom II on the front lawn of the museum at 4343 Seventy-third Street North, 2 blocks east of the airport. Aviation buffs can spend hours here delving into the mystery and history of flying. This outstanding facility features a reproduction of a 1910 Curtis "Pusher," the second powered plane to follow on the heels of the Wright brothers' success; a 1925 crop duster that launched Delta Airlines; a dozen Cold War aircraft from the F-84 and F-86 through the A-12 Blackbird, including a MiG-15 and MiG-21; and hundreds of models that trace aviation's history. You'll see decades of memorabilia relating to Amelia Earhart, Gen. Claire Chenault's Flying Tigers, and the infamous Red Baron.

"We've doubled our collection during the last four years," said a staff member, and expansion continues. Visitors can view short movies, shown continuously, on such subjects as the Tuskegee Airmen and women in aviation as well as humorous newsreels on early attempts to fly. Take time to look through the Alabama Aviation Hall of Fame and the Air Force's Fiftieth Anniversary Collection of Aircraft Art on the second floor. The museum, which also offers an aviation reference library, is open from 9:30 A.M. to 4:30 P.M. Tuesday through Saturday and from 1:00 to 4:30 P.M. on Sunday. Modest admission.

Afterward return downtown to the Birmingham-Jefferson Civic Center for a spectator outing at the *Alabama Sports Hall of Fame* (205–323–6665). Located at 2150 Richard Arrington Jr. Boulevard, this unique two-floor facility focuses on some of the state's greatest sports figures. Walls of bronze plaques pay tribute to athletes from Olympic diving champion Jenni Chandler to Joe Louis, who boxed his way to the world heavyweight title. You'll also see displays on such sports luminaries as John Hannah, Joe Namath, Bo Jackson, Pat Sullivan, Bart Starr, Ozzie Newsome, Hank Aaron, Willie Mays, Jesse Owens, Hubert Green, Bobby Allison, Pat Dye, and Bear Bryant. Wall cases and displays feature trophies, uniforms, photographs, and other memorabilia from the sports world.

Even though exhibits cover Hall of Fame inductees who made names for themselves in archery, auto and harness racing, golf, baseball, boxing, track, and waterskiing, the name of the game in Alabama is Football (and yes, with a capital F). A black-and-white photo exhibit, depicting unhelmeted players in skimpy uniforms, captures some historic moments during the first Alabama–Auburn clash on February 22, 1893, in Birmingham. Football fever rages in many other parts of the country, but the intensity seems several degrees higher in the South and reaches a boiling point in Alabama during the annual collegiate battle between the Crimson Tide and the War Eagles. You can visit the Hall of Fame Monday through Saturday from 9:00 A.M. to 5:00 P.M. Check out www.ashof.org for more information. Admission.

Nearby at 2000 Eighth Avenue North stands the *Birmingham Museum of Art* (205–254–2565), noted for its excellent Wedgwood collection, the finest outside England. The museum houses a diverse collection of more than 25,000 paintings, pieces of sculpture, prints, drawings, and examples of the decorative arts dating from ancient to modern times. You'll see works by Monet, Sargent, Corot, Cassatt, Bierstadt, Motherwell, Stella, Chihuly, and others.

Mark your calendar now for a blockbuster exhibit scheduled to open in October 2007 and run for twelve to fourteen weeks. "Pompeii: Stories from an Excavation" will feature some 500 objects including furniture, statues, jewelry, coins, frescoes, and body casts buried during the volcanic eruption of Mount Vesuvius in A.D. 79. The Birmingham Museum of Art is one of only three U.S. museums chosen to host this exhibition. Other museum treasures include the Kress collection of Renaissance paintings and the largest collection of Asian art in the South.

Check with the staff regarding current offerings. Don't miss the multilevel Charles W. Ireland Sculpture Garden, which provides a splendid backdrop for outdoor exhibits. Kathy G's Terrace Cafe serves lunch from 11:00 A.M. to 2:00 P.M. Tuesday through Saturday and features a jazz brunch the first Sunday of each month. Stop by the Museum Store for an extensive selection of books, posters, jewelry, crafts, and unique gift items. Except for major holidays, the museum is open from 10:00 A.M. to 5:00 P.M. Tuesday through Saturday and noon to 5:00 P.M. Sunday. Check on current exhibits and other happenings at www.artsBMA.org. Free admission.

Continue south on Twenty-first Street to University Boulevard and take a right to reach the *University of Alabama at Birmingham* campus. One of the nation's top-ranked medical centers, UAB practices a triple-thrust program of education, research, and service. Tucked in the heart of this much-trodden complex on the third floor of the Lister Hill Library Building, you'll find the *Alabama Museum of Health Sciences* and the *Reynolds Historical Library*

Christmas in Nauvoo

When Gene McDaniel planned a Christmas celebration in Nauvoo, population 249, he expected maybe 250 to 500 people. Between 2,000 to 3,000 people showed up for that first holiday festival in 1989, and that's how it's been ever since. Christmas in Nauvoo takes place the first Saturday in December with an open house at the **Old Harbin Hotel** (205–697–5652), myriad lights, attendant festivities, and parade led by Miss Alabama, who makes the hotel her overnight base.

Other special events in Nauvoo include an Antique Car and Truck Show in June and the Train Station Bluegrass Festival in April and September.

Once a booming coal-mining town, Nauvoo takes its name from a Hebrew word meaning "pleasant." A railroad worker, who said the place reminded him of his hometown in Illinois, christened it Nauvoo. After two mines and a lumber mill closed in the 1950s, Nauvoo started to shrivel and dry up. The town's largest structure, the two-story brick Old Harbin Hotel, stands on the corner of McDaniel Avenue and Third Street. Built in 1923 at a cost of $24,574, the hotel boasted sixteen furnished rooms and seventy-six electric lights. The structure, which retains its original pine walls, downstairs pressed-tin ceilings, and four center rooms with skylights, was added to the Alabama Landmark Register in 1990.

Owners Gene and Earlene McDaniel, who live on the premises, have collected a variety of furnishings, antiques, and memorabilia to decorate each of the nine guest rooms individually.

"We don't advertise for customers," said Gene, a retired union coal miner and hardware store owner. "Don't expect a person on duty at the desk. Most weekends in summer, we're booked with family reunions because the whole clan can gather here." Gene, who owns several other buildings in Nauvoo, said he's had from 20,000 to 25,000 visitors at the hotel since 1989. Breakfast is included, and rates are standard. Visit www.nauvooalabama.com to check out special events in town.

About a mile from the hotel on the Carbon Hill and Nauvoo Road, you'll find some of the best barbecue in these parts at the **Slick Lizard Smokehouse** (205–697–5789). Named for a local mine, the eatery's walls are made of rough lumber edged with bark. Iced tea arrives in quart-size fruit jars with handles, and the decor features light fixtures made of wagon wheels. Farm implements, a wash pot, rub board, Buffalo Rock Cola signs, Alabama football memorabilia, old photos, and newspaper clippings add to the atmosphere.

The menu explains what's behind the name: "You're as slick as a lizard!" one miner said to another as they crawled out of the mine. That's how mining was done—on your belly through slick clay portals that were only about 25 inches high. This mine was located behind the present cafe in the mid-1920s.

"As the story continues, the name 'Slick Lizard' stuck with us. We were a coal-mining town, and we are very proud of our heritage and community. Welcome to Slick Lizard Smokehouse!" The staff invites you to "fill your gizzard at the Slick Lizard" on Thursday and Sunday from 11:00 A.M. to 8:00 P.M. and on Friday and Saturday from 11:00 A.M. to 9:00 P.M. Economical prices.

(205–934–4475). (But you probably won't find a nearby parking place, so wear your walking shoes.) With a rare and valuable collection of medical books and manuscripts (some predate the printing press), the library houses one of the country's foremost collections of its type—on par with similar collections at Harvard, Yale, Johns Hopkins, and other prestigious institutions. Incredible as it sounds, you can read actual letters (pertaining to dental matters) handwritten by George and Martha Washington. The library also owns original correspondence of Louis Pasteur, Sir William Osler, Pierre Curie, and Florence Nightingale. These letters, of course, are safely locked up, but you can ask the curator to don white gloves and show them to you.

The library owes its existence to radiologist Lawrence Reynolds, an Alabamian who grew up in a family of physicians and devoted much of his lifetime to acquiring rare medical books and manuscripts (once spending a month's salary of $600 on a single volume). In 1958 Dr. Reynolds donated his impressive collection of some 5,000 items (now doubled in size) to his alma mater. The library's collection features richly illustrated vellum manuscripts, rare first editions such as Vesalius's 1543 textbook on human anatomy, the earliest known treatise on wine, and a 1517 handbook of surgery (written in German instead of Latin) with extraordinary hand-executed illustrations. Another work, William Harvey's 1628 *De motu cordis,* accurately describes the body's blood circulation for the first time. Also, the library owns a comprehensive collection of primary and secondary resource material relating to Civil War medicine. Other interesting items include antique maps, a sizable collection of Nobel Prize Papers, and a set of two Chinese anatomical charts that date to 1668 and delineate the body's acupuncture points. Don't miss the display of exquisite ivory miniature mannequins (physicians' dolls used for medical instruction) dating from the seventeenth and eighteenth centuries. Another room contains displays of various medical instruments and equipment along with changing exhibits. The library and museum are open from 9:00 A.M. to 5:00 P.M. Monday through Friday, and admission is free. You can find more information at www.uab.edu/historical with links to the Reynolds Historical Library, the Alabama Museum of Health Sciences, and the UAB Archives.

Don't miss the ***Birmingham Civil Rights Institute*** (205–328–9696), located at 520 Sixteenth Street North. The focal point of the Civil Rights District, which also embraces historic Sixteenth Street Baptist Church and Kelly Ingram Park, the facility features innovative exhibits, which re-create in graphic fashion a sad chronology of segregation's inequities. Visitors start their journey through darkness with a film, followed by a startling entrance to the "Barriers" Gallery, where exhibits trace the struggle that led to the passage of civil rights laws. The new Richard Arrington Jr. Resource Gallery offers an interactive multimedia experience and creates a "living library" honoring persons who participated in the civil rights struggle. Video segments from the institute's Oral History Project interviews are available for learning and research. Admission. Hours are 10:00 A.M. to 5:00 P.M. Tuesday through Saturday and 1:00 to 5:00 P.M. Sunday. Visit www.bcri.org for more information.

While exploring the Magic City, take in nearby Homewood, where you'll find a delightful neighborhood market and cafe specializing in Mediterranean fare. **Nabeel's Cafe** (205–879–9292) at 1706 Oxmoor Road offers a menu with a global theme and a market filled with imported herbs, coffees, teas, olive oil, beans, nuts, and more. Vats of olives, bins of spices, and wedges of Greek, Italian, Bulgarian, Russian, and Lebanese cheeses tempt the shopper here.

The Krontiras family, John and Ottavia with their son Anthony, own and operate this establishment, housed in the white-painted brick building with an exterior wall mural and green canopies. The cafe evokes the intimacy of a European dining experience with a leisurely sharing of food and drink. Wine barrels and a wooden rack for wine storage along the dining-room wall suggest the old country. Anthony, Nabeel's chef, focuses on family recipes and prepares food with home-cooked flavor. Nabeel's numerous awards include "Birmingham's Favorite Restaurant" in a former readers' poll conducted by *Birmingham Magazine*. "We try to treat customers as if they were guests at our home," said John.

Sip some of the cafe's celebrated and refreshing mint tea and scoop up some taramasalata dip, made of red caviar and salted carp roe, with a pita wedge while you decide what to order. From homemade soups and piquant Greek salads to sandwich specialties like *fior di latte* (made with fresh mozzarella cheese, roasted peppers, and fresh basil), Nabeel's crew prepares everything fresh daily. Favorites include eggplant parmesan and a spinach pie *(spanakopita)*. Made of fresh spinach and layered with phyllo, Greek feta cheese, and herbs, *spanakopita* is served with a salad and pita bread. Other popular menu items include grouper Greek style and filet mignon. End your meal on a sweet note with baklava, cannoli, butter cookies, or honey crescents. Hours run from 9:30 A.M. to 9:30 P.M. Monday through Saturday. Click on www.nabeels.com for more information and some mouth-watering recipes.

Another interesting dining experience awaits at 195 Vulcan Road in Homewood. Here, at **The Restaurant at Culinard** (205–271–8228), you can dip into progressive American cuisine prepared by aspiring chefs and gourmands as they perfect their skills in chopping, whisking, sautéing, and serving their way through a two-year culinary course—longer if they add a baking stint to the core curriculum. Someday, you might say, "I knew that chef when . . ."

Menus, prepared by senior-level students, change seasonally, and you could start your dinner with something like seared diver scallops with sour apple endive risotto or grilled foie gras bruschetta with a morel and leek compote. A second round could translate to something like asparagus and crispy oyster

The Bright Star Celebrates Its One-Hundredth Anniversary in 2007

Bring on the champagne. Light the candles. Start the celebration. The Bright Star has been the setting for countless birthday, engagement, and anniversary parties plus myriad special events and holiday galas. In 2007, the legendary restaurant in Bessemer will hit the century mark—a milestone calling for more festivities, but this time with The Bright Star as honoree.

Kick off your own celebration and make the restaurant's signature bread pudding. Hooray for the Bright Star and a century of stellar dining!

The Bright Star's New Orleans–Style Bread Pudding with Whiskey Sauce

2 cups granulated sugar

2 tablespoons ground cinnamon

1 tablespoon ground nutmeg

12 eggs

1 quart heavy cream

1 tablespoon pure vanilla extract

12 slices French bread, cut in halves

½ cup raisins

In a small mixing bowl, blend sugar, cinnamon, and nutmeg. Mix with spatula or wire whip. In a medium mixing bowl, whip 12 eggs. To same bowl add 1 quart heavy cream and mix well. Add 1 tablespoon pure vanilla extract. Mix all ingredients. Slowly blend ingredients from small mixing bowl into mixture in medium mixing bowl.

In an appropriate size pan, 2 inches to 4 inches deep, place French bread halves. Add ½ cup raisins. Pour pudding mix (medium bowl) over bread and raisins. Allow pudding mix to soak into bread.

To bake, submerge pan in water bath and bake approximately 3 hours at 300 degrees Fahrenheit until golden brown and firm.

Whiskey Sauce

1 pint half-and-half cream

½ cup sugar

1 teaspoon pure vanilla extract

2 tablespoons bourbon

In a boiler, mix half-and-half, sugar, and vanilla. Bring to a boil, then thicken slightly with cornstarch. Add bourbon and stir. Spoon over bread pudding.

bisque. Entrees feature items like grilled rib-eye steaks, veal, roasted striped bass, prawns, leg of lamb and chop, or free-range stuffed chicken breast. Dessert lovers can anticipate temptations like Seville orange tart soufflé with strawberry anglaise or warm chocolate fondant with berries, coriander sauce, and blue ginger ice cream. The chef's table features three-course lunch menus and four-course dinner menus. Most a la carte items fall in the moderate range, and gratuities go to the student scholarship fund. Lunch hours are 11:00 A.M. to 1:00 P.M. Monday through Friday. The dinner schedule is 6:00 to 8:00 P.M. Monday through Thursday and until 9:00 P.M. Friday. Reservations are recommended. Check out www.therestaurantatculinard.com for more information.

Before leaving the Birmingham area, stop by ***The Bright Star*** (205–424–9444) in nearby Bessemer. Housed in a tall brick building at 304 North Nineteenth Street, this restaurant beckons diners with an extensive menu prepared with Greek flair. Brothers Jimmy and Nicky Koikos continue a family culinary tradition that started in 1907.

The attractive interior features roomy brass and glass-topped booths and murals dating from 1915, painted by a European artist traveling through the area. The Bright Star offers daily luncheon specials, such as fresh trout amandine or Greek-style beef tenderloin tips with such side dish choices as fresh fried eggplant, corn on the cob, and candied yams.

For dinner start with a cup of the restaurant's scrumptious gumbo. (All fish dishes here feature fresh seafood straight from the coast.) For the main course, you might choose broiled snapper (Greek style) or the beef tenderloin. Other enticing entrees include lobster and crabmeat au gratin, a broiled seafood platter, and a tasty blackened snapper, prepared New Orleans style, with a creamy wine sauce. Top off your meal with a slice of fresh homemade pineapple-cheese or lemon icebox pie. Economical to moderate prices. Lunch hours start at 10:45 A.M. daily and end at 3:15 P.M., and dinner hours start at 4:30 P.M. and go to 9:00 P.M. except for Thursday through Saturday when the closing time changes to 10:00 P.M. View the property at www.thebrightstar.com.

The Capstone

Traveling southwest from Birmingham about 50 miles takes you to ***Tuscaloosa.*** This college town, rich in tradition, served as Alabama's capital from 1826 to 1846.

Before exploring the area's many attractions, you might like to fortify yourself with a slab of ribs at ***Dreamland*** (205–758–8135), 2 miles from the intersection of U.S. Highway 82 and Interstate 59, off Jug Factory Road in Jerusalem Heights at 5535 Fifteenth Avenue East. Here you don't have to agonize over what to order—the choice is ribs along with slices of white bread to sop up the sauce. You'll also get a bib that says AIN'T NOTHIN' LIKE 'EM—NOWHERE, a stack of napkins, and a wet paper towel to assist you in this gustatory project that must be performed with no inhibitions. If you want more variety in your meal, get a bag of potato chips. Beer or soft drinks, followed by toothpicks, complete the feast.

True, Dreamland stays crowded and the noise level runs high, but regulars say these things add to the place's appeal. Dreamland's hours are 10:00 A.M. to 9:00 P.M. Monday through Thursday. On Friday and Saturday the restaurant is open from 10:00 A.M. to 10:00 P.M. and Sunday from 11:00 A.M. to 9:00 P.M. Rates are economical to moderate.

Continue to nearby *Cypress Inn* (205–345–6963) at 501 Rice Mine Road North. Located on the Black Warrior's banks, this restaurant offers fresh seafood, prime steaks, and traditional Southern fare as well as a relaxing river view. House specialties include Hoppin' John (a combination of black-eyed peas, rice, scallions, and bacon), smoked chicken with white barbecue sauce, crispy fried catfish, and fresh broiled red snapper. Also popular are the homemade yeast rolls, fresh raisin-bran muffins, and peanut butter pie. The Cypress Inn serves lunch from 11:00 A.M. to 2:00 P.M. Sunday through Friday; dinner hours run from 5:00 to 9:00 P.M. Sunday through Thursday and 5:00 to 10:00 P.M. Friday and Saturday. Economical to moderate prices.

alabamatrivia

Founded in 1819 near the site of an early Indian village, Tuscaloosa occupies the highest navigable point on the Black Warrior River.

Art lovers will want to search out a rare museum near NorthRiver Lodge, at 8316 Mountbatten Road. *The Westervelt Warner Museum of American Art* (205–343–4540) showcases Jack W. Warner's remarkable assemblage resulting from four decades of collecting. In addition to paintings and sculpture, the collection includes American decorative arts and antiques such as furniture by Duncan Phyfe, silverware by Paul Revere, exquisite porcelain, early American firearms, and more. "Most of the furniture dates to the period between 1820 and 1840," said Warner, "and every piece is museum quality."

Here, you'll view portraits of Washington, Jefferson, and Lafayette all painted from life as you wend your way through galleries and color-coordinated suites in the Blue, Yellow, Green, and Salmon Rooms. Visitors to the Gulf States Paper offices will remember seeing some of the works previously exhibited there. Now, former CEO and chairman Warner has created a single venue as a backdrop for his extensive collection, which has been called an "unparalleled assembly of 18th, 19th and 20th century American art."

Artists represented include Andrew Wyeth, Frederic Remington, George Catlin, Mary Cassatt, and Georgia O'Keeffe. Also, you'll see works by John Singer Sargent, Winslow Homer, Albert Bierstadt, James McNeil Whistler, Childe Hassam, James Peale, Thomas Cole, Asher B. Durand, and many others.

Be sure to visit the ladies' room (if you're the right gender, that is) to see a series of etchings and other works by Mary Cassatt. The men's room decor features photographs depicting Robert E. Lee and his horse, Traveler, as well as Lee's funeral.

"I often like the little studies better than the big finished painting," said Warner, whose world-class collection can be viewed by the public noon to 5:00 P.M. Tuesday through Friday; 10:00 A.M. to 5:00 P.M. Saturday; and 10:00 A.M. to 5:00 P.M. on Sunday. Admission. For more information check out the museum's Web site at www.warnermuseum.org.

Linked to the museum by a scenic footbridge, the **Westervelt Warner Lodge** (205–343–4215) at 2700 Yacht Club Way, Northeast, offers lovely views in a get-away-from-it-all setting with waterfalls, private garden tours, tennis, swimming, golf, and more. Moderate to deluxe.

Afterward head for the **University of Alabama campus,** the site of a beautiful historic district as well as the home of the Crimson Tide. Since student William Gray Little organized the college's first football club in 1892, Alabama has celebrated "A Century of Champions." A good place to learn about the school's more than one-hundred-year football history is the **Paul W. Bryant Museum** (205–348–4668). To reach the museum from US 82, take the University Boulevard exit and follow the signs. If you arrive via I–59, exit onto Interstate 359, take the Thirty-fifth Street exit to Tenth Avenue, go north to Bryant Drive, and then turn east. You'll find the museum on campus at 300 Paul W. Bryant Drive next to the Four Points Hotel Tuscaloosa-Capstone by Sheraton.

alabamatrivia

Educator Julia Tutwiler, born in 1841 in Tuscaloosa, worked to secure the admission of women to the University of Alabama.

For some background on the legendary figure called "The Bear," the man who became college football's most acclaimed coach, start your museum visit by viewing *The Bryant Legacy,* a film narrated by sports commentator Keith Jackson. While browsing among the displays, you'll see a replicated setting of Bear Bryant's office and a dazzling version of his famous hat. Sculptor Miraslav Havel translated the familiar crimson-and-white houndstooth pattern into a multifaceted Waterford crystal showpiece. A courier transported the real hat from Tuscaloosa to Ireland for its magic rendering—and back again.

Although dedicated to the memory of Bryant, who headed Alabama's football teams from 1958 to 1982, the museum also pays tribute to other coaches and players prominent in the school's history. You'll see photos, memorabilia, and audiovisual displays pertaining to such superstars as Joe Namath, Kenny Stabler, Cornelius Bennett, and Bart Starr. To supplement vintage film clips, montages, and recordings, the museum offers taped highlights of recent games.

In addition to the large exhibit hall, the museum houses a comprehensive library of media guides, game programs, photographs, books, films, scrapbooks, and other materials covering Southeastern Conference and college sports. Modest admission. Except for major holidays, hours run from 9:00 A.M. to 4:00 P.M. daily.

While exploring the campus, stop by the ***Gorgas House*** (205–348–5906) on Capstone Drive. One of four university buildings to survive the Civil War, this 1829 two-story brick Federal-style cottage with a curving cast-iron staircase originally served as a college dining hall. Inside you'll see period furnishings, an outstanding collection of Spanish Colonial silver, and memorabilia of William Crawford Gorgas, who was noted for his work in the prevention and cure of yellow fever. Modest admission. The Gorgas House is open Tuesday through Friday from 10:00 A.M. to 4:00 P.M. Tap into http://amnh.ua.edu and link to Gorgas House. for more details.

Housed at nearby Smith Hall, the ***Alabama Museum of Natural History*** (205–348–7550) features extensive fossil and mineral collections. Entering this 1909 Classical Revival building, you'll see a spacious hall and a sweeping marble staircase with iron railings. Exhibits include pottery, tools, weapons, and various artifacts from South Pacific and Central and South American cultures.

On display in the gallery upstairs, you'll find the Hodges meteorite—an outer-space missile weighing eight-and-a-half pounds that struck a Sylacauga woman in 1954. Featured fossils include mammoth, mastodon, mosasaur, and marine turtle, along with a recently acquired 65-foot whale fossil. You'll also see a Studebaker buggy from the 1880s and a free-standing exhibit illustrating the research methods used by Professor Eugene Allen Smith, for whom the building is named, in gathering his geological and biological collections. Except for major holidays, you can visit the museum Tuesday through Saturday from 10:00 A.M. to 4:30 P.M. Modest admission. Check amnh.ua.edu for more background.

Downtown at 2300 University Boulevard in a building that dates to the 1890s, you'll find ***DePalma's*** (205–759–1879). This Italian cafe is noted for its pizzas, calzones, and dishes such as pine nut–crusted salmon, veal Marsala, or pasta DePalma—angel-hair pasta baked in a cream sauce with garlic, cheeses, and Italian herbs and topped with mushrooms, mozzarella, and a choice of ham, Italian sausage, artichokes, and more. Tiramisu ranks at the top of the dessert list, and the crew offers a great wine selection, too. In fact, the owners make regular scouting trips to Italy for their selections. Here, messages don't come *in* a bottle—but *on* a bottle—because the staff invites you to sign and date your wine label and pen an appropriate message. Then your special bottle joins a long line of others on the booth-level shelf. DePalma's is open from 11:00 A.M. to 10:00 P.M. Sunday through Thursday and until 11:00 P.M. Friday and Saturday. Prices are economical to moderate.

After your campus tour take time to explore Tuscaloosa (a Choctaw name that means "black warrior"). While downtown, stop by the **Battle-Friedman House** (205–758–6138), a handsome Greek Revival mansion located at 1010 Greensboro Avenue. Built in 1835, this structure now serves as a house museum and city cultural center. The home may be visited Tuesday through Saturday between 10:00 A.M. and noon and 1:00 to 4:00 P.M. and Sunday from 1:00 to 4:00 P.M. Admission.

Continue to 1512 Greensboro Avenue, where you'll find **The Waysider Restaurant** (205–345–8239) in a small early-twentieth-century house. Because this is *the* place for breakfast in Tuscaloosa, you may have to stand in line, so bring along a newspaper to read while you wait for a table. No wimpy affair, breakfast at The Waysider means homemade biscuits (with a deserved reputation), eggs, grits (get the cheese version), and a meat of your choice: from sugar-cured ham to grilled pork chops or steak. An order of real country-cured ham with two eggs and red-eye gravy runs in the economical range. You can also opt for pancakes.

The Waysider opens at 5:30 A.M. Tuesday through Saturday. Sunday breakfast hours run from 6:30 A.M. to 1:00 P.M. Lunch hours are 11:00 A.M. to 1:30 P.M. Tuesday through Friday.

Consider cruising the Black Warrior River aboard the **Bama Belle** (205–339–1108), a paddlewheel riverboat replica. Owner Nikki Medeiros offers scenic, dinner, and holiday cruises plus private party charters. For information on rates and the current cruise schedule, call or click on www.bama belle.com. "We're docked at #1 Greensboro Avenue in Tuscaloosa's new Riverwalk Park," said Nikki, "and the park is a great place for biking, jogging, and roller blading."

Next, head to nearby **Northport,** just a short drive across the Black Warrior River. Once called Kentuck, Northport has developed into an important craft center with a complex of studios and galleries. Each fall the **Kentuck Festival of the Arts** features more than 300 selected artists and craftspeople from all over the country. Celia O'Kelley, Steve Davis, Justin Robinson, Ann Betak, and a number of other artists maintain individual studios at **Kentuck Art Center** (205– 758–1257), located at 503 Main Avenue. The gift shop, which offers photography, pottery, glass, jewelry, musical instruments, textiles, baskets, and other items, is open Monday through Friday from 9:00 A.M. to 5:00 P.M. and Saturday from 10:00 A.M. to 4:30 P.M. Call for information on the center's artists, exhibits, or Kentuck Museum's gallery or visit www.kentuck.org.

While exploring Northport, stop by **The Globe** (205–391–0949) at 430 Main Avenue, where you'll find a menu with an international focus. As for the restaurant's name, founding partners Jeff Wilson and Gary Wise, who met during a university production of *Richard II,* chose The Globe in reference to Shakespeare's famous London theater; moreover, back in the 1820s and '30s, Northport was home to a hotel called The Globe, located nearby. Spotlighting the Bard, the decor features framed page reproductions of woodcuts from the *First Folio.* Drawings of Shakespearean characters share billing with photos of downtown Northport in earlier years.

A brisk business made it necessary to enlarge the restaurant, accomplished by knocking a hole through the wall to the adjoining structure, a former dry-goods store. Both buildings date to 1909, and an archway permits easy access between them. (Some people claim a ghost roams The Globe's premises during the wee hours.)

Jeff and his wife, Kathy, later bought Gary's interest in the business, and describe the cuisine as ranging from "traditional French to fusion." The ever-popular Athenian pasta salad consists of orzo and vegetables in a balsamic vinaigrette, topped with feta cheese, Kalamata olives, and grilled shrimp. Another favorite lunch item, The Globe's special quesadillas come in a vegetarian version or with grilled chicken, shrimp, Creole crawfish, or jumbo lump crabmeat. The menu's global influence manifests itself in such items as scallops Madrid and Jamaican jerk chicken served over a mango rum compote and topped with red onions and fresh basil mustard. Lunch hours run from 11:00 A.M. to 3:00 P.M. Thursday through Saturday, and dinner is served from 5:00 to 10:00 P.M. Monday through Saturday. Rates are economical to moderate.

If you have a green thumb, be sure to stop by the Potager (205–752–4761), next door at 428 Main Avenue. The shop offers everything from books and tools to gardening accessories. Zebra finches provide the chirping background music. Afterward step through the connecting door to Adams' Antiques for more browsing. Both shops are open from 10:00 A.M. to 4:30 P.M. Tuesday through Saturday.

After your Northport excursion, head for **Moundville,** called by *National Geographic* "the Big Apple of the 14th century." To reach **Moundville Archaeological Park** (205–371–2572 or 205–371–2234), located about 15 miles south of Tuscaloosa, take State Route 69 South. Said by archaeologists to be the best-preserved prehistoric settlement east of the pueblos, Moundville is an internationally known archaeological site with more than twenty flat-topped earthen mounds, plus other less prominent ones, spread over a 317-acre setting on the

Black Warrior River. For a sweeping overview of the grounds, you can climb to the top of a 60-foot ceremonial mound. At the ***Jones Archaeological Museum,*** you'll see hundreds of Mississippian artifacts, ceremonial vessels, and tools made by the advanced group of prehistoric people who occupied this area between A.D. 1000 and 1450. Don't miss the Rattlesnake disc, the most famous artifact ever found at Moundville. Although scholars disagree on the meaning of the entwined rattlesnakes on the disc, the hand with the eyelike motif in the palm is common in Mississippian art.

The park, open daily, may be visited from 8:00 A.M. to 8:00 P.M. Except for major holidays, the museum is open 9:00 A.M. to 5:00 P.M. The museum closes at 4:00 p.m. from November through February. Camping, hiking, and picnicking facilities are available. Modest admission. The annual four-day ***Moundville Native American Festival,*** featuring southeastern Native American crafts and cultural activities, takes place during the first week in October. For more information, click on http://moundville.ua.edu.

After your ancient history junket, you'll probably be ready for a present-day meal, and you can find a tasty one in downtown Moundville at ***Miss Melissa's Café*** (205–371–9045). Located at 384 Market Street, the restaurant serves "a meat and two or three," vegetable plates, chicken salad, homemade pies and cakes, and more. Current hours are 6:00 A.M. until 2:00 P.M. Monday through Saturday. Economical.

Afterward return north to US 82, and travel west toward Pickensville and the Tennessee-Tombigbee (Tenn-Tom) Waterway, which offers exceptional fishing, hunting, and recreational facilities.

Tenn-Tom Terrain

Don't miss the ***Tom Bevill Visitor Center*** (205–373–8705) at Pickensville, ½ mile south of the junctions of State Routes 14 and 86. The white-columned Greek Revival–style mansion you see here looks as if it dates from the mid-1800s but actually was completed in 1986. Definitely not your average rest stop, this facility primarily represents a composite of three historical homes in the vicinity, and you'll see portraits of these grand mansions in the central hall. Ascend the sweeping stairway to the second floor, where various exhibits interpret the Tennessee-Tombigbee Waterway's history. A 22-foot relief map illustrates the waterway's course through several locks and dams, and a model display demonstrates the lockage process. Even better, you can climb to the roof level and perhaps watch a vessel pass through the Tom Bevill Lock and Dam. Whether or not said event happens during your visit, the splendid view from the cupola justifies the climb.

Strange as It Sounds

Carrollton offers a unique site—a face imprinted on a windowpane at the *Pickens County Courthouse.* To learn the strange story behind the image of a prisoner's face preserved here since 1878 (the visage remains despite repeated scrubbings and harsher attempts at removal), step inside the courthouse and pick up a leaflet that provides some background information. You can also read an intriguing account of the mysterious face in Kathryn Tucker Windham's book *13 Alabama Ghosts and Jeffrey* (published by the University of Alabama Press in Tuscaloosa).

After your house tour, stop by the U.S. Snagboat *Montgomery* near the visitor center. Recently declared a National Historic Landmark, this steam-powered sternwheeler once kept Southern rivers navigable by removing tons of debris, such as fallen trees and sunken logs, that impeded river traffic. Except for some federal holidays, and weekends during January and February, the center is open daily year-round. Summer hours are 9:00 A.M. to 5:00 P.M., and winter hours are 8:00 A.M. to 4:00 P.M.

Next, head south to *Aliceville,* home of a unique museum, a lovely bed-and-breakfast, and fine Southern fare at *Plantation House Restaurant* (205–373–8121). The eatery, located at 102 Memorial Parkway on the State Route 17 bypass across from the Piggly Wiggly supermarket, features two homemade soups daily and plenty of ethnic variety with Cajun, Italian, and Mexican selections. You'll enjoy a variety of homemade desserts at this restaurant, which dates to 1905 and is listed on the Alabama Register of Historic Landmarks and Heritage. The restaurant opens daily at 11:00 A.M. and closes at 9:00 P.M. Monday through Saturday and 2:00 P.M. on Sunday. Prices are moderate.

Don't miss the *Aliceville Museum* (205–373–2363), downtown at 104 Broad Street. During World War II some 6,000 German prisoners—most from Field Marshall Erwin Rommel's Afrika Korps—were interned at Camp Aliceville, site of the present-day *Sue Stabler Park* about 2 miles due west of town on State Route 17. In 1993 the city hosted its fifty-year Prisoner of War Reunion. During this three-day event, officials, residents, and visitors—including fifteen German ex-POWs and their families—gathered to dedicate the only World War II German POW museum in the United States. A fifteen-minute video, featuring first-person interviews with the camp guards and prisoners, provides background on the museum's focus. Historians will want to view a forty-five-minute video produced by the History Channel. Exhibits include drawings, paintings, sculpture, musical instruments, furniture, newspapers, photos, and other artifacts from Camp Aliceville. Also, visitors can see an American military collection from World War II in the adjacent building and a 1948 Coca-Cola bottling works. Museum hours are 10:00 A.M. to 4:00 P.M. Monday through Friday and 10:00 A.M. to 2:00 P.M. Saturday. Modest admission.

You can enjoy some warm hospitality at *Myrtlewood* (205–373–2623 or 866–409–7523), a bed-and-breakfast at 602 Broad Street. Owned by Jeanne and Jerry Cockrell, this 1909 home features sun porches, stained glass, and Victorian furnishings. Be sure to notice the coffee table's display of memorabilia in a front parlor. Guests can opt for an early Continental breakfast or a full plantation breakfast in the dining room. Standard to moderate rates.

From Aliceville you can either dip southeast via State Route 14 to Eutaw (a charming town covered in the Southwest section of this book) or return east to tour Tannehill, about midway between Birmingham and Tuscaloosa.

Peach Country

To reach *Tannehill Historical State Park* (205–477–5711) near McCalla, take exit 100 off I–59 and follow the signs. This 1,500-acre wooded park spills into Tuscaloosa, Jefferson, and Bibb Counties. On the grounds you'll see the remains of the Tannehill Iron Furnaces and more than forty pioneer homes and farm outbuildings. A cotton gin, blacksmith shop, and gristmill (that grinds cornmeal one weekend a month from March to November) add to the authenticity of this mid-1800s re-creation. Exhibits at the Iron and Steel Museum of Alabama spotlight the history of technology prior to 1850. The facility offers hiking trails and camping. The park is open from 7:00 A.M. to dark year-round. Museum hours run from 8:30 A.M. to 4:30 P.M. except during daylight savings time, when they change to 9:00 A.M. to 5:00 P.M. Modest admission.

Before leaving the park, stop by *Furnace Master's Restaurant* (205–477–7707) to enjoy a comfortable and rustic atmosphere and view the world from a rocking chair. Try the seafood buffet, served Friday and Saturday, starting at 5:00 P.M., and sample the Greek-style coleslaw. A breakfast buffet is served on the weekends. Hours are 11:00 A.M. to 8:00 P.M. Tuesday through Thursday, 11:00 A.M. to 9:00 P.M. Friday, 7:00 A.M. to 9:00 P.M. Saturday, and 7:00 A.M. to 9:00 P.M. Sunday. Economical prices.

Afterward you might like to shift south to *Montevallo,* located in the middle of Alabama. Here the *University of Montevallo,* situated on a beautiful campus complete with brick streets, tree-lined drives, and historical buildings such as the 1823 King House and Reynolds Hall, makes a pleasant stopover. An arbor walk features a variety of trees labeled by their common and scientific names. Better yet, pick up a *Red Brick Walking Tour* guide, available in versions highlighting several interests—from architectural and horticultural to ghosts. These guides and other information on local sites are available

Reynolds Hall at the University of Montevallo

at the chamber of commerce office (205–665–1519) and the Montevallo Welcome Center, both based at the historic Will Lyman House at 720 Oak Street, adjacent to the campus. The public can also attend campus concerts, plays, films, lectures, art exhibits, and sporting events; most activities are free. Call the university's public relations office at (205) 665–6230 to check on current happenings during the time of your visit

For overnighters, the on-campus *Ramsay Conference Center* (205–665–6280) offers double rooms (with TV but no phones) on a space-available basis, seven days a week during the school term, at bargain rates. A short stroll away you'll find the college dining hall with cafeteria-style meals. Pay-at-the-door prices for breakfast, lunch, and dinner are economical.

While in Montevallo spend some time browsing among the treasures at *The House of Serendipity.* Housed in a downtown vintage building with a pressed-tin ceiling and wraparound balcony, this unique establishment is located at 645 Main Street. Owned by Jane and Bruce McClanahan, this shop, where "the unexpected is found," features everything from antiques, greeting cards, and art supplies to Basket Case creations by basketry instructors Faye Roberts and Mimi Lawley. Jane also offers a matching service for discontinued patterns in American crystal and dinnerware. Store hours are 9:00 A.M. to 5:00 P.M. Monday through Saturday.

The *McKibbon House Bed and Breakfast Inn* (205–665–1275) at 611 East Boundary Street offers bed-and-breakfast accommodations and a beckoning front porch with comfortable swing and wicker seating. This Queen Anne Victorian, which dates to 1900, makes a lovely base while you visit local attractions in the

Montevallo area. After a day of sightseeing, you can look forward to relaxation and warm hospitality plus wine and cheese in the late afternoon.

New owner Lyle Cunningham, originally from Shelby County but more recently Napa Valley, returned to her roots and bought this attractive property complete with 80 percent of the home's furnishings from the Dew family. Lyle previously worked as a chef on a dude ranch in Wyoming and operated a log cabin vacation rental in Napa Valley. She often prepares her breakfast specialty, vanilla French toast, for guests.

Lyle's sister, Leigh Hardin, serves as business partner and lives in a cottage behind the main house. Trooper, "a black lab who thinks he's a person in a dog outfit, will welcome you because he thinks you came only to see him," says Lyle. You can also pay a visit to www.mckibbonhouse.com, but you won't get the vanilla French toast. Moderate rates.

A Revolutionary Experience

Prepare yourself for a revolutionary experience and step into the action at *The American Village* (877–811–1776), located 4 miles off I-65 at exit 234 in Montevallo. Actually, you don't have to do much preparation if your visit coincides with that of school groups because their teachers have already primed them to participate and appreciate the exciting turn of events that brought about a struggling young nation's independence.

Authentically costumed interpreters bring to life the fervor of that time when our forebears made choices that formed the fabric of our lives today. You'll get caught up in such events as the Stamp Act Rally and interact with colonial residents expressing their growing resentment against the mother country. You'll hear Patrick Henry's fiery oratory and attend the 1787 Philadelphia Convention to form a new national government. You'll voice your opinions, vote, and maybe even sit behind the desk in the Oval Office.

The backdrop for this revolutionary experiment is a complex of various colonial buildings including the centerpiece Washington Hall, inspired by Mount Vernon, and a Williamsburg-style courthouse. But this 113-acre development is not about buildings—handsome though they are—it's about ideas. And the dreamer who envisioned this place, Tom Walker, who serves as executive director, wants citizens of today and tomorrow to realize they also have choices—just as our early leaders did. The village's mission of strengthening and renewing the foundations of American citizenship can be witnessed in action weekdays from 10:00 A.M. to 4:00 P.M. Call for the summer schedule. Tours start on the hour, and the day's final tour begins at 3:00 P.M. You can pay a virtual visit via www.americanvillage.org. Admission.

Village visitors can anticipate another treat with the completion of a Southern Living Showcase House in October 2006. Patterned after the Philadelphia residence occupied by George and Martha Washington and then John and Abigail Adams, the President's House will add another facet to the on-site history lesson. Admission.

Before leaving town, visit Orr Park, where you can stroll along Shoal Creek, a natural habitat for Tim Tingle's life-size wood carvings of birds, animals, and wizard faces.

Continuing south to **Clanton** in the heart of peach country, you'll find several places to purchase this locally grown fruit. Peach Park, for instance, features fresh peaches (in season) along with homemade peach ice cream, milk shakes, yogurt, and other delicious desserts as well as pecans and boiled peanuts.

While in the area, plan a visit to **Confederate Memorial Park** (205–755–1990), just off U.S. Highway 31 near I–65. The site of a former home for Confederate veterans and their widows, the park features a museum with historical displays, Civil War relics, flags, Confederate uniforms, and weaponry. On the grounds you'll also find two cemeteries, a chapel, the old Mountain Creek Post Office, picnic pavilions, and hiking trails. Except for major holidays, the museum is open from 9:00 A.M. to 5:00 P.M. daily with the exception of a lunch hour. The park may be visited year-round from 6:00 A.M. to dusk.

Head back north to **Calera** to see several antiques shops and the **Heart of Dixie Railroad Museum** (205–668–3435). From I–65 take exit 228 and travel less than a mile west on State Route 25, following signs to the museum. Exhibits include World War II photos, framed timetables, waiting room benches, old railroad lanterns, signal equipment, special tools used to repair steam locomotives, a caboose stove, and an arrival/departure board from the demolished Birmingham Terminal. A glass case contains dishes made by Marshall Field and Company in 1925 for the Rock Island Lines. You'll see a centralized train control board (CTC) with which one person, a railroad counterpart of the airline's air traffic controller, managed a large section of tracks and the trains that traveled it. Locomotives, guard cars (the museum owns four of only six in existence), passenger and freight cars, and the state's largest railroad crane stand outside the green depot museum. Hours are 9:00 A.M. to 4:00 P.M. Monday through Saturday. The museum sponsors train rides and special events. Call for more information on the museum and train ride schedule with excursion rates. Trains generally run from mid-March until the weekend before Christmas. Museum admission is free, but donations are accepted. Click on www.heartofdixie rrmuseum.org for more information.

Continue a few miles northeast via State Route 25 to **Columbiana,** where you'll discover hundreds of prized possessions from the country's *first* First Family. "People can't believe we have all these things that belonged to George Washington, and they are amazed to find such a collection here in central Alabama instead of Virginia," says Bonnie Atchison, curator of the **Karl C. Harrison Museum of George Washington** (205–669–8767). Housed in a newly constructed building that adjoins the Mildred B. Harrison Library's right side, the facility provides spacious quarters for the extensive collection and permits previously stored pieces to be exhibited. Located at 50 Lester Street, the museum stands behind the handsome Shelby County Courthouse.

The foyer's focal point, a commanding bust of George Washington, was created by French sculptor Jean Antoine Houdan from a life mask. Nearby, a glass case topped by a handsome pair of pink Sevres vases contains family correspondence, documents, jewelry, and a writing instrument from Washington's survey case. "One of our finest possessions is Martha's prayer book. We also have an original letter, written about a year before her death," said former curator Nancy Harrison, whose father established the museum in 1982.

Two dining room tables feature beautiful settings with exquisite porcelain pieces and coin-silver utensils used at Mount Vernon. A prized 207-piece set of Minton porcelain is displayed on a table and buffet and also fills the shelves of a walnut cabinet signed by William Elfie.

Other treasures include family portraits, various personal items, an original 1787 Samuel Vaughn sketch of Mount Vernon's grounds, and some seventy letters and documents dating to the Revolutionary War period. You can read correspondence from James Madison, Lord Cornwallis, John Adams, Aaron Burr, and other historic figures. The collection's oldest item is the 1710 handwritten will of Col. Daniel Parke, the grandfather of Martha Washington's first husband. You'll also see an original tintype made by Civil War photographer Mathew B. Brady that depicts Robert E. Lee in uniform for the last time.

Amassed by Eliza Parke Custis Law, Martha Washington's granddaughter, the collection passed through six generations of Washington heirs down to Shelby County's Charlotte Smith Weaver. After giving her grandchildren selected items, Mrs. Weaver offered the remainder of the family collection for public preservation. Columbiana banker Karl Harrison acquired two-thirds of it for this museum, and the rest went to Mount Vernon. The Columbiana museum procured additional family pieces from the estate of George Washington's half brother, Augustin, in 1989. Except for major holidays, the museum is open 10:00 A.M. to 3:00 P.M. Monday through Friday. Guided tours, which take about an hour, are available Wednesday through Friday. Admission is free. Visit online at www.washingtonmuseum.com.

Woodland and Water

Continue east to **Sylacauga,** sometimes called Marble City. While many cities contain marble monuments and buildings, here the entire town rests on a marble bed about 32 miles long and more than a mile wide. Sylacauga marble was used in the U.S. Supreme Court Building in Washington, D.C., Detroit's General

Motors Building, and in many other distinctive edifices. "The Sylacauga area has some of the whitest marble in the world," says a local quarrying company official.

Stop by the **Isabel Anderson Comer Museum and Arts Center** (256–245–4016) at 711 Broadway Avenue North. At the museum, housed in a former library building dating from the 1930s, you'll see a big chunk of calcite quartz, unusual because it came from the middle of a local marble quarry. The museum owns several pieces by Giuseppe Moretti, the Italian sculptor who designed Birmingham's statue of *Vulcan*. Moretti came to Sylacauga in the early 1900s to open a marble quarry.

The museum's displays cover everything from beaded evening bags and Victorian hat pins to a reproduction of the Hodges meteorite that hurtled down on Sylacauga from outer space and struck a local woman in 1954. Here, you'll find a gallery of Native American artifacts, antique toys, handmade fabrics from the 1830s, and an extensive collection of photos and scrapbooks on local history. Pioneer exhibits are housed in the basement. One section features albums, awards, photos, costumes, and other memorabilia of native son Jim Nabors, who starred as TV's Gomer Pyle on *The Andy Griffith Show*.

alabamatrivia

More than two dozen albums showcase the singing talent of Sylacauga native Jim Nabors of *The Andy Griffith Show* and *Gomer Pyle, USMC* fame.

The museum is open 10:00 A.M. to 5:00 P.M. Tuesday through Friday or by appointment. Although there's no admission charge, donations are accepted.

Don't leave town without treating yourself to some ice cream at **Blue Bell Creameries** (256–249–6100 or 888–573–5286) at 423 North Norton Avenue. What's your pleasure? Choices range from lemon, triple chocolate, chocolate chip, caramel pecan fudge, and banana split to pecan praline and cream, cherry vanilla, and black walnut—and the list goes on. In addition to watching ice cream being made, you can relax (after you finish agonizing over which flavor to order) in the old-fashioned ice-cream parlor or browse in the Country Store. Tours, which last about forty-five minutes, take place Monday through Friday. Call ahead for information on how to schedule or join a tour. The Country Store is open from 9:00 A.M. to 5:00 P.M. Monday through Friday.

After leaving Sylacauga, follow U.S. Highway 280 southeast to **Alexander City,** home of the Russell Corporation. Employing about four-fifths of the local workforce, Russell outfits the sports world all the way from Little League through hundreds of college teams to most of the National Football League. This company handles every step of the process from cotton production to finished product. The sweat suit you don for your jog around the block may well have come from Alex City, as the locals call it.

The *Russell Retail Store* (256–500–4464), a big cheese-wedge of a building at 3562 US 280, sells sweatpants and tops, T-shirts, cardigans, and other leisure wear—maybe even your favorite team's togs. In addition to a university section (that carries mostly Atlantic Coast Conference and Southeastern Conference athletic apparel), the outlet offers casual clothing for ladies and children. Cross-Creek and HIGH Cotton lines feature an array of items in both heavyweight and lightweight knits. You may want to personalize your purchases with selected transfers—from SAVE THE EARTH to holiday and hunting themes—that can be applied by heat press in fifteen seconds.

Clothing sells here for one-third off the retail value. Also, a back room contains discounted items. The store's hours are 9:00 A.M. to 5:30 P.M. Monday through Saturday and 1:00 to 5:00 P.M. Sunday.

While in the Alex City area, you might like to explore nearby *Horseshoe Bend National Military Park,* the site of the final battle of the Creek War. Located about 12 miles north of Dadeville on State Route 49, the 2,040-acre park features a visitor center with exhibits on the battle, Creek Indian culture, and frontier life.

Other local options include boating, swimming, and fishing at *Lake Martin,* which offers a 750-mile shoreline against a backdrop of wooded hills. This body of water spills over the southern half of Tallapoosa County and even splashes into neighboring Elmore and Coosa Counties. Depending on the season and local weather conditions, anglers haul in largemouth and striped bass, bream, bluegill, crappie, and catfish from this lake. For more outdoor recreation continue south to Elmore County.

Places to Stay in Central Alabama

ALEXANDER CITY

Holiday Inn Express
2945 U.S. Highway 280
(256) 234–5900 or
(800) HOLIDAY

Horseshoe Inn
3146 U.S. Highway 280
(256) 234–6311

Jameson Inn
4335 U.S. Highway 280
(256) 234–7099 or
(800) 526–3766

ALICEVILLE

Myrtlewood
602 Broad Street Northeast
(205) 373–2623 or
(866) 409–7523

ANNISTON

The Victoria
1600 Quintard Avenue
(256) 236–0503 or
(800) 260–8781

ASHVILLE

Roses and Lace Country Inn
20 Rose Lane
(205) 594–4366

BIRMINGHAM

Birmingham Marriott
3590 Grandview Parkway
(205) 968–3775 or
(800) 627–7468

**Crowne Plaza,
The Redmont**
2101 Fifth Avenue North
(205) 324–2101 or
(800) 2–CROWNE

Pickwick Hotel
1023 Twentieth
Street South
(205) 933–9555 or
(800) 255–7304

**Renaissance Ross Bridge
Golf Resort and Spa**
4000 Grand Avenue
(205) 916–7677 or (800)
593–6419
www.rossbridgeresort.com

**Sheraton
Birmingham Hotel**
2101 Richard Arrington Jr.
Boulevard North
(205) 324–5000 or
(888) 627–7095

The Tutwiler
2021 Park Place North
(205) 322–2100 or
(866) 850–3053

The Wynfrey Hotel
1000 Riverchase Galleria
(205) 987–1600 or
(800) WYNFREY

DELTA

Cheaha State Park
2141 Bunker Loop
(256) 488–5115 or
(800) 846–2654

MONTEVALLO

**McKibbon House
Bed & Breakfast Inn**
611 East Boundary Street
(205) 665–1275

**Ramsay
Conference Center**
University of Montevallo
(205) 665–6280

MUNFORD

The Cedars Plantation
590 Cheaha Road
(256) 761–9090

NAUVOO

Old Harbin Hotel
131 Third Street
(205) 697–5652

OXFORD

**Holiday Inn Express
Hotel & Suites**
160 Colonial Drive
(256) 835–8768
(800) HOLIDAY

PELHAM

Oak Mountain State Park
200 Terrace Drive
(205) 620–2524 or
(800) ALA–PARK

STERRETT

Twin Pines Resort
1200 Twin Pines Road
(205) 672–7575

SYLACAUGA

Jameson Inn
89 Gene Stewart Boulevard
(256) 245–4141 or
(800) 526–3766

TUSCALOOSA

Comfort Inn
4700 Doris Pate Drive
(205) 556–3232 or
(800) 311–3811

Courtyard by Marriott
4115 Courtney Drive
(205) 750–8384 or
(800) 321–2211

**Four Points Hotel
Tuscaloosa–Capstone
by Sheraton**
320 Paul Bryant Drive
(205) 752–3200 or
(800) 477–2262

Westervelt Warner Lodge
2700 Yacht Club Way, NE
(205) 343–4215

VINCENT

Blue Spring Manor
2870 Highway 83
(205) 672–9955

Places to Eat in
Central Alabama

ALEXANDER CITY

Cecil's Public House
243 Green Street
(256) 329–0732

Sinclair's Kowaliga
295 Kowaliga Marina Road
(334) 857–2889

ALICEVILLE

**Plantation House
Restaurant**
102 Memorial Parkway
(205) 373–8121

ANNISTON

Betty's Bar-B-Q, Inc.
401 South Quintard Avenue
(256) 237–1411

FOR MORE INFORMATION ABOUT CENTRAL ALABAMA

**Alexander City Area
Chamber of Commerce**
120 Tallapoosa Street
P.O. Box 926
Alexander City 35011-0926
(256) 234-3461
www.alexandercity.org
receptionac@charterinternet.com

**Anniston/Calhoun County
Chamber of Commerce**
1330 Quintard Avenue
P.O. Box 1087
Anniston 36202
(256) 237-3536 or (800) 489-1087
www.calhounchamber.com
info@calhounchamber.com

**Greater Birmingham
Convention and Visitors Bureau**
2200 Ninth Avenue North
Birmingham 35203-1100
(205) 458-8000 or (800) 458-8085
www.birminghamal.org
info@birmingham.org

Montevallo Chamber of Commerce
720 Oak Street
Montevallo 35115
(205) 665-1519

**Tuscaloosa Convention and
Visitors Bureau**
1305 Greensboro Avenue
P.O. Box 3167
Tuscaloosa 35403
(205) 391-9200 or (800) 538-8696
www.visittuscaloosa.com
tuscacvb@dbtech.net

Classic on Noble
1024 Noble Street
(256) 237-5388

Top O' the River
3330 McClellan Boulevard
(256) 238-0097

The Victoria
1600 Quintard Avenue
(256) 236-0503

ASHVILLE

Ashville House
35 Third Street
(205) 594-7046

BESSEMER

The Bright Star
304 North Nineteenth Street
(205) 424-9444

BIRMINGHAM

Bombay Cafe
2839 Seventh Avenue South
(205) 322-1930

Highlands Bar & Grill
2011 Eleventh Avenue South
(205) 939-1400

Hot and Hot Fish Club
2180 Eleventh Court South
(205) 933-5474

The Olive Tree
2030 Little Valley Road
(205) 823-5825

The Restaurant at Culinard
195 Vulcan Road
(205) 271-8228

Restaurant G
Fourth Avenue North and
Nineteenth Street
(205) 323-1820

The Silvertron Cafe
3813 Clairmont Avenue
(205) 591–3707

CALERA
Zapopan Restaurant
4416 U.S. Highway 31
(205) 668–4008

HOMEWOOD
Nabeel's Cafe
1706 Oxmoor Road
(205) 879–9292

IRONDALE
The Irondale Cafe
1906 First Avenue North
(205) 956–5258

JACKSONVILLE
Old Henry Farm
Restaurants
(aka The Barn)
301 Henry Road Southwest
(256) 435–0673

MAYLENE
Fox Valley Restaurant
County Road 17
(205) 664–8341

McCALLA
Furnace Master's
Restaurant at Tannehill
Historical State Park
12632 Confederate Parkway
(205) 477–7707

MONTEVALLO
Zapopan Restaurant
4551 State Route 25
(205) 665–7404

MOUNDVILLE
Miss Melissa's Café
384 Market Street
(205) 371–9045

MOUNTAIN BROOK
Chez Lulu
1909 Cahaba Road
(205) 870–7011

NAUVOO
Slick Lizard Smokehouse
Carbon Hill and
Nauvoo Road
(205) 697–5789

NORTHPORT
The Globe
430 Main Avenue
(205) 391–0949

OXFORD
China Luck
503 Quintard Drive
(256) 831–5221

SPRINGVILLE
Gulf Seafood
140 Laster Drive
(205) 467–9348

SYLACAUGA
LaCosta Mexican
Restaurant
215 North Broadway Avenue
(256) 249–3360

TRUSSVILLE
Chocolate Biscuit Tearoom
335 Main Street
(205) 655–0119

TUSCALOOSA
Cafe Venice
2321 University Boulevard
(205) 366–1209

Cypress Inn
501 Rice Mine Road North
(205) 345–6963

DePalma's
2300 University Boulevard
(205) 759–1879

Dreamland
Off Jug Factory Road in
Jerusalem Heights
(205) 758–8135

Evangeline's
Galleria of Tuscaloosa
1653 McFarland
Boulevard North
(205) 752–0830

Kozy's
3510 Loop Road
(205) 556–0665

The Waysider Restaurant
1512 Greensboro Avenue
(205) 345–8239

Arlington Antebellum Home and Gardens

331 Cotton Avenue Southwest
Birmingham
(205) 780–5656
This circa 1850 Greek Revival mansion contains a fine collection of period antiques.

Birmingham Zoo

2630 Cahaba Road
(205) 879–0408 or (205) 879–0458
Both big and little kids enjoy outings to this facility, the home of some 900 animals from all over the globe.

International Motorsports Hall of Fame and Talladega Superspeedway

Off Interstate 20, Talladega
(256) 362–5002
This unique facility, which occupies a complex of circular-shaped buildings, captures the speed of movement and thrill of competitive racing. You'll see the Budweiser Rocket Car, a missile on wheels that broke the sound barrier, and record-breaking vehicles once guided by Richard Petty, Bill Elliott, Bobby Allison, and other racing greats. Additional exhibits include vintage autos, drag racers, motorcycles, trophies, photos, and a simulator that puts you in the driver's seat. You can also tour the adjacent Talladega Superspeedway, the world's fastest speedway. For more information check out www.motorsportshalloffame.com and www.talladegasuperspeedway.com.

McWane Science Center

200 Nineteenth Street North
Birmingham
(205) 714–8300
Definitely not off the beaten path, this science-adventure museum occupies the historic Loveman's department store building in the heart of downtown. Youngsters will especially enjoy the IMAX theater's presentations and simulated space-flight experiences offered by the Challenger Center for Space Science Education, a nonprofit organization founded by the families of the seven *Challenger* crew members who died in the tragic 1986 space shuttle explosion. The Ocean Pool, World of Water, and various interactive science exhibits all add to the excitement. Visit the museum's Web site at www.mcwane.org.

VisionLand

Interstate 20/59 near Interstate 459
Bessemer
(205) 481–4750
This fun-filled family park spreads across one hundred rolling acres in Bessemer, just southwest of Birmingham. With a theme dedicated to Birmingham's early iron and steel industry, the amusement park features multiple thrills aboard a $4.5-million wooden roller coaster, The Rampage, plus rides galore. Other attractions include a splash beach and Magic Adventure theme park. Visit the park's Web site at www.visionland.com.

Southeast Alabama

The Plains

On your way to "The Plains" (home of Auburn University) in the historic Chattahoochee Trace's upper section, you may want to swing south to *Tallassee,* just north of Interstate 85 at State Routes 14 and 229, for some home-style mouth-watering food and a yesteryear experience at *Hotel Talisi* (334–283–2769). Located at 14 Sistrunk Avenue, this 1920s hotel brims with antiques and nostalgia—from its red-carpeted lobby with ceiling fans and crystal chandeliers to the second-floor hall-way's wooden "Superman" phone booth. Three baby grand pianos (including a 1924 version), three uprights, and a player spinet add to the ambience.

In the spacious upstairs hall, you'll see Western Union writing desks, interesting reading material, and an array of seating areas—great for conversation or for curling up with a mystery. Furnished in eclectic fashion with finger vases, parlor lamps, and antiques from the early 1900s, the rooms possess a uniqueness noticeably absent in today's world. Standard rates.

Continuing the hotel's famous family-style buffet tradition, Bob Brown, Roger Gaither, and crew offer a daily feast featuring fried chicken, baked chicken with dressing, sweet potato soufflé,

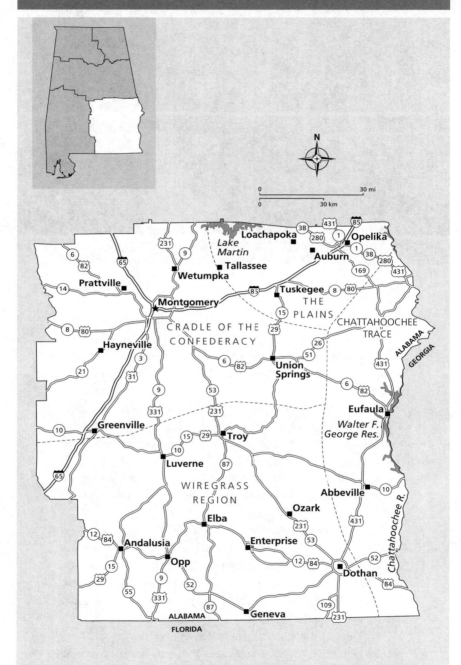

a medley of fresh vegetables, corn bread, hush puppies, and homemade pies accompanied by piano/organ dinner music. Except for Sunday, when the feast ends at 2:50 P.M., hours are 11:00 A.M. to 7:50 P.M. daily. Standard to moderate rates.

South of Tallassee in the Shorter area, search out the ***Back Forty*** (334–727–0880), a farm restaurant at 5001 County Road 30. Marjorie and Ted Johnson allocated the back forty acres of their Hillcrest Farms operation to this tranquil out-of-the-way eatery with a warm country atmosphere. Learn the legend of the hush puppy while enjoying a few with your meal of grilled or fried catfish or a combination platter of shrimp, frog legs, crab claws, and/or oysters. The Back Forty also serves rib-eye steaks, chicken, salads, and sandwiches plus Sunday specials. Top off your meal with cheesecake, which comes from Notasulga's Bulger Creek Farm. Grandma's banana pudding is another popular dessert here. Prices are economical to moderate. The restaurant opens at 5:30 P.M. on Friday and at 4:30 P.M. on Saturday and closes at 9:00 P.M. It is also open the first Sunday of each month from 11:00 A.M. to 2:00 P.M.

Next, strike out east to ***Tuskegee.*** Stop by the ***Tuskegee Human & Civil Rights Multicultural Center*** (334–724–0800), which also serves as a welcome center. Located in a former bank building at 104 South Elm Street, the facility houses exhibits on the history of Macon county, including one on the Tuskegee Syphilis Study and local civil rights activities. Here, you can pick up tourist

GAY'S TOP PICKS IN SOUTHEAST ALABAMA

Alabama Shakespeare Festival,
Montgomery

First White House of the Confederacy,
Montgomery

The Jule Collins Smith Museum of Art,
Auburn

Landmark Park,
Dothan

Lovelace Athletic Museum and Hall of Honor,
Auburn

Old Alabama Town,
Montgomery

Pioneer Museum of Alabama,
Troy

Rosa Parks Library and Museum,
Montgomery

State Capitol,
Montgomery

Town of Eufaula

Tuskegee Institute National Historic Site,
Tuskegee

U.S. Army Aviation Museum,
Fort Rucker

The Intrepid Tuskegee Airmen

During the early 1940s, Moton Field served as the training grounds for the Tuskegee Airmen, who overcame formidable odds to serve their country with bravery and distinction in a segregated America. As escorts to World War II bombing missions in North Africa and Southern Europe, these African-American aviators compiled an enviable combat record and ranked among the military's best pilots. The 332nd Fighter Group never lost a bomber to enemy fighters while escorting the 15th Air Force on bombing missions. Revered by American bomber crews (who called them the "Red-tail Angels" because of their aircrafts' distinctive markings), these flying heroes also commanded the respect of the German Luftwaffe.

At the United States Air Force Academy, the Tuskegee Airmen statue acknowledges their extraordinary contribution: "They rose from adversity through competence, courage, commitment, and capacity to serve America on silver wings, and to set a standard few will transcend."

Lending her support to Tuskegee Institute's civilian pilot training program, First Lady Eleanor Roosevelt visited here in March 1941. She requested to be taken on a flight by Charles Alfred "Chief" Anderson, who inspired the founding of Tuskegee's School of Aviation, and newspapers across the country carried a photo of this unprecedented event.

The Tuskegee group's achievements represent a turning point in the role of African-Americans in the U.S. military and factored into President Harry S. Truman's signing Executive Order 9981 in 1948, setting the stage for the military's desegregation and later the Civil Rights Movement.

In 1998, Congress designated the Tuskegee Airmen National Historic Site as a unit of the National Park System. Although it is still in the developmental stages, visitors can see the remaining hangar, which will later be restored to its original World War II appearance, and other structures such as the the airfield taxiway, control tower, reservoir, gasoline pits, and fuel storage facilities from that period. The modest airport terminal also features exhibits of photos that chronicle the history of Black aviation and the Tuskegee Airmen.

The National Park Service Visitor Center is located on the outskirts of Tuskegee at 1616 Chappie James Avenue. Except for major holidays, the site is open daily from 9:00 A.M. to 4:30 P.M. Free admission. To reach the "Home of Black Aviation," take exit 38 off I–85. For more information call (334) 727–6390 or (334) 724–0922.

information. The staff will answer your questions and suggest nearby off-the-beaten-path spots to visit. Hours are Monday through Saturday from 10:00 A.M. to 3:00 P.M. Admission is free.

For a look at historic farm implements, home furnishings, and exhibits relating to local history, you'll want to visit Tuskegee's downtown square. Beside a florist shop at 109 Westside Street stands the ***Tuskegee Heritage Museum,*** formerly called Kirk's Old Farm Museum. Charles Kirk owns both buildings, and he gives tours of the museum on a reservations basis. To schedule one, call Flowers by Margie (334–727–6200), where you'll probably find Kirk busy helping his wife and making deliveries. Beyond the storefront entrance, you'll see Creek Indian artifacts and memorabilia from Booker T. Washington, Dr. George Washington Carver, and the Tuskegee Airmen. Also on display are hundreds of agricultural tools and appliances used before the advent of electricity, along with merchandise from a 1902 edition of the Sears, Roebuck & Company catalog. Admission.

You'll smell printer's ink when you walk into ***Charlie Tee's*** (334–724–9770) at 119 Westside Street. Former coach and owner Charles Thompson promises "the best screen printing and embroidery on earth," and you can choose a souvenir T-shirt from a selection of designs, including some featuring the famed Tuskegee Airmen. Originally the home of Brown's Dry Goods and Department Store, the building dates to the 1850s. Believed to be the state's oldest commercial building still retaining its original interior, this structure has been added to the list of Alabama's Most Endangered Historic Places. Hours generally run from 9:00 A.M. to 5:00 P.M. Monday through Friday.

To keep up your energy level, stop by H. A. Vaughan Feed and Seed Company (334–727–5700) at 106 Lee Street for a bag of peanuts (warm from the oven) to munch on while exploring.

Next make your way to West Montgomery Road and ***Tuskegee Institute National Historic Site*** (334–727–3200), where even peanut-butter buffs will be amazed to learn about the peanut's potential. The Carver Museum pays tribute to the creative genius of the agronomist, artist, and inventor who helped change the course of Southern agriculture. George Washington Carver's agricultural experiments with peanuts, pecans, sweet potatoes, and cotton

alabamatrivia

George Washington Carver invented peanut butter during his experiments at Tuskegee Institute.

resulted in a more educated approach to farming—not to mention hundreds of new products, many featured among the museum's exhibits. You'll also see some of Carver's artwork and a model of the first lab he used to launch research that resulted in the transformation of sweet potatoes into after-dinner mints, a coffee substitute, lemon drops, starch, synthetic ginger, tapioca, library paste, medicine, writing ink, and a multitude of other items. As for the multipurpose peanut, the legendary scientist's list of possible uses ranges from beverages, foods, cosmetics, dyes, and medicines to diesel fuel, laundry soap, and insecticide. Before you leave the museum, be sure to visit the gift section. I bought a copy of a booklet (first published in June 1925) entitled *How to Grow the Peanut and 105 Ways of Preparing It for Human Consumption,* containing recipes from peanut bisque to peanut pudding. Museum admission is free. Except for Thanksgiving, Christmas, and New Year's Day, the museum is open daily from 9:00 A.M. to 4:30 P.M.

Later take a campus stroll to see some of the handmade brick buildings, which students constructed during the institute's early years. You'll also want to tour *The Oaks,* home of Booker T. Washington, who served as first president of Tuskegee Institute, which was founded in 1881. The home is furnished as it was during the time the Washington family lived there. Admission is free. However, due to renovation, tours are available on a limited basis only. For the current status call (334–727–3200).

Head north to the "land where turtles live"—a former Creek Indian settlement called *Loachapoka* that once also thrived as a stagecoach junction. Seven miles west of Auburn on State Route 14, you'll find the *Loachapoka Historic District,* which features several structures dating from the decade 1840 to 1850. *The Lee County Historical Society Museum,* housed in the old Trade Center building, contains items ranging from a unique hand-carved cedar rocking chair and an 1840s accounting desk to an oak map case, an antique medical bag, and a punch bowl and dipper made from gourds.

Upstairs, rooms with individual themes feature vintage costumes such as an 1877 wedding dress, an exhibit on Ella Smith's Roanoke doll creations, antique quilts, and a melodeon. Other displays include military uniforms and equipment, kitchen utensils and gadgets, and an almost complete section of Auburn annuals that date to the 1890s.

On the grounds you'll see a steam-powered cotton gin, gristmill, working blacksmith shop, bandstand, doctor's buggy, and dogtrot cabin (moved here from rural Tallapoosa County and reconstructed). If you visit in October, don't miss the *Historical Fair and Ruritan's Syrup Sop* in Loachapoka. Folks at this event, harking back to yesteryear, demonstrate the entire process of converting sugar cane into syrup—from cane crushing by mule-drawn press to syrup sampling on homemade sweet potato biscuits (sometimes called "cat head biscuits" because of their large size). For information on making an appointment to see the museum, call the Auburn-Opelika Tourism Bureau at (866) 880–8747 or (334) 887–8747.

Afterward continue east to "sweet Auburn, loveliest village of the plain." This line from Oliver Goldsmith's poem "The Deserted Village" inspired the university town's name. Founded by the Alabama Methodist Conference in 1856, the school later became a land-grant institution. (Incidentally, if you enter *Auburn* by way of I–85, a trail of big orange tiger paws takes you all the way to the university campus.)

GAY'S FAVORITE ANNUAL EVENTS IN SOUTHEAST ALABAMA

Rattlesnake Rodeo
Opp, first Saturday and Sunday
in April
(334) 493–4572 or (800) 239–8054

Azalea-Dogwood Trail and Festival
Dothan, late March or early April
(334) 615–3700 or (888) 449–0212

Auburn Floral Trail
Auburn, late March or early April
(334) 887–8747 or (866) 880–8747

Spring Pilgrimage
Eufaula, first weekend in April
(888) 383–2852

A-Day Football Game
Auburn, April
(334) 844–4040 or (800) AUB–1957

Auburn CityFest
Auburn; April
(866) 880–8747 or (334) 887–8747

Jubilee Cityfest
downtown Montgomery
Memorial Day weekend
(334) 834–7220

Alabama Highland Games
Wynton M. Blount Cultural Park at the
Alabama Shakespeare Festival
Montgomery, fourth Saturday in
September
(334) 272–2174

Riverfront Arts & Food Festival
Train Shed at Union Station
Montgomery, early October
(334) 240–4092

On the Tracks Food & Wine Festival
Opelika, October
(866) 880–8747 or (334) 887–8747

**Historical Fair and Ruritan's Syrup
Sop in Loachapoka**
Loachapoka, October
(334) 887–8747 or (866) 880–8747

National Peanut Festival
Dothan, November
(334) 793–4323 or (888) 449–0212

Start your tour of the *Auburn University Historic District* at Toomer's Corner, a busy intersection that gets layered so deeply with toilet tissue after each Tiger victory that sometimes vehicles cannot pass through for an hour or two while a celebration takes place. (Auburn is the only city in the world to have a line item in the city budget for the removal of toilet paper.) Before embarking on your campus trek, you might like to step into Toomer's Drugstore, a local landmark, to see the antique marble soda fountain and to order a lemonade.

This section of campus features several buildings that date from the 1850s to the early 1900s. You'll see the Gothic Revival University Chapel, Langdon Hall, and Samford Hall. The latter, a four-story brick structure of Italianate design, dates to 1888 and stands on the site of Old Main, a building that burned the year before.

To explore a tucked-away corner on campus, search out the Donald E. Davis Arboretum, with pavilion, lake, and some 200 labeled botanical specimens ranging from red Japanese maples and chinquapin oaks to Southern magnolias and chinaberry trees.

Don't miss the *Lovelace Athletic Museum and Hall of Honor* (334–844–4750), located at the corner of Samford and Donahue in the Athletic Complex. Honoring Auburn's athletes, the museum recognizes their sports achievements with high-tech interactive exhibits, life-size figures in talking dioramas, and a cavalcade of fascinating displays. Trip along the Tiger Trail and experience a vicarious but thrilling football victory with the crowd's roar and take a look at a replicated Toomer's Corner, triumphantly decorated with toilet paper.

Athletes represented include Heisman Trophy winner and football/baseball hero Bo Jackson, NBA star Charles Barkley. star baseball player Frank Thomas, Heisman Trophy winner/coach Pat Sullivan, and legendary coaches Pat Dye and Shug Jordan. Museum hours are 8:00 A.M. to 4:30 P.M. Monday through Friday, 9:00 A.M. to 4:00 P.M. Saturday and the Sundays of home games and 8:00 A.M. to kickoff on Football Saturdays. Check out www.lovelacemuseum.com and see some Auburn legends.

To visit a jewel of a museum, head to 901 South College Street. Here you'll find *The Jule Collins Smith Museum of Art* (334–844–1484) overlooking a three-acre lake. Constructed of travertine stone from Italy, the handsome new facility features eight exhibition galleries, a museum shop, an auditorium, and a cafe (open for lunch Tuesday through Friday). On entering, you'll see a stunning glass chandelier created for the vaulted rotunda by internationally known glass artist Dale Chihuly.

Other treasures include one of the world's largest collections of Victorian Belleek porcelain, outstanding Tibetan bronzes, and more than one hundred of Audubon's most acclaimed prints. But the big story here centers on a collection of thirty-six paintings and drawings that had remained homeless for more than half a century.

Originally assembled by the U.S. State Department in 1946, the collection features works by John Marin, Georgia O'Keeffe, Ben Shahn, Arthur Dove, Ralston Crawford, Yasuo Kuniyoski, and others. Because of its abstract nature and the political leanings of a few of the artists, the traveling exhibit met with so much criticism on the home front that it was recalled, stored, and labeled government "surplus property," thus allowing tax-supported institutions like Auburn to receive a 95 percent discount when the collection was subsequently offered at auction. An Auburn professor with foresight, Frank Applebee, spearheaded "the art bargain of the century" when he persuaded art department instructors to pool their yearly salary increase and enter the announced auction. As a result, Auburn University's Advancing American Art Collection was acquired in 1948 for an unthinkable $1,072. Experts call this body of works, now valued somewhere between $7 and $10 million, one of the most important collections of American art from the post–World War II era.

After viewing the exhibits, take time to enjoy the museum's botanical gardens with walking paths. Hours are 10:00 A.M. to 5:00 P.M. Tuesday through Saturday and 11:00 A.M. to 5:00 P.M. on Sunday. Admission (except for students) is charged. For more information, click on www.julecollinssmithmuseum.com.

While in Auburn consider headquartering at *Crenshaw House Bed and Breakfast* (334–821–1131 or 800–950–1131), 2 blocks north of Toomer's Corner. Shaded by giant oak and pecan trees, this blue Victorian gingerbread–style house stands at 371 North College Street in Auburn's Old Main and Church Street Historic District. Owners Fran and Peppi Verma, who furnished their two-story 1890 home with lovely antiques, offer eight units for overnight guests. The Vermas wanted to start a small family business and purchased the house "knowing it would lend itself well to a bed-and-breakfast facility," Fran says, adding that her husband had enjoyed bed-and-breakfast lodging while traveling in Europe. As for breakfast, guests receive a room-service menu and indicate their choices along with a serving time. The Web site is www.auburnalabama.com. Standard to moderate rates.

Also, golfers will want to check out *Auburn Links at Mill Creek* (334–887–5151), a $5-million facility that occupies 274 acres located about 3 miles south of town near the intersection of U.S. Highway 29 and I–85 at exit 51. (The eighteenth hole's sand traps form a giant tiger paw print.)

Auburn's sister city, *Opelika,* makes a good place to continue your area exploration. In Opelika's "olden days," passengers traveling through by train sometimes saw shootouts across the railroad tracks. Fortunately, today's visitors don't have to dodge stray bullets, so you can relax as you explore the Railroad Avenue Historic District.

As a result of Opelika's participation in Alabama's Main Street program (a project of the National Trust for Historic Preservation), many once-forgotten structures have been rescued and reincarnated as charming shops such as *Easterday Antiques* at 805 South Railroad Avenue. Helen Easterday, who's been called "the quintessential town person," and her husband, Kenneth, have embraced the local downtown revitalization program to the point of converting the enormous upper level of their shop into a wonderful home. Mrs. Easterday's passion for art may be observed in the exquisite antique furnishings, oriental rugs, paintings, and accessories displayed in her shop. For health reasons, she limits her schedule and operates by appointment only. For more information or an appointment, call (334) 749–6407.

After your Railroad Avenue stroll, head to *The Museum of East Alabama* (334–749–2751), located nearby at 121 South Ninth Street. Here you'll see a dugout canoe of white cypress that dates back as far as 3,500 B.C. Other exhibits consist of glass milk bottles, baby bonnets, Shirley Temple and Roanoke dolls, toys, collections of vintage typewriters, pianos, farm implements, war memorabilia, and surgical instruments. Other unusual exhibits include a foot X-ray machine (typical of those once used in shoe stores) and a bicycle-propelled ice-cream cart. The museum's collection also includes an early-twentieth-century kitchen and a full-size fire truck. Hours are 10:00 A.M. until 4:00 P.M. Tuesday through Friday and 2:00 to 4:00 P.M. on Saturday. Admission is free.

Looking to the right as you exit the museum, you'll see the lofty clock tower of the Lee County Courthouse, a half block away. Listed on the National Register of Historic Places, the handsome, white-columned, two-story brick structure dates to 1896 and features marble floors and decorative arched windows.

Take time to drive around a bit to see Opelika's lovely homes, which exemplify a wide range of architectural styles. Better yet, make reservations to stay in one of them—***The Heritage House Bed and Breakfast Inn*** (334–705–0485), at 714 Second Avenue. Barbara Patton, Opelika's former mayor and an advocate of historic preservation, appealed to various parties to step in and preserve this fine old 1914 Neoclassical tan brick home during the years it stood vacant. Finding no volunteers, she called a family conference to discuss its purchase. With the help of her son Richard, Barbara turned the thirteen-room home into a bed-and-breakfast. In January 2004, Carole and Steve Harrison purchased the property and continue to welcome overnight visitors. They offer five lovely rooms for guests and serve a full Southern breakfast. See www.opelika heritagehouse.com. Moderate rates.

While in the area, golfers will enjoy playing the ***Grand National,*** one of Alabama's fine courses on the Robert Trent Jones Golf Trail. For more information on this award-winning course, built on 1,300 acres encompassing a 650-acre lake, call (334) 749–9042 or (800) 949–4444.

Chattahoochee Trace

After touring War Eagle country, head south toward Eufaula. Along the way you'll see Pittsview (if you don't blink). Stop by the mayor's office (334–855–3568) on U.S. Highway 431 for a friendly chat with Frank Turner (who's the unofficial mayor) and a look at his folk art gallery. You'll find paintings by an area folk artist, signed "Mr John Henry Toney" along with his age. Frank also features the work of Butch Anthony, James (Buddy) Snipes, and other folk artists. Hours are by chance or appointment.

Afterward continue south toward ***Eufaula,*** sometimes called the "Natchez of Alabama." You may want to make your base at lovely ***Lakepoint Resort*** (334–687–8011 or 800–544–LAKE), about 7 miles north of town just off US 431.

Located on the shores of Lake Eufaula (also known as Lake George), this complex offers accommodations ranging from campsites, cabins, and cottages to resort rooms and suites along with a restaurant, coffee shop, lounge, and gift shop. Recreation options include swimming, golfing, tennis, hiking, picnicking, biking, waterskiing, and boating—not to mention fishing in a 45,200-acre lake known as the Big Bass Capital of the World. Room rates are standard.

Continue to Eufaula, a city filled with multiple versions of the perfect Southern mansion. Located on a bluff above the Chattahoochee River, Eufaula boasts the state's second-largest historic district and offers a feast for architecture aficionados. During the *Eufaula Pilgrimage,* an annual event that takes place the first full weekend in April, visitors can enjoy home tours, antiques shows, concerts, and other festivities. For more information, contact the Eufaula Heritage Association at (334) 687-3793 or go to www.eufaulapilgrimage.com.

Stop by the *Hart House* (334-687-9755) at 211 North Eufaula Avenue, an 1850 Greek Revival structure that serves as headquarters for the Historic Chattahoochee Commission. Here you can pick up visitors information about the Trace, a river corridor running through portions of Alabama and Georgia. Throughout this bistate region, travelers will discover a wealth of historic sites, natural attractions, and recreation facilities. Except for holidays, the Hart House may be visited from 8:00 A.M. to 5:00 P.M. Monday through Friday.

Continue to *Shorter Mansion* (334-687-3793) at 340 North Eufaula Avenue. This elegant structure dates to 1884 and features seventeen Corinthian-capped columns and an elaborate frieze of molded acanthus leaves and scrolls beneath its lofty balustraded roof. Be sure to notice the front door's beveled leaded glass and the entrance hall's parquet floor and molded plaster cornices. This Neoclassical Revival mansion, furnished in fine Victorian period pieces, houses the Eufaula Historical Museum and serves as headquarters for the Eufaula Heritage Association.

One upstairs room contains portraits of six state governors who were either born in or later lived in Barbour County. Another upstairs room pays tribute to retired Adm. Thomas H. Moorer, a Eufaula native who served two terms as chairman of the Joint Chiefs of Staff. Displays include Admiral Moorer's portrait, uniform, awards, and mementos from his naval career.

You'll also see Waterford crystal and cut-glass chandeliers, antiques, Confederate relics, period wedding dresses, Alabama memorabilia, and decorative arts. You may browse through the mansion at your leisure or take a guided tour. Admission. Except for major holidays, the home is open Monday through Saturday from 9:00 A.M. to 4:00 P.M.

Before leaving Eufaula be sure to visit *Fendall Hall* (334-687-8469), at 917 West Barbour Street. Built between 1856 and 1860, the home features stenciled walls and ceilings painted by a nineteenth-century Italian artist, and the original decor with High Victorian colors remains relatively unchanged. Also noteworthy are the entrance hall's striking black-and-white marble floor and the home's early plumbing system, supplied by attic cisterns. Rumor has it that a ghost named Sammy makes his presence known here from time to time. Currently the house is open for tours Monday, Tuesday, and Thursday through Saturday from 10:00 A.M. to 4:00 P.M. Admission.

After touring this town of lovely mansions, head to *Clayton,* a small town with some unique attractions, such as the *Octagon House* at 103 North Midway Street. Listed on the National Register of Historic Places, this unusual structure is the state's sole surviving antebellum octagonal house. The ground floor served as the original kitchen (and also as the setting for a mystery, *The Rusty Key,* written by one of the home's owners). Four chimneys extending above the cupola enclose the staircase of this eight-sided structure. The first floor features four main rooms, two small rooms, and two halls that open to the surrounding porch. To arrange a tour call (334) 775–3254. Modest admission.

At nearby Clayton Baptist Church Cemetery (also on North Midway Street), you'll find the *Whiskey Bottle Tombstone,* once featured on *Ripley's Believe It or Not!* television show. The bottle-shaped headstone and footstone, which mark the final resting place of William T. Mullen (1834–1863), still contain their original removable stone stoppers. Such a memorial obviously tells a story, and the story behind the stone goes something like this: Mr. Mullen, a local accountant, acquired a reputation as a heavy drinker. His wife, Mary, a devout teetotaler, threatened that if he drank himself to death, she would let the world know by erecting an appropriate memorial. The Whiskey Bottle Tombstone testifies that she kept her promise.

Wiregrass Region

Continuing south along the Chattahoochee Trace takes you to *Dothan,* in the state's southeastern corner. Here, in a region called the Wiregrass, early settlers battled the odds to cultivate this large stretch of land once completely covered by clumps of stiff, dry grass growing under longleaf pines. To learn more about the Wiregrass region's roots, stop by *Landmark Park* (334–794–3452), in Dothan on US 431, about 3 miles north of Ross Clark Circle. At this living-history farmstead, you may be greeted by sheep, goats, pigs, chickens, cows, and a mule. You'll see a blacksmith shop, pioneer log cabin, smokehouse, cane-mill syrup shed, and other authentic outbuildings of an 1890s farm.

"We want to preserve the natural and cultural heritage of the Wiregrass region," says William Holman, Landmark Park's executive director, who calls the one-hundred-acre park an outdoor classroom. The cozy clapboard farmhouse looks as if its occupants just stepped out to milk the cows and may return any minute. An apron hangs on a cupboard door, and a shaving mug and brush wait beside the wash stand.

The park offers a full schedule of special events with demonstrations of seasonal farming activities, pioneer skills, and various crafts. In addition to the farmstead, you'll see a country store, church, one-room schoolhouse, drugstore, gazebo, interpretive center, planetarium, nature trails, boardwalks, beaver ponds, and picnic areas. Youngsters will especially enjoy the playground with its barnyard theme. Modest admission. Hours are 9:00 A.M. to 5:00 P.M. Monday through Saturday and noon to 5:00 P.M. Sunday (or 6:00 P.M. during daylight savings time).

Continue to downtown Dothan, the area's major trade center. Proclaimed "Peanut Capital of the World," this region produces one-fourth of the nation's peanuts. Each fall Dothan stages the *National Peanut Festival* with a full calendar of events, from demonstrations of square dance rounds by the Goober Gamboleers to a contest for prize-winning peanut recipes. Look for the large peanut sculptures, individually decorated and placed throughout town.

Across the street from the Civic Center, you'll see the *Wiregrass Museum of Art* (334-794-3871) at 126 Museum Avenue. This three-level facility features a full schedule of rotating exhibits attractively displayed in various galleries. The museum contains a classroom/studio and a children's hands-on gallery. Youngsters will find the activity area entertaining as well as educational. The museum's hours are 10:00 A.M. to 5:00 P.M. Tuesday through Saturday. Admission is free, but donations are accepted.

First known as Poplar Head, Dothan took its present biblical name in 1885. Around that time, concerned citizens decided to tone down the town's rowdy image and hired a marshal and deputies to enforce new laws designed to terminate the saloons' regular Saturday-night brawls.

While driving around town, you'll see local history depicted in colorful murals on various city buildings. The Mule Marker in Poplar Head Park pays tribute to the animal that played a major role in the Wiregrass region's early development. Nearby at North Saint Andrews Street, you'll notice the impressive Dothan Opera House, a Neoclassical Revival structure that dates from 1915. Another downtown historic site, Porter Hardware, with its rolling ladders, still exudes the nostalgic flavor of its late-1800s origin.

Afterward head to nearby Ozark, home of the Claybank Church on East Andrews Avenue just off State Route 249. This 1852 log church with hand-split board shingles and original pews is open daily during daylight hours.

You might like to continue your exploration of the Wiregrass region with a visit to *Enterprise.* If so, don't miss the *Boll Weevil Monument.* Actually, you can't miss this memorial because it stands in the middle of Main Street. And if you aren't sure you'd recognize a boll weevil (a bug about a quarter-inch long with a snout half the length of its body), just watch for a statue of a woman clad in classic drapery who stands on an ornamented pedestal and holds a magnified version of the pest high above her head. A streetside plaque explains that in 1919 the citizens of Enterprise and Coffee County erected the statue IN PROFOUND APPRECIATION OF THE BOLL WEEVIL AND WHAT IT HAS DONE AS THE HERALD OF PROSPERITY. After the boll weevil demolished two-thirds of Coffee County's cotton in 1915, local farmers started to diversify, planting other crops such as sugar cane, corn, hay, potatoes, and peanuts. Particularly suited to the Wiregrass, peanuts played a primary role in saving the local economy after the boll weevil's destruction and soon became the region's principal cash crop.

About half a block from the Boll Weevil Monument stands the venerable *Rawls Hotel* (334–308–9387) at 116 South Main Street. Listed on the National Register of Historic Places, the hotel dates to 1903 and makes a great head-

Boll Weevil Monument

quarters while checking out the local sites. A hub for civic and social events until it closed in the early 1970s, the recently refurbished property once again lures travelers. In addition to several businesses, the hotel houses a fine dining restaurant, meeting rooms, Hayden's Tavern, and four handsome rooms and suites. Call the Rawls Bed and Breakfast at (334) 406–2817 for reservations. Rates are standard to moderate.

Behind the hotel on Railroad Street, you'll find the former Enterprise Depot. In railroad's golden days, passengers simply stepped off a train here, and a short stroll took them to the Rawls. Today's visitor can browse through the depot's rooms and large freight area filled with historical artifacts. "Many of the arrow and spear points in the Indian Room were discovered by local farmers, while plowing their land," said a volunteer.

History buffs can dip into more local lore at Pea River Genealogical Library on Main Street. A stroll along Main Street takes you past eateries like the Magnolia Room Café and antiques shops.

Before or after exploring downtown, stop by the Enterprise Welcome Center and Little Red Schoolhouse (complete with pot-bellied stove and slate boards) near the U.S. Highway 84 bypass.

At the Boll Weevil Soap Company, you'll find Southern Belle, Camellia Flower, High Cotton, Gardener's Love, Southern Romance, and other herbal products made by Rosemary Howell, a nurse by profession. Visit www.bwsoap.com or stop by 600 Boll Weevil Circle, Suite 3, and make someone happy with a fine selection of soaps.

Golfers will want to play Tartan Pines, a challenging eighteen-hole course on the town's west side. The facility, with a restaurant on the premises, opened in 2000 and offers club memberships but also welcomes the public.

Opp, in neighboring Covington County, hosts a unique annual event: the *Rattlesnake Rodeo.* This spring festival, scheduled the first full weekend in March, features the world's only rattlesnake race along with arts and crafts (including several made from rattlesnake skins), a buck dancing contest, and programs on rattlesnake education and safety. For specific information call (334) 493–4572. You can also write to the Opp Jaycees at P.O. Box 596, Opp 36467 or contact the chamber of commerce at (800) 239–8054.

To reach *Troy* follow State Route 87 north from Enterprise. On the southern outskirts of this town, the home of Troy State University, you'll find the *Mossy Grove School House Restaurant* (334–566–4921) just off U.S. Highway 231 at 1902 Elba Highway. Set among moss-draped trees, this rustic structure started out as a one-room schoolhouse in 1856. Later enlarged and renovated, the building still contains its original stage, now part of the back dining room.

Diners can order fried dill pickles to nibble on while waiting for their entrees and admire memorabilia ranging from Confederate money, swords, and a cannonball to antique tools, barrels, and even bear teeth. Also displayed here are an old-fashioned telephone, cheese cutter, barber chair, and many other items.

Popular entrees include broiled shrimp scampi, charbroiled chicken tenders, and charbroiled rib eye. All dinners include hush puppies, coleslaw or salad, wedge fries or baked potato, and white beans with a special pepper relish. Moderate prices. Hours are 5:00 to 9:00 P.M. Tuesday through Saturday.

Continuing north through Troy takes you to *Pioneer Museum of Alabama* (334–566–3597), located at 248 US 231. Situated on thirty wooded acres, this fascinating folk museum contains some 18,000 items from the past two centuries. You'll find extensive collections, all well organized and attractively displayed, plus fifteen outbuildings. Household items range from lemon squeezers, sausage stuffers, and butter molds to cookware, fluting irons, spittoons, and an Edison phonograph with a morning glory–shaped speaker. Although the lovely period furnishings of the three Bass Rooms reflect an upper-class lifestyle, the museum's collections focus on items that played a part in the daily existence of the community's middle- and lower-class members.

Other exhibits include newspaper typesetting and printing machines, an enormous collection of farm equipment, blacksmith and carpenter shop displays, and several horse-drawn vehicles, including an antique hearse. One exhibit, "When Cotton Was King," features a mule with "a lean and hungry look." Upon seeing the sculptor's interesting armature, museum officials had the artist stop working at once to preserve the unique look of the unfinished piece. Other objects on display include a portable boll weevil catcher, a peanut sheller, and a moonshine still.

Don't miss the early-twentieth-century street setting featuring storefronts of barber and millinery shops, a bank, and offices for a dentist, doctor, and lawyer— all appropriately equipped. Save plenty of time for exploring the grounds, too. On your way to see the furnished dogtrot log cabin and nearby tenant house, you'll pass a loblolly pine known as the Moon Tree—the seed from which it grew journeyed to the moon and back with the Apollo astronauts. Before leaving the museum, stop by the country store stocked with essentials such as snuff, castor oil, patent medicines, and bone buttons. You'll also find a restored 1928 schoolhouse, a working gristmill, a corncrib made of hand-hewn logs, a covered bridge, a nature trail, and a picnic area on the grounds. Other interesting exhibits include Native American artifacts and a coal-burning train engine. Thursday visitors can watch quilters at work, and weaving demonstrations take place Friday and Saturday. Except for major holidays, hours are 9:00 A.M. to 5:00 P.M. Monday through Saturday. Admission. Preview the property at www.pioneer-museum.org.

Cradle of the Confederacy

For a really great meal at *Red's Little School House* (334-584-7955), located at blink-and-you've-missed-it Grady, travel north from Troy on US 231, then turn onto State Route 94 in the direction of Dublin and Ramer. At the intersection of Route 94 and Gardner Road, look for a tall water tower, labeled PINE LEVEL, with a small red structure beside it. At this restaurant, housed in a former school and owned by Debbie Deese, you'll find a buffet selection of all-you-can-eat, fresh, home-cooked vegetables such as sweet potato soufflé, fried okra, and collards. (Red, Debbie's father and the former owner, grows acres and acres of vegetables each season and reaps a huge harvest.) The menu also features fried corn bread, chicken and dumplings, barbecue, and fried chicken. If you manage to save room for dessert, the choices are listed on the blackboard.

Even though the nation's presidents look sternly from their frames over the chalkboard and old maps suggest geography-test anxiety, this is a place to relax.

Schoolmarm Debbie banters with the customers, who obviously enjoy both the food and the friendly surroundings. Debbie, who calls herself "a half-decent guitar player," sometimes sings for the crowd. "Everyone brags on the food, and laughs at the entertainment," she writes in the preface of her cookbook.

Debbie converted two school buses into traveling kitchens and takes her catering show on the road for large gatherings. She has cooked for five governors and one president. "I think food is the answer to everything," she says. School starts at 11:00 A.M. and ends at 9:00 P.M. Wednesday through Saturday and closes at 3:00 P.M. on Sunday. Prices are economical to moderate.

Afterward continue north on one of several roads that lead to **Montgomery,** about thirty minutes away. Montgomery offers a wealth of attractions appealing to all interests. In the past the city has been home to such luminaries as Tallulah Bankhead, Hank Williams, and Nat King Cole. Montgomery served as a launching ground for the Wright brothers, who gave early flying lessons here; a playground for Zelda and F. Scott Fitzgerald; and a battleground in the Civil Rights Movement. This city also pioneered the nation's first electric trolley system, the Lightning Route, which made its successful trial run in 1886.

alabamatrivia

Nat King Cole was born at the Cole-Samford House on St. John Street in Montgomery.

Make the new **Montgomery Area Visitor Center** (334–262–0013) at 300 Water Street your first stop in the city. Housed in historic Union Station that dates to 1898, the center offers a handsome medley of exhibit panels on area attractions along with maps and information on accommodations, restaurants, festivals, and more. Take a virtual thirteen-minute city tour in the minitheater and collect some souvenirs in the gift shop. Hours are 8:00 A.M. to 5:00 P.M. Monday through Saturday and noon to 4:00 P.M. Sunday.

Here you can also pick up a trolley map for the Lightning Route, an easy way to see the city with no parking problems. An all-day pass costs $1.00 (50 cents for seniors). Passengers can board at twenty-minute intervals along the route, and the trolleys run from 9:00 A.M. to 5:45 P.M. Monday through Saturday.

On the city's southeast side, you'll find the **Alabama Shakespeare Festival (ASF)** (334–271–5353 or 800–841–4ASF). Just off East Boulevard on Woodmere Boulevard in the Wynton M. Blount Cultural Park, ASF presents works ranging from familiar classics to world-premiere Southern Writers' Project productions. You can take in a performance of works by such writers as Sir Noel Coward, Anton Chekhov, Eugene O'Neill, George Bernard Shaw, Tennessee Williams, and, of course, the Bard. The only American theater invited to fly the same flag as that used by England's Royal Shakespeare Company, ASF attracts more than 300,000 visitors annually from all fifty states and sixty foreign countries and is the world's fifth-largest Shakespeare festival.

Situated in a 250-acre, landscaped, English-style park, the $21.5 million performing-arts complex houses two stages, rehearsal halls, and a snack bar along with costume, prop, and gift shops. The grounds, perfect for strolling or picnicking, feature a reflecting lake complete with gliding swans. Wend your way through Shakespeare Gardens, with a 325-seat amphitheater against a setting that brings to life the Bard's botanical references to flowers and herbs, such as rosemary "for remembrance" (and great as a garnish for most meat dishes, too).

alabamatrivia

A life-size statue of Hank Williams stands in Montgomery's Lister Park across from the City Auditorium, where Williams's funeral service took place.

Linger awhile and enjoy the park's various colors, textures, and smells. For information, brochures, or tickets, call or write to Alabama Shakespeare Festival, One Festival Drive, Montgomery 36117-4605. You can visit www.asf.net to check on current productions.

Before leaving the park take time to browse through the ***Montgomery Museum of Fine Arts*** (334–244–5700). Located at One Museum Drive, this facility features the fine Blount Collection with works representing more than 200 years of American art. Also, you'll see Old Master prints, outstanding porcelain and glass collections, nineteenth- and twentieth-century American paintings and sculpture, and art of the American South. View www.mmfa.org for current exhibitions and more information on the museum's holdings. Admission is free. Except for major holidays, the museum's hours are 10:00 A.M. to 5:00 P.M. Tuesday through Saturday. Thursday hours extend to 9:00 P.M. The Sunday schedule is noon to 5:00 P.M. Enjoy a lunch break in the museum at Café M, an artful bistro that serves from 11:00 A.M. to 2:00 P.M. Tuesday through Saturday. Sample the Mediterranean chicken salad and flourless fudge cake. Then save a bit of bread to toss to the ducks, who cruise by regularly with great expectations. Rates are economical to moderate.

Sometime during your Montgomery visit, consider searching out an off-the-beaten-path place called ***Dawson's at Rose Hill*** (334–215–7620), in the Mt. Meigs community at 11250 U.S. Highway 80 East. A winding tree-lined driveway leads to the restaurant, which occupies a white frame Colonial-style home on the rolling grounds of an 1814 plantation northeast of Montgomery. Originally a 4,000-acre estate, Rose Hill was built by Henry Lucas, a wealthy landowner in Montgomery County. The surrounding forty acres of rose gardens gave the estate, listed on the Alabama Historical Register, its name.

Typical dinner selections feature medallions of beef with wild rice and portobello mushrooms or sole on angel-hair pasta with lemon butter. Lunch is served from 11:30 A.M. to 2:00 P.M. Tuesday through Friday (reservations only). Dinner hours run from 5:00 to 9:00 P.M. Tuesday through Saturday. Moderate to expensive.

Back in downtown Montgomery, across the street from Cloverdale Park, stands the former home of a famous couple who personified the Jazz Age. Housed in the lower right section (Apartment B) of a circa-1910 two-story brown structure at 919 Felder Avenue, you'll find the **Scott and Zelda Fitzgerald Museum** (334-264-4222). Francis Scott Key Fitzgerald met Zelda Sayre, a native of Montgomery and daughter of an Alabama Supreme Court judge, at a local dance in 1918. The couple married in 1920, soon after Scott published his first novel, *This Side of Paradise.*

alabamatrivia

The Wallace Foundation in Montgomery honors Lurleen Wallace, the third woman ever elected governor of a state.

The Fitzgeralds and their daughter, Scottie, lived here from October 1931 to April 1932. While here Scott worked on his novel *Tender Is the Night* and the screenplay for a Jean Harlow movie. At the same time Zelda, whose writings include a play as well as several short stories and articles, started her only novel, *Save Me the Waltz.* Beautiful, flamboyant, and driven, Zelda also excelled at painting and ballet. Unfortunately, her recurring mental collapses played havoc with the family's lives and prevented her from realizing more of her creative potential.

You'll see eight pieces of Zelda's original artwork including paintings and a self-portrait in pencil along with her personal cigarette holder, family photos, autographed books, letters, and other memorabilia. Plans were afoot to tear down this historic home until local attorney Julian McPhillips and his wife, Leslie, purchased it and set about creating this museum. In the sunroom you can watch a twenty-five-minute video that provides some glimpses into the lives of the author of *The Great Gatsby* and his talented but tormented wife. A donation of $5.00 per adult is requested. Hours are 10:00 A.M. to 2:00 P.M. Wednesday through Friday and 1:00 to 5:00 P.M. Saturday and Sunday.

Afterward head downtown to Montgomery's capitol complex, where you can easily spend a full day. If you enjoy digging into the past, you'll find this area fascinating to explore. From here Jefferson Davis telegraphed his "Fire on Fort Sumter" order, beginning the Civil War. Rising impressively above its surroundings on Dexter Avenue, the 1851 capitol reflects the period's prevailing architecture—Greek Revival. In this building Jefferson Davis took his presidential oath for the Confederacy, and a six-pointed brass star now marks the spot.

At 644 Washington Avenue, just across the street from the capitol, stands the *First White House of the Confederacy* (334–242–1861). Occupied by the Jefferson Davis family during the early days of the War Between the States, this Italianate-style home built by William Sayre dates to the early 1830s. Elegant downstairs parlors and second-floor bedrooms (including a charming nursery) contain Davis family possessions and period antiques. Other displays include Civil War relics, letters, and glass-cased documents. Hours are 8:00 A.M. to 4:30 P.M. Monday through Friday. Admission is free.

Next door to the Davis home, you'll find a treasure-filled museum, the Alabama Department of Archives and History. This building houses an enormous manuscript collection and exhibits spanning the gap from the Stone Age to the Space Age.

A short jaunt takes you to the *Dexter Avenue King Memorial Baptist Church* (334–263–3970). Located at 454 Dexter Avenue, the church became a National Historical Landmark in 1974. It was at this church, pastored by Dr. Martin Luther King Jr., that the Montgomery bus boycott was organized on December 2, 1955, launching the American Civil Rights Movement.

A forty-five-minute tour covers the church's early history as well as the more recent role it played as a rallying place for civil rights activists. On the ground floor, a six-section folk mural illustrates major events from Dr. King's life. Hours are 10:00 A.M. to 4:00 P.M. Tuesday through Friday and 10:00 A.M. to 2:00 P.M. on Saturday. Admission.

Nearby, in front of the Southern Poverty Law Center at 400 Washington Avenue, stands the *Civil Rights Memorial.* Designed by Maya Lin, who also served as the architect for the Vietnam Memorial in Washington, D.C., this black granite memorial documents major events in the struggle for civil rights.

Don't miss the *Rosa Parks Library and Museum* (334–241–8615), a state-of-the-art facility at 252 Montgomery Street. This site marks the spot where Mrs. Parks was arrested in 1955 and offers an in-depth look at the event that launched the Montgomery bus boycott. A project of Troy State University Montgomery, the interpretive museum features original exhibits, including historical papers from that era and a replica of the public bus, complete with a unique treatment of the scene in which Mrs. Rosa Parks played her significant role in shaping history to become "Mother of the Civil Rights Movement." The new Children's Wing features the Cleveland Avenue Time Machine, which takes riders on a unique trip to the past with an overview of events that led to the modern day Civil Rights Movement. On the second floor visitors will find extensive historical information with kiosk, panel, and computer presentations detailing events before and during the Montgomery Bus Boycott. For more background on this pivotal event in the city's (and nation's) civil rights heritage, visit http://

montgomery.troy.edu/museum. Museum hours run from 9:00 A.M. to 5:00 P.M. Monday through Friday and from 9:00 A.M. to 3:00 P.M. on Saturday. Admission.

Also downtown, at 301 Columbus Street, you can step back into the nineteenth century at *Old Alabama Town* (334–240–4500 or 888–240–1850). This fascinating concentration of historically restored buildings provides glimpses of city and country living in the nineteenth and early twentieth centuries. Start your tour at the Loeb Center, where you can also visit the museum store. Continue your excursion into the past at Lucas Tavern and other buildings in this history-filled complex. You'll see an 1850s dogtrot house (a dogtrot is a form of Southern architecture that features an open central hall connecting two rooms, sometimes called pens). Other stops include such buildings as a carriage house, grocery store, church, country doctor's office, and a one-room schoolhouse—complete with *McGuffey's Readers* and slates.

You'll also see the nearby Rose-Morris House, where you can enjoy music on the dogtrot, and the *Ordeman House,* a handsome townhouse with elegant furnishings and backyard dependencies. Guided tours here take place at 10:30 A.M. and 1:00 P.M. Monday through Friday. Also, visitors can walk through the home on their own between 10:00 A.M. and 2:00 P.M. Admission. Except for major holidays, the center's hours are 9:00 A.M. to 3:00 P.M. Monday through Saturday. Check out www.oldalabamatown. com to learn more.

"Your Cheatin' Heart" immediately brings Hank Williams to mind for all country music lovers, and fans from throughout the world travel to Montgomery to pay tribute at his grave site. Set in Oakwood Cemetery, the marble memorial is sculpted in the shape of two large music notes and a cowboy hat.

Ordeman House

You can also see a life-size bronze statue of the musician in Lister Hill plaza, across from City Hall.

Stop by 118 Commerce Street for an in-depth look at the legacy of Alabama-born Hank Williams. Paying tribute to the memory of this country music legend, the *Hank Williams Museum* (334–262–3600) contains recordings, albums, musical instruments, clothing, a saddle with silver trim, family photos, and other personal items. The museum's focal point is the baby-blue 1952 Cadillac convertible in which the singer/songwriter died while being driven to his scheduled performance in Canton, Ohio, on January 1, 1953. Eight rooms and thirty-five showcases feature memorabilia of family members and associates. A carved Kowliga, like the wooden Indian that inspired Williams's song, "Kowaliga" and created by the Wood Chippers (with a time investment of 559 hours), looms 8½ feet tall. Museum hours are 9:00 A.M. to 6:00 P.M. Monday through Saturday (or 9:30 A.M. to 4:30 P.M. Monday through Saturday from November 1 to April 1) and 1:00 to 4:00 P.M. on Sunday. Admission. Tap into www.thehankwilliamsmuseum.com for more details and some toe-tapping music.

alabamatrivia

Life magazine ranked Hank Williams as Number One in the "100 Most Important People in Country Music."

Across the street at 551 Clay Street, you'll find a warm welcome at *Red Bluff Cottage* (334–264–0056 or 888–551–CLAY), a perfect place to headquarter in Alabama's capital city. In fact, the upstairs porch of this raised cottage offers fine views of the state capitol and the Alabama River. Bonnie and Barry Ponstein, who purchased the inn from previous owners Anne and Mark Waldo, share the cooking and dispense Southern hospitality—Alabama style. "We have a good time down here," says Barry, quoting his three rules: No smoking, no pets, and no grumpy people. Pay a virtual visit via www.RedBluffCottage.com and check for special packages. Moderate rates.

After exploring the capital of the Old South, head north to *Wetumpka,* a charming town with a unique setting. Not only situated on the Coosa River's banks, Wetumpka also sits in the bowl of a 4-mile-wide crater created by the impact of a meteorite about eighty-three million years ago. Head first to the Wetumpka Area Chamber of Commerce (334–567–4811), located at 110 East Bridge Street in the heart of downtown. While collecting travel information at the chamber office, housed in a former bank building that dates to 1905, notice the original brass chandelier with a Greek key design that repeats the ceiling motif. "Wetumpka comes from an Indian word that means 'tumbling waters,'" said executive director Jan Wood.

Spanning the Coosa River, you'll see the town's focal point, a picturesque arched bridge built in 1937. Named for a former governor, the Bibb Graves Bridge allegedly is the only one south of the Mason/Dixon Line suspended by reinforced concrete. After crossing the bridge, notice the historic First Presbyterian Church, organized in 1834. It was here that soldiers in the Wetumpka Light Guard gathered on April 16, 1861, before leaving to confront their destinies in the Civil War.

If you saw the movie *Big Fish,* filmed in and around Montgomery and starring Jessica Lange, Albert Finney, Ewan McGregor, and Danny DeVito, then the town might look vaguely familiar although the film crew made several exterior changes.

Before leaving town, be sure to visit ***Our Place Café*** (334–567–8778) for a delectable dinner. Located at 809 Company Street, the restaurant occupies a brick building once owned by the Graham family. Back in the 1930s, the structure housed a grocery store with an apartment above and later served as an office for the family's wholesale gasoline business.

Owners David and Mona Funderburk offer casual elegance in dining and an ambience-filled restaurant with seating on two levels. Try the signature crab cakes, served with a special dill sauce, or the evening special. David describes his cuisine as "more Creole than Cajun," and his menu features six seafood selections nightly as well as steaks. The restaurant opens at 4:30 P.M. Tuesday through Saturday. Prices are moderate.

Save time to explore nearby ***Fort Toulouse–Jackson Park*** (334–567–3002). To reach the park, the site of two forts from different centuries, take US 231 North and watch for the turnoff sign across from the Food World supermarket. Continue 2.4 miles down this road to the main gate. After entering the park you'll see the visitor center on the left. Inside, displays of artifacts unearthed in archaeological digs, from brass uniform buttons and silver earrings to French wine bottles and cannonballs, provide background on the site's history.

The original 1717 French fortress, named for Count Toulouse (son of Louis XIV), served as a trading post where Native Americans exchanged furs and deerskins for European goods. This French outpost also helped keep the British at bay. Gen. Andrew Jackson's forces later built a larger nineteenth-century counterpart while fighting the Creek Indians. From here Old Hickory plotted his campaign against the British and Spanish that ended with the Battle of New Orleans.

Fort Toulouse and Fort Jackson living-history programs, staged monthly on the park's grounds, permit visitors to dip a bit deeper into the forts' earlier days. "We usually have something going on here three out of four weekends," said site director Jim Parker.

The Elms

While driving around the Millbrook area in Elmore County north of Montgomery, search out The Elms (334–290–ELMS) with a backdrop of camellias, roses, spirea, wisteria, and magnolias. Located at 360 Lindsey Road in Coosada, the historic home once served as the centerpiece of a cotton plantation that covered 16,000 acres. Here you'll be greeted by owner Jeanne Hall Ashley and Boomer, a friendly bearded collie. "One thing that's so special about this property," said Jeanne, "is that we have the original pioneer home, the second home, a cemetery, and early family correspondence." The Elms recently appeared in a movie as well as on a DVD called *The Haunted South*.

Built for Absalom and Emma Bolling Hall Jackson in 1836, the handsome two-story home with Greek Revival architectural influences contains "antiques, family portraits, memorabilia, and maybe a ghost or two," said Jeanne. Mary Louisa Crenshaw Hall, Jeanne's great-grandmother, gave Millbrook its name.

Although she grew up in Colorado, Jeanne spent her childhood summers in Alabama with her grandmother here at The Elms and gladly shares some of the area's rich history and fascinating anecdotes with visitors. Now on a mission to rescue The Elms as well as nearby Ellerslie (built in 1818 and the area's oldest home), Jeanne left northern Virginia and a career as an aviation disaster planning consultant to preserve these ancestral treasures. Call ahead for an appointment to take a house tour. Admission.

This 164-acre park also offers a picnic area, campground, and launching ramp. Another attraction is the thirty-acre arboretum with walkway, foot-bridges, and study decks. Nearby, the Coosa and Tallapoosa Rivers—with their cache of bass, bream, catfish, and crappie—beckon anglers. (A state fishing license is required.) Modest admission. Except for major holidays, the park is open from sunup to sundown year-round, and the visitor center hours run from 8:00 A.M. to 5:00 P.M. daily. For more information visit www.preserveala.org.

After your park outing follow State Route 14 west to **Prattville.** Daniel Pratt, for whom the town was named, came here from New Hampshire in the 1830s and established an industrial center—still the site for the manufacture of cotton gins. A drive through **Old Prattvillage** takes you past a section of restored nineteenth-century buildings. For a driving tour map, which highlights about forty homes in the historic district along with area churches and industrial sites, stop by the chamber of commerce on Court Street or City Hall at 101 West Main Street.

Better yet, a walking tour of the village lets you get up close and personal. At Prattvillage Gardens you'll see a small 1800s plantation chapel surrounded by a profusion of plants and a butterfly walk. Open the gate and stroll past theme gardens devoted to herbs, perennials, and old-fashioned favorites like hollyhocks, dianthus, and oak-leaf hydrangeas.

Stop by the ***Prattaugan Museum*** (334–361–0961), which houses the Heritage Center. Located at 102 East Main Street, this circa 1848 home showcases antiques, exhibits on area history, Indian artifacts, and genealogical records. In the backyard, notice the artesian well with a dipper hanging nearby. Prattville acquired its "Fountain City" title because it boasts a number of artesian wells. Except for city holidays, hours are Monday through Friday from 10:00 A.M. to 4:00 P.M. Admission is free, and donations are accepted.

Heritage Park, which features a three-tiered fountain, overlooks the town's focal point, Daniel Pratt's big brick gin factory. From this scenic spot, you can watch water spilling over the dam into Autauga Creek. A short stroll takes you to Tichnor Street Antiques & Interiors with a large selection of interesting pieces.

Wander along historic West Main Street past Red Arrow Hardware with its nostalgic inventory and The Elephant Walk, which houses a boutique and garden cafe. Across the street, you can see all sorts of timepieces awaiting repair at The Village Clocksmith. Check out A Carousel of Shops with an impressive inventory of "antiques, boutiques, and uniques."

Nature lovers will enjoy trekking through Wilderness Park on Upper Kingston Road. Located inside the city limits, the park could be a world away— in central China by the looks of it. Instead of a typical Southern forest's foliage, the paved half-mile path leads through a thick stand of towering bamboo.

alabamatrivia

Alabama's forest acreage ranks as third largest in the nation and second largest in the South.

While exploring Prattville, head to Pratt's Mill Shopping Center at 2096 State Route 14 East, where the staff of ***Chocodelphia*** produces things celestial and chocolate—milk chocolate, white chocolate, and dark chocolate, the favorite of chocoholics. Assortments of hand-dipped candies fill glass cases, and the friendly folks here will wrap up your choices. Owners Laura Hart and Cathy Coker invite you to relax in the coffee shop here and sample some specialties. Hours are 6:45 A.M. to 6:00 P.M. Monday through Friday and 8:00 A.M. to 6:00 P.M. Saturday. To order a selection of your favorite chocolates, call Chocodelphia (334–361– 2106 or 877–246–2633) or visit on the Web at www.chocodelphia.com.

For some scrumptious Southern cooking, make reservations (required) at ***The Guest House*** (334–365–7532) at 209 Doster Street. With the motto "If you leave here hungry, it's your own fault," you can guess what's in store: turkey and dressing, roast beef with rice and gravy, ham with raisin sauce, oven-roasted chicken, squash croquettes, sweet potato casserole, baked pineapple, curried fruit, and more. The dessert tray features an alluring array of cheese-cakes, meringues, and pies. Heaping dishes of food are passed around the table, family-style. In 1990, Linda and Doug Blackwell took over this business, which Miss Floy Burton founded and operated for almost four decades. For some recipes straight from The Guest House kitchen, pick up a cookbook called *Miss Floy's Finest*.

Search out nearby ***Buena Vista*** (334–365–3690 or 334–361–0961), an early plantation home, located on Autauga County Road 4 between US 31 and State Route 14. Fronted by four Ionic columns and constructed of heart pine, the Greek Revival–style structure stands on a sweeping lawn studded with camellias and magnolias. A striking circular staircase spirals from the large entrance hall to the third-floor banquet room. Originally built in the Federal style and known as Montgomery House, the home is listed on the National Register of Historic Places. Some historians claim the house dates to 1822, but other sources say circa 1830 would be more accurate. You'll see some period furnishings and a beautiful white quilt stitched in patterns that repeat the home's architectural accents. Created by Flavin Glover, a contemporary quilter based in Auburn, the Buena Vista quilt was featured in an issue of *Decorating and Crafts* magazine. Owned by a local corporation and operated by the Autauga County Heritage Association, Buena Vista is open to the public for tours on Tuesday between 10:00 A.M. and 2:00 P.M. or by appointment. Admission is free, but donations are accepted.

Head to ***Lowndesboro,*** south of Prattville. This small town, founded by cotton planters in the 1830s, contains some thirty surviving antebellum structures. If you'd like to visit ***Marengo*** (334–278–4442), an 1835 plantation home with an interesting history, take US 80 west. At the flashing caution light 13 miles past Dannelly Field Airport, turn right and travel 1.3 miles. You'll find Marengo on the left. Owned by the Lowndesboro Landmarks Foundation, this historic home serves as an events venue for special functions. Operated by Tammy and Kirk Meadows, the facility opens when a minimum of twenty-four guests make a dinner party reservation. Once that quota is reached, individual diners are accepted by reservation.

Guests arrive around 6:00 P.M. for appetizers, drinks, socializing, and a tour of the historic home. When the dinner bell rings about an hour later, the staff serves a multicourse dinner starting with homemade soup that's followed by a seasonal salad. The entree might be a chargrilled tenderloin filet, pecan-encrusted salmon, or beef en croute with homemade rolls, vegetables, and dessert. Guests can opt for a menu of four or five courses. After dinner, Tammy (dressed in vintage clothing) tells the group about the history of Marengo as well as the town of Lowndesboro and shares some intriguing ghost stories. Call for reservations and rates. Tammy, who lives nearby, offers day tours of the historic home, where an exhibit such as art, vintage clothing, or needlework is often in progress. Call for an appointment. Admission. For more background, see www.marengoplantation.com.

Want to visit the best little town in Alabama? Then head about 40 miles (or minutes) south of Montgomery, take the Greenville exit 130 off Interstate 65, and turn left. Ditto if you're looking for the best small town in America.

It's true—**Greenville,** with a population of some 8,000—outscored every other U.S. city with fewer than 100,000 residents in a national home towns index that measures the power of place using statistical data compiled by academic researchers.

Known as "Camellia City," Greenville promises plenty for flower lovers, history buffs, and golfers. Founded in 1820, the town boasts lovely homes, churches, and public buildings, many on the Register of Historic Places. Cambrian Ridge, one of the award-winning courses on the Robert Trent Jones Golf Trail, beckons only minutes away with the famed RTJ course, Capitol Hill, in easy driving distance.

Stop by the Greenville Area Chamber of Commerce (334–382–3251 or 800–959–0717) housed in the old CSX depot on Bolling Street to pick up a brochure called *Historic Main Street Greenville*, which details a self-guided tour of the town's interesting sites. Shady streets, brick paving, and gas lights make Commerce Street an attractive place to stroll.

"People are walking downtown as part of their exercise program—you'd be amazed at the number of people downtown in the evenings," says Nancy Idland, executive director of Greenville's Main Street Program, which promotes downtown revitalization.

A jaunt takes you past a local landmark, the **_Ritz Theatre._** Dating to 1935, the former movie house built in the then-popular Art Deco style later fell into disrepair. Now rescued and restored, the Ritz serves as the venue for a variety of productions from theater to music and dance. Other sites of interest include Greenville's circa-1936 City Hall, a WPA project and the city's best example of Colonial Revival civic architecture. Continue your stroll through Confederate Park, established in 1897. With a fountain as its centerpiece, this block-size space is sometimes the setting for evening concerts.

You'll see several handsome churches such as First Presbyterian, Greenville's oldest brick church. Search out the Pioneer Cemetery with its ornate cast-iron fence and elaborate monuments. Unusual cast-iron covers, an invention patented in 1874 by Greenville native Joseph R. Abrams, top several graves, and others are covered with giant cockleshells, a Victorian custom. Many of the area's early settlers, including Capt. William Butler for whom the county is named, are buried here.

Spend some time browsing through some of Greenville's one-of-a-kind boutiques and gift shops such as The Pineapple at 132 West Commerce Street, which offers unusual flags and banners, photo frames, hand-decorated clothing, and collectibles. In a beautifully restored building at 112 West Commerce, Karen Rainey Interiors showcases antiques and accessories and provides decorator services for interiors from Gulf Coast condos to Atlanta townhouses. Grayson's in Greenville at 850 Fort Dale Road specializes in antiques, accent pieces, and gifts.

With a wooded recreation area plus playgrounds and pavilions for picnickers, **Sherling Lake** about 4 miles west of Greenville via exit 130 off I–65, offers plenty of recreation options, including camping and fishing. August visitors can take in the annual Watermelon Jubilee with arts, crafts, food, and fun.

From Greenville, a short drive south takes you to Georgiana and the **Hank Williams, Sr., Boyhood Home and Museum** (334–376–2396). Located at 127 Rose Street, the home contains six rooms filled with walls of family photos, original posters, albums, 78 rpm recordings, a church pew, piano, and 1923 Victrola. Also, visitors will see one of the singer's Stetson hats and two suits. Fans from all over the world donated many of the items on display. Draperies, custom made for the musician's Nashville home, feature an overall design of lyrics and music from "Your Cheatin' Heart." Hours are 10:00 A.M. to 5:00 P.M. Monday through Saturday during daylight savings months. Otherwise, the museum closes at 4:00 P.M. Modest admission. During the first Friday and Saturday in June, Georgiana hosts an annual Hank Williams Day Celebration with country music concerts, food concessions, and street dances.

Places to Stay in Southeast Alabama

AUBURN/OPELIKA

Auburn Marriott Opelika Hotel and Conference Center at Grand National
3700 Sunbelt Parkway
(334) 741–9292 or
(866) 846–4655

Auburn University Hotel and Dixon Conference Center
241 South College Street
(334) 821–8200 cr
(800) 228–2876

Chewacla State Park
124 Shell Toomer Parkway
(334) 887–5621 cr
(800) ALA–PARK

Crenshaw House Bed and Breakfast
371 North College Street
(334) 821–1131 or
(800) 950–1131

The Heritage House Bed and Breakfast Inn
714 Second Avenue
(334) 705–0485

Hilton Garden Inn
2555 Hilton Garden Drive
(334) 502–3500 or
(800) HILTONS

CLAYTON

The Four Seasons Bed & Breakfast
62 West Louisville Avenue
(334) 775–9758

DOTHAN

Best Western Dothan Inn & Suites
3285 Montgomery Highway
(334) 793–4376 or
(800) 528–1234

Courtyard by Marriott
3040 Ross Clark Circle
(334) 671–3000 or
(800) 321–2211

Hampton Inn & Suites
4684 Montgomery Highway
(334) 671–7672

Holiday Inn South
2195 Ross Clark Circle
(334) 794–8711 or
(800) 777–6611

ENTERPRISE

Enterprise Inn & Suites
630 Glover Avenue
(334) 347–6262

Rawls Hotel
116 South Main Street
(334) 308–9387

EUFAULA

Comfort Suites
12 Paul Lee Parkway
(334) 616–0114

Jameson Inn
136 Towne Center Boulevard
(334) 687–7747 or
(800) 526–3766

Lakepoint Resort
U.S. Highway 431 North
(334) 687–8011 or
(800) 544–LAKE

GREENVILLE

Jameson Inn
71 Jameson Lane
(334) 382–6300 or
(800) 526–3766

MONTGOMERY

Drury Inn and Suites
1124 Eastern Boulevard
(334) 273–1101

Embassy Suites
300 Tallapoosa Street
(334) 269–5055 or
(800) 362–2779

MAINSTREAM ATTRACTIONS WORTH SEEING IN SOUTHEAST ALABAMA

Montgomery Zoo
2301 Coliseum Parkway
Montgomery
(334) 240–4900
Observe more than 800 animals from five continents in the zoo's naturalistic settings and take a train ride around the park. Relocated from its former home in Opelika and housed next to the zoo, the Mann Museum allows you to get acquainted with bears, wolves, moose, and more mounted specimens of North American wildlife, all presented in realistic settings. The natural history museum's life-size exhibits numbered more than 300 at last count. Both attractions are open from 9:00 A.M. to 5:00 P.M. daily. Admission.

U.S. Army Aviation Museum
Andrews Avenue and Novosel Street
Fort Rucker
(334) 255–3036, (334) 598–2508, or
(888) 276–9286

This museum is in Fort Rucker, a training base for military helicopter pilots located 5 miles west of Ozark. Covering the complete history of Army Aviation, this complex contains one of the world's largest collections of helicopters. Exhibits include maps and photos of Army Aviation's role in the Louisiana Maneuvers through Operation Desert Storm, a full-scale model of the Wright B Flyer, and unusual pieces such as a Sopwith Camel and a Nieuport 28. You can even walk through a Chinook (CH-47-A) and view today's high-tech Apache combat helicopter. The Army Aviation Museum is free and open to the public from 9:00 A.M. to 4:00 P.M. Monday through Saturday and from noon to 4:00 P.M. on Sunday. Visit the museum's Web site at www.armyavnmuseum.org.

Fairfield Inn
5601 Carmichael Road
(334) 270–0007 or
(800) 228–2800

Holiday Inn East
1185 Eastern Boulevard
(334) 272–0370 or
(800) HOLIDAY

Red Bluff Cottage
551 Clay Street
(334) 264–0056 or
(888) 551–CLAY

Studio Plus
5115 Carmichael Road
(334) 273–0075

Wingate Inn
2060 Eastern Boulevard
(334) 244–7880

PRATTVILLE

**Montgomery Marriott
Prattville Hotel and
Conference Center**
2500 Legends Circle
(888) 250–3767 or
(334) 290–1235

TALLASSEE

Hotel Talisi
14 Sistrunk Avenue
(334) 283–2769

Places to Eat in Southeast Alabama

AUBURN/OPELIKA

Ariccia
241 South College Street
(334) 821–8200 or
(800) 228–2876

Auburn City Limits
2450 State Route 14 West
(334) 821–3330

Hamilton's
174 East Magnolia Avenue
(334) 887–8780

J. Williams
277 S. Gay Street
(334) 501–5656

The Lakeview Room
3700 Sunbelt Parkway
(334) 741–9292

Mellow Mushroom
128 North College Street
(334) 887–6356

Warehouse Bistro
105 Rocket Avenue
(334) 745–6353

DOTHAN

**Hunt's Steak, Seafood,
and Oyster Bar**
177 Campbellton Highway
(334) 794–5193

Old Mexico
2920 Ross Clark Circle
(334) 712–1434

The Old Mill Restaurant
2557 Murphy Mill Road
(334) 794–8530

Serafino
111 West Troy Street
(334) 671–7627

ENTERPRISE

Carlisle's on Main
401 South Main Street
(334) 347–8108

Cutt's
417 East Lee
(334) 347–1110

Rawls Hotel
116 South Main Street
(334) 308–9387

EUFAULA

Allie's at the Airport
1720 North Eufaula Avenue
(334) 687–3132

Cajun Corner
114 North Eufaula Avenue
(334) 616–0816

Lakepoint Resort
104 Lake Point Drive
(334) 687–8011

Old Mexico
1248 South Eufaula Avenue
(334) 687–7770

River City Grill
209 East Broad Street
(334) 616–6550

GRADY

Red's Little School House
20 Gardner Road
(334) 584–7955

GREENVILLE

Bates' House of Turkey
1001 Fort Dale Road
(334) 382–6123

LOWNDESBORO

Marengo
100 North Broad Street
(334) 278–4442

MILLBROOK

Fantail Restaurant
2060 Downing
(334) 285–7255

Smokehouse Barbecue
2461 Main Street
(334) 285–0006

MONTGOMERY

Bonefish Grill
7020 East Chase Parkway
(334) 396–1770

Dawson's at Rose Hill
11250 U.S. Highway 80 East
(334) 215–7620

Gracie's English Tearoom
1734 Mulberry Street
(334) 240–2444

Lek's Railroad Thai
Union Station,
300 B Water Street
(334) 269–0708

Leslie Bailey's Silver Spoon
222 North McDonough
Street
(334) 264–1116

Martha's Place
458 Sayre Street
(334) 263–9135

**Montgomery Brewing
Company**
12 West Jefferson Street
(334) 834–BREW

The Olive Room
121 Montgomery Street
(334) 262–2763

Sinclair's (Cloverdale)
1051 East Fairview Avenue
(334) 834–7462

Vintage Year, Inc.
405 Cloverdale Road
(334) 264–8463

PRATTVILLE

The Guest House
209 Doster Street
(334) 365–7532
(reservations only)

**Marriott Legends at
Capitol Hill**
2500 Legends Circle
(334) 290–1235 or
(888) 250–3767

SHORTER

Back Forty
5001 County Road 30
(334) 727–0880

TALLASSEE

Hotel Talisi Restaurant
14 Sistrunk Avenue
(334) 283–2769

TROY

**Mossy Grove School
House Restaurant**
1902 Elba Highway
(334) 566–4921

WAVERLY

**The Yellowhammer
Restaurant**
1465 Patrick Street
(334) 887–5800

WETUMPKA

Our Place Café
809 Company Street
(334) 567–8778

FOR MORE INFORMATION ABOUT SOUTHEAST ALABAMA

Auburn/Opelika Tourism Bureau
714 East Glenn Avenue
Auburn 36830
(334) 887–8747 or (866) 880–8747
www.aotourism.com
rlbridges@aocvb.com

Dothan Area Convention & Visitors Bureau
3311 Ross Clark Circle Northwest
P.O. Box 8765
Dothan 36304
(334) 794–6622 or (888) 449–0212
www.dothanalcvb.com
dothancvb@mail.ala.net

Enterprise Chamber of Commerce
553 Glover Avenue
P. O. Box 310577
Enterprise 36331-0577
(334) 347–0581 or (800) 235–4730
www.enterprisealabama.com
chamber@entercomp.com

Eufaula/Barbour County Chamber of Commerce
333 East Broad Street
Eufaula 36027
(334) 687–6664 or (800) 524–7529
www.historiceufala.com
info@eufalachamber.com

Historic Chattahoochee Commission
P.O. Box 33
Eufaula 36072-0033
(334) 687–9755
www.hcc-al-ga.org
hcc3@earthlink.net

Montgomery Convention & Visitors Bureau
300 Water Street
P.O. Box 79
Montgomery 36101
(334) 261–1100 or (800) 240–9452
www.visitingmontgomery.com
tourism@montgomery chamber.com

Tuskegee Area Chamber of Commerce
121 South Main Street
Tuskegee 36083
(334) 727–6619
www.tuskegeeareachamber.com
tachwa@earthlink.net

Southwest Alabama

Black Belt

Alabama's Black Belt, so called because of a strip of dark, rich soil that stretches across part of the state's south-central section, covers 4,300 square miles. This fertile farmland became the setting for a host of plantations prior to the Civil War, and you'll see many antebellum structures throughout the area. From **Selma,** which retains a lingering flavor of the Old South's cotton-rich aristocratic past, you can easily make a loop of several small Black Belt towns with their treasure troves of architecture. Situated on a bluff above the Alabama River, Selma served as a major munitions depot, making battleships as well as cannonballs, rifles, and ammunition for the Confederate cause.

Soon after arriving in Selma, make a point to stop by the ***Crossroads Visitor Information Center*** (334–875–7485), conveniently located at 2207 Broad Street. Here, you can ask George "Cap" Swift your local questions and collect plenty of literature on city and area attractions. The facility houses a Book Nook with publications by Alabama authors, a variety of gift items, driving-tour brochures, and more. Hours run from 8:00 A.M. to 8:00 P.M. daily.

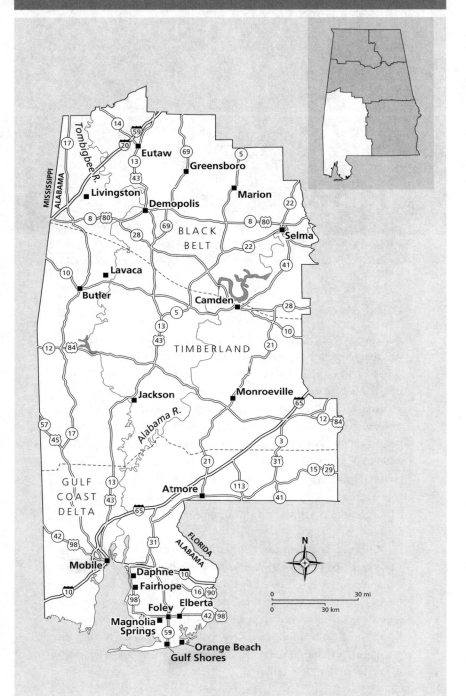

U.S. Highway 80 west from Montgomery to Selma leads across the *Edmund Pettus Bridge,* a landmark that figured prominently in the civil rights struggle. In 1965 marchers followed Martin Luther King Jr. across this bridge on their trek to Montgomery during voting-rights demonstrations.

Located near the bridge, the *National Voting Rights Museum* (334–418–0800) at 1012 Water Avenue presents a visual history of the Selma-to-Montgomery march and related events. Upon entering, viewers see themselves reflected in a mirrored "I Was There" wall with a display of cards recording firsthand observations by individuals. A series of rooms focus on reconstruction, suffrage, and other aspects of the voting-rights struggle. A large window, etched with the names Andrew Young, Martin Luther King Jr., Thurgood Marshall, Dick Gregory, and other museum Hall of Fame inductees, provides a fitting vantage point for viewing the historic Pettus Bridge. Hours are 9:00 A.M. to 5:00 P.M. Tuesday through Friday, 10:00 A.M. to 3:00 P.M. Saturday, and Sunday by appointment. Admission.

Take time to stroll along historic Water Avenue, a restored nineteenth-century riverfront warehouse district with brick streets, arcades, and parks overlooking the river. Nearby, at 1124 Water Avenue, you'll find a minimall with an eatery and several interesting shops.

Settle into a room at the newly restored *St. James Hotel* (334–872–3234 or 866–965–2637) and map out your Selma itinerary. One of the country's few remaining antebellum riverfront hotels, the St. James occupies a corner at 1200 Water Avenue. Lacy iron grillwork traces the balconies of the camel-colored structure, which surrounds a courtyard with fountain. The original 1837 hotel served passengers from paddle wheelers and steamboats that plied the Alabama River and also those from the nearby railroad station. Jesse and Frank James (under assumed names) once stayed at the St. James.

GAY'S TOP PICKS IN SOUTHWEST ALABAMA

Battleship USS *Alabama,*
Mobile Bay

Bellingrath Gardens and Home,
Theodore

Fort Morgan,
Mobile Bay

Gulf Coast beaches

Mobile's historic districts

Mobile Museum of Art,
Mobile

Old Cahawba Archaeological Park,
Cahaba

Town of Demopolis

Town of Fairhope

Town of Marion

Town of Selma

Many of the rooms' balconies overlook the historic Edmund Pettus Bridge. Furnished with antebellum and Victorian pieces, the hotel boasts a ballroom; elegant guest rooms and suites; a Drinking Room with handsome, marble-topped mahogany bar; and a white-tablecloth dining room. Standard to moderate.

At the ***Bridgetenders House*** (2 Lafayette Park, off Washington Street; 334–875–5517), a cottage that dates to 1884, you can sit on the porch in the shadow of the Edmund Pettus Bridge, sip cider, and contemplate Selma's history. Television camera crews stationed themselves here, plugging into the house's electrical outlets while reporting on the Selma-to-Montgomery march.

To welcome travelers, owners Kathi and George Needham offer two guest suites with kitchens, bedrooms, and sitting rooms and provide a continental breakfast with plenty of snacks and goodies plus a selection of historic photos, periodicals, and background materials as a frame of reference for this unique site. You can e-mail the property at Bridgtendr@aol.com. Rates are standard.

During your waterfront excursion, saunter into ***The Restaurant on Grumbles Alley*** (334–872–2006), named for a local character in Selma's storybook of history. You'll find this eatery at 1300 Water Avenue, a few steps from the Bridgetenders House. Be sure to notice the restaurant's two original black iron gates (believed to be slave doors) that weigh about 400 pounds each. And don't get the wrong idea from the century-old skeleton, attired in a Confederate uniform, seated on the stair landing—starving is not something you have to worry about here.

Everything served here, including the bread for sandwiches and the dressings for salads, is made from scratch. Some customers claim this restaurant serves the best Reuben sandwiches they ever ate. You might instead opt for the restaurant's justly famous marinated chicken-breast sandwich; hearty red bean and rice soup; or a variety of steak cuts. Economical to moderate prices. Restaurant hours are 11:00 A.M. to 9:00 P.M. on Monday through Thursday, 11:00 A.M. to 10:00 P.M. Friday, and 11:00 A.M. to 3:00 P.M. Saturday.

To dip into more of the city's interesting history, stop by the handsome ***Old Depot Museum*** (334–874–2197), located on the corner of Martin Luther King Street and Water Avenue. Built in 1891 by the Louisville and Nashville Railroad, this arched and turreted two-story redbrick structure stands on the site of the Confederate Naval Foundry, which Union troops destroyed during the Battle of Selma in 1865. The museum houses everything from a 1908 portrait camera used by psychic Edgar Cayce (who once lived in Selma and operated a photography studio here) to Victorian hair combs, plantation records, quilts, Confederate bills, cannonballs, early medical equipment, and antique tools.

In the Black Heritage Wing, you'll see sculpture by Earl Hopkins, nationally recognized for his wood carvings and leather crafts. Hopkins, who uses

GAY'S FAVORITE ANNUAL EVENTS IN SOUTHWEST ALABAMA

Mardi Gras
Mobile, February
(800) 5MOBILE

Arts & Crafts Festival
Fairhope, March
(251) 621–8222

Azalea Trail Run and Festival
Mobile, March
(800) 5MOBILE

Festival of Flowers
Mobile, March
(877) 777–0529 or (800) 5MOBILE

Historic Selma Pilgrimage
Selma, March
(800) 45-SELMA

The Original German Sausage Festival
Elberta, last Saturday in March
and October
(251) 986–5805

Crawfish Festival
Faunsdale, last weekend in April
(unless Easter)
(334) 628–3240

Blessing of the Fleet
Bayou La Batre, May
(251) 824–2415

To Kill a Mockingbird
Monroeville, last weekend of April and
first three weekends in May
(251) 575–7433
www.tokillamockingbird.com

Alabama Deep Sea Fishing Rodeo
Dauphin Island, July
(800) 5MOBILE
www.adsfr.com

Alabama Tale Tellin' Festival
Selma, second weekend in October
(800) 45–SELMA

Bayfest Music Festival
Mobile, first weekend in October
(251) 470–7730

Fishing Rodeo
Orange Beach, October
(251) 974–1510

National Shrimp Festival
Gulf Shores, October
(251) 968–6904 or (800) 745–SAND

Riverfront Market
Selma, second Saturday of October
(800) 45SELMA

Frank Brown International Songwriters Festival
Gulf Shores, November
www.fbisf.com

Pow Wow
Atmore, November
(251) 368–9136

Heritage Harbor Days
Foley, November
(251) 943–1200

Magic Christmas in Lights
Bellingrath Gardens & Home
late November through December
(251) 973–2217

Christmas on the River
Demopolis, December
(334) 289–0270

exotic woods in his creations, worked at Colonial Williamsburg before retiring to his native Selma. A not-to-be-missed rare display of photographs, made between 1895 and 1905 by Selmian Mary Morgan Keipp, depicts daily life on a Black Belt plantation. Curator Jean Martin calls this wonderful series "one of the finest and most complete collections of photos covering that period in history."

Behind the museum you'll see a Firefighters Museum plus a boxcar, caboose, and old farm equipment. Monday through Saturday the museum is open from 10:00 A.M. to 4:00 P.M. or by appointment. Modest admission.

Nearby at 410 Martin Luther King Street, stands **Brown Chapel African Methodist Episcopal Church,** another significant structure in Selma's history. This 1908 Byzantine-style building served as headquarters for the civil rights activists who played a pivotal role in bringing about the passage of the National Voting Rights Act during the turbulent decade of the 1960s. Visitors may take a self-guided walking tour of the surrounding historic area.

Sometime during your local tour, be sure to stop at 109 Union Street to tour the white-columned, three-story, brick **Vaughan-Smitherman Museum** (334–874–2174), named for the local hospital (once housed here) and in honor of Selma's former mayor, who played an active role in historic preservation. Crowning Alabama Avenue, this impressive building opened its doors in 1848 as the Central Masonic Institute and later served as a hospital for wounded Confederates (escaping the fate of many Selma buildings when Union general John Harrison Wilson's raiders, disobeying orders, embarked on a wholesale campaign of wanton destruction in April 1865). The building later served as a courthouse, military school, and private hospital. Inside you'll see a large collection of Civil War relics, Confederate money, medical artifacts, and period furnishings from the mid-1800s. Hours are 9:00 A.M. to 4:00 P.M. Tuesday through Saturday or by appointment. Modest admission.

On a drive through the Old Town Historic District, you'll see block after block of antebellum and Victorian architecture. The **Historic Selma Pilgrimage** provides visitors with opportunities to tour many of the city's outstanding homes each spring (see http://pilgrimage.selmaalabama.com for more information). A reenactment of the Battle of Selma is another popular springtime event.

For a memento of your visit, consider purchasing a cookbook called *Tastes of Olde Selma,* available in several places throughout the city. Compiled by Selma's Olde Towne Association, the book contains line drawings and brief histories of many of the town's significant structures along with a selection of wonderful recipes. The front cover features a color illustration of **Sturdivant Hall** (334–872–5626), a Neoclassical mansion located at 713 Mabry Street. Designed by Thomas Helm Lee (Robert E. Lee's cousin), this magnificent home that took three years to build boasts elaborate ceilings and decorative moldings with a motif of intertwined grape leaves and vines. You'll also see a spiral staircase, marble mantels, and servant pulls—each with a different tone. Other treasures include period furnishings, portraits, silver, crystal, china, and a rare French-made George Washington commemorative clock of ormolu and gold—one of only seven in existence.

Coral vines climb the home's back walls, and mock lemons perfume the air. You may be presented with a sprig or cutting of lavender, mint, or sage from the mansion's herb garden outside the backyard kitchen. The home's formal gardens, which feature a variety of native flowers, shrubs, and trees, serve as a lovely backdrop for the pilgrimage's annual grand ball. Except for major holidays, Sunday, and Monday, Sturdivant Hall is open from 10:00 A.M. to 4:00 P.M. Admission.

By the way, some Selmians say the ghost of John McGee Parkman, one of Sturdivant Hall's former owners, roams the mansion. You may or may not see house ghosts here, but you can certainly find several in Sturdivant Hall's gift shop—sandwiched between the covers of some of Kathryn Tucker Windham's books, such as *13 Alabama Ghosts and Jeffrey* or *Jeffrey's Latest 13*. For a souvenir or gift, you might like to buy *Alabama—One Big Front Porch,* an engrossing collection of stories compiled by Mrs. Windham. To hear her in person—along with other famous Southern storytellers—plan

alabamatrivia

Currency issued in Louisiana before the Civil War ($10 notes bearing the word *dix*, French for the number ten) led to the South being called "Dixie Land" and gave Alabama her nickname, "Heart of Dixie."

your visit to coincide with the **Alabama Tale Tellin' Festival,** an annual fall event staged in Selma. (In great demand as a speaker, Alabama's famous First Lady of Folk Tales and Ghost Stories travels frequently, so if you see someone behind the wheel of a Dodge Spirit with a license plate that reads JEFFREY, be sure to wave.)

Driving along Dallas Avenue (which becomes State Route 22), you'll pass the **Old Live Oak Cemetery,** filled with ancient trees festooned by Spanish moss. During spring, dogwoods and azaleas make this site even more spectacular. A number of Confederate graves and unique monuments may be seen here, including the mausoleum of William Rufus King, who named Selma and planned its layout. King, on the Democratic ticket with Franklin Pierce, died shortly after being elected vice president of the United States.

For dinner strike out for the **Tally-Ho Restaurant** (334–872–1390), located at 507 Mangum Avenue, just off Summerfield Road in the northern section of town. Owner Bob Kelley's entrees run the gamut from seafood and chicken to prime rib au jus. A board features daily specials, which might include grilled pork chops with rosemary sauce. Homemade zucchini muffins accompany entrees. For dessert try the chocolate cheesecake or amaretto soufflé. The restaurant's hours are 5:00 to 10:00 P.M. Monday through Saturday. Prices are moderate.

During your Selma visit, swing southwest about 9 miles on State Route 22 toward *Cahaba* ("Cahawba" is the historical spelling). Watch for a sign that says TO CAHABA, then turn left and travel 3½ miles. When you reach a dead end, turn left again and continue 3 miles to *Old Cahawba Archaeological Park* (334–872–8058), the site of Alabama's first permanent state capital. Here, near the place where the Cahaba and Alabama Rivers merge, once stood a thriving town. Today's visitors will have to use some imagination to visualize the remaining ruins as grand mansions that surrounded a copper-domed capitol, completed in 1820. A large stone monument and interpretive signs in conjunction with old street markers, brick columns, cemeteries, and domestic plants growing wild offer the few clues that this off-the-beaten-path spot once flourished as a political, commercial, and cultural center. You'll also see an artesian well (where watercress grows), the source of water for the elaborate gardens surrounding the Perine family mansion, which once stood nearby.

The visitor and education centers provide information on Cahaba's glory days. In 1825 legislators voted to move Alabama's capital to Tuscaloosa. While local lore holds that frequent flooding caused Cahaba to lose its position as the state's seat of government, evidence suggests that sectional politics probably played a larger role. Gradually Cahaba became a ghost town, and by 1900 most of its buildings had disappeared. The park offers a handicapped accessible nature trail. Except for major holidays, the park is open daily from 9:00 A.M. to 5:00 P.M., and the visitor center is open from noon to 5:00 P.M. Admission is free.

Afterward follow US 80 west from Selma until you reach Dallas County Road 45; then turn north to *Marion,* one of Alabama's oldest towns and a leading cultural center for planter society. The city is home to both Judson College and Marion Military Institute. The latter's chapel, Old South Hall, and Lovelace House on campus served as hospitals during the Civil War. The graves of more than a hundred Southern and Union soldiers were later relocated from campus to Confederate Rest, a cemetery behind St. Wilfrid's Episcopal Church. The Old Marion City Hall (moved to MMI's campus from the downtown square) houses the Alabama Military Hall of Honor. For an appointment to see the exhibits, call (334) 683–2346.

Downtown you'll see several historical churches and the handsome Perry County Courthouse dating from the early 1850s. Be sure to drive down Green Street, the setting for a number of antebellum residences, including the Lea-Griffith Home (circa 1830), where Texas hero Sam Houston married Margaret

Lea (their marriage license is recorded in the courthouse). With some 200 sites (in a wide variety of architectural styles) listed on the National Register of Historic Places, Marion promises plenty to see.

During your Marion excursion take a stroll across the Judson College campus and stop by the *Alabama Women's Hall of Fame,* which occupies the first floor of Bean Hall. Formerly the school's library, this Carnegie-built structure stands on the corner of Bibb and East Lafayette Streets. Bronze plaques pay tribute to Helen Keller, Julia Tutwiler, Lurleen Burns Wallace, Tallulah Bankhead, Zelda Sayre Fitzgerald, her daughter Frances Scott Fitzgerald Smith, and many other women of achievement with Alabama connections. Former first ladies Barbara Bush and Rosalynn Carter have spoken at past induction ceremonies. Except for major holidays, hours are 8:00 A.M. to 5:00 P.M. Monday through Friday. For a tour call (334) 683–5100. Admission is free.

At 303 and 305 West Lafayette Street, you'll find *Myrtle Hill* (334–683–9095), which consists of neighboring antebellum homes surrounded by twelve acres of Victorian gardens. Elegantly furnished with period antiques, the homes offer spacious accommodations for bed-and-breakfast guests and the option of a Continental or plantation breakfast. Owners Wanda and Gerald Lewis sometimes treat guests to ghost-story and folk-tale sessions. Moderate rates.

Marion's early-twentieth-century train depot serves as a visitor center complete with walking trail along the former railroad tracks. For more information on Marion, call the chamber of commerce at (334) 683–9622 or stop by 1200 Washington Street.

After exploring Marion follow State Route 14 west to Alabama's Catfish Capital, *Greensboro.* Because this Black Belt town managed to escape the Civil War's ravages, a large number of its antebellum homes and churches have been preserved. In fact the entire downtown district, featuring some 150 nineteenth-century structures, is on the National Register of Historic Places. More than sixty of the town's homes predate the Civil War. Be sure to drive along Main, Tuscaloosa, and South Streets, all of which offer interesting architecture. At Market and South Streets, you'll see the Noel-Ramsey House. Built between 1819 and 1821, this is the only remaining residence of French settlers from nearby Demopolis's Vine and Olive Colony.

Don't miss *Magnolia Grove* (334–624–8618), a two-story Greek Revival house built around 1840 by a wealthy cotton planter, Col. Isaac Croom. Located at 1002 Hobson Street, the home stands among lovely magnolia trees and landscaped gardens on a twelve-acre setting. Magnolia Grove was also the home of Croom's nephew, Rear Adm. Richmond Pearson Hobson, a Congressional Medal of Honor winner. A naval hero in the Spanish-American War, Hobson later served in Congress and introduced legislation (the Hobson Amendment) that became the basis for the Constitution's prohibition amendment. The Museum Room contains memorabilia from Hobson's military and political careers.

The house also features family portraits, heirlooms, and furnishings from the 1830s to the early 1900s. You'll see an 1866 piano, a Persian rug from the late 1800s, a chaperon's bench, and antique quilts. Outbuildings include a kitchen, slave cottage, and a structure that probably served as Isaac Croom's office. Hours are 10:00 A.M. to 4:00 P.M. Tuesday through Friday, and the first and third Saturdays of each month or other times by appointment. The grounds may be visited from noon to 4:00 P.M. on Sunday. Admission.

From Greensboro head south on State Route 25 toward *Faunsdale,* population ninety-eight. Housed in an 1890s mercantile building on the town's main street, *Ca-John's Faunsdale Bar & Grill* (334–628–3240) serves great steaks and seafood, and owner John (Ca-John) Broussard, originally from Louisiana, offers a variety of crawfish specialties in season. The food speaks for itself, attracting diners from distant towns. Windows sport red-and-white checkered cafe curtains. A pot-bellied stove and fireplace add to the ambience. Saturday night patrons can enjoy live music until the wee hours. Hours are 5:00 to 10:00 P.M. Friday and 11:00 A.M. to 10:00 P.M. on Saturday. From Faunsdale return to US 80 and head west toward Demopolis.

alabamatrivia

An immense 1833 meteor shower inspired the song, "Stars Fell on Alabama."

Sometime during your visit to the area, make an outing to *Prairieville,* the site of *St. Andrews Episcopal Church.* Located a short distance off US 80, this red Carpenter Gothic structure dates from 1853 and is a National Historic Landmark. Nearby you'll see a picturesque old cemetery, where many of this area's early settlers are buried.

Peter Lee and Joe Glasgow, master carpenters and slaves of Capt. Henry A. Tayloe, supervised a crew of slaves belonging to church members in the construction of this edifice, built to serve settlers from the Atlantic seaboard.

Craftspeople created the mellowed appearance of interior wood walls by applying a brew made from the stems of tobacco plants. Pokeberry weeds provided color for some portions of the lovely stained-glass windows. Ragweed, chewed and molded, forms the decorative relief letters of a biblical quotation near the altar. Be sure to notice the pipe organ (which is still playable) and the choir gallery. Closed as a regular parish in 1927, the church hosts a special service the first Sunday in October followed by a picnic dinner on the grounds. Group tours can be arranged by appointment; call (334) 289–3363.

St. Andrews Episcopal Church

Traveling 9 miles west on US 80 takes you to ***Gaineswood*** (334–289–4846), a gorgeous cream-colored mansion with white-columned porticos. Once the centerpiece of a huge plantation, the home now stands in the suburbs of the town of ***Demopolis*** at 805 South Cedar Avenue. Gen. Nathan Bryan Whitfield, a gifted inventor, musician, artist, and architect, started construction on the house in 1843. He spent almost two decades planning and building this elegant Greek Revival home and continued to refine it until the Civil War's outbreak.

Stepping into the columned ballroom, you'll see yourself reflected thirteen times in the vis-à-vis mirrors. Be sure to notice the glass-ceiling domes and the elaborate friezes and medallions. The home contains its original furnishings, family portraits, and accessories. Don't miss the flutina (invented by Whitfield), a one-of-a-kind musical instrument that sounds something like a riverboat calliope.

In many ways Gaineswood reminded me of Thomas Jefferson's splendid Monticello, and my guide said visitors often make that observation. Except for major holidays, Gaineswood is open Tuesday through Friday from 9:00 A.M. to 4:00 P.M. Tours start on the hour with other times by appointment for groups. Admission.

Continue to downtown Demopolis, "the City of the People," a town with an interesting origin that goes back to 1817 when 400 aristocrats, fleeing France after Napoleon's exile, landed here at the white limestone bluffs overlooking the Tombigbee River. They acquired a large tract of land along the river and set about establishing the ***Vine and Olive Colony.*** The agricultural experiment, however, yielded little more than frustration for the colonists, who lacked essential farming skills and found the local climate and soil unsuitable for cultivating their imported grape vines and olive trees.

You'll see a display on this early colony in the French Room at ***Bluff Hall*** (334–289–9644). Located at 407 North Commissioners Avenue next to the Civic Center, this 1832 brick home takes its name from its position overlooking the Tombigbee River. Originally built in the Federal style, the home took on a Greek Revival appearance after later additions. Furnishings are Empire and mid-Victorian.

As you start upstairs notice the newel post's amity button, symbolizing a state of harmony between the owner and builder. In addition to documents, crystal, silver spoons, cannonballs, portraits, and other memorabilia of the Vine and Olive Colony, you'll see a room filled with period costumes, such as an 1831 wedding dress. Bluff Hall is noted for its extensive collection of vintage clothing.

The kitchen's interesting gadgets range from an egg tin, sausage stuffer, and fluting iron to the "humane" rat trap on the hearth. Adjacent to the home, the Canebrake Craft Corner offers a choice selection of items including posters depicting a European artist's imaginative conception of the early Vine and Olive Colony, handmade split-oak baskets, and eye-catching pottery by Susan Brown Freeman. Bluff Hall is owned and operated by the Marengo County Historical Society. (The county's name was inspired by Napoleon's victory at the Battle of Marengo in northern Italy.) Except for major holidays, Bluff Hall is open Tuesday through Saturday from 10:00 A.M. to 5:00 P.M. and on Sunday from 2:00 to 5:00 P.M. During January and February, the home closes at 4:00 P.M. Admission.

Dip into more history at ***Laird Cottage*** (334–289–0282), which also houses the Geneva Mercer Museum and the Marengo County Historical Society headquarters. Located at 311 North Walnut, the circa-1870 home reflects a Greek Revival–Italianate style of architecture. Here you'll see works by Mercer, a gifted Marengo County artist and sculptor, who studied and worked with Giuseppe Moretti, the Italian sculptor who designed Birmingham's statue of Vulcan. Call for hours or an appointment. Admission is free.

While sightseeing stop by the Demopolis yacht basin on US 43 for a meal at ***New Orleans Bar & Grill*** (334–289–2668). If you sit near a window, you can still see a portion of the white chalk bluffs where the French Bonapartists landed. (This landmark is less prominent since the Demopolis Lock and Dam raised the river level by 40 feet in 1954.)

Here you can meet and eat with "the boat people," members of the city's maritime community who live aboard their yachts and play active roles in the town's civic and social life. The restaurant serves a variety of sandwiches, salads, and dinner entrees. Try the Jack Daniels steak and chicken salad. Hours are 11:00 A.M. till 2:00 P.M. and 4:00 to 9:00 P.M. Monday through Thursday. The

Grill is open from 11:00 A.M. to 9:30 P.M. Friday and noon to 9:30 P.M. Saturday. Prices are moderate. When you leave, take along some bread to feed the fish and turtles that congregate below the boardwalk—they expect it.

Demopolis offers more than mansions and water recreation. You'll find plenty of interesting places to shop, too. Downtown, at 109 West Washington Street, The Mustard Seed offers fine gifts, china, crystal, housewares, collectibles, dolls, and toys. Maison de Briques, a flower and gift shop at 102 US 80 East, stocks a variety of decorative items.

Local festivals include a July the Fourth celebration, Freedom on the River at City Landing, and December's *Christmas on the River,* which features a weeklong festival of parades, tours, and events culminating in an extravaganza of decorated, lighted boats gliding down the Tombigbee River. For more information on these or other special events, including productions by the Canebrake Players (a local theater group) or on other area attractions, call (334) 289–0270.

Traveling north takes you to *Eutaw,* a charming hamlet situated around a courthouse square that dates from 1838. The town boasts fifty-three antebellum structures, with many on the National Register of Historic Places. Head first to the chamber of commerce office on the courthouse square, where you'll find information on both Eutaw and Greene County.

Beside the historic Vaughn Morrow House on Main Street stands the First Presbyterian Church. Organized in 1824 as Mesopotamia Presbyterian Church, the congregation's current home dates from 1851. This white-steepled structure looks as if it belongs on a Christmas card (without the snow, of course—a rare commodity in most of Alabama). Original whale-oil lamps, stored for a time in the slave gallery, have been wired for electricity and again grace the church's interior. For a tour, inquire at the church office in the adjacent Educational Building.

Nearby, on the corner of Main Street and Eutaw Avenue, stands St. Stephen's Episcopal Church. The handsome brick structure features a hand-carved lectern, an elegant white marble baptismal font, and beautiful stained-glass windows. To see the lovely interior, check with the church office.

Don't miss *Kirkwood Mansion* (205–372–2694) at the intersection of State Route 14 and Kirkwood Drive. Topped by a belvedere, this impressive 1860 American Greek Revival home features eight massive Ionic columns, Carrara marble mantels, and Waterford crystal chandeliers. Owners Danky and Al Blanton have furnished the home with museum-quality antiques. Built by Foster Mark Kirksey, the mansion was on the verge of completion when the Civil War brought construction to a halt. After a century of neglect, the house was rescued by Mary and Roy Swayze, who moved here from Virginia and set about transforming Kirkwood. In 1982 Nancy Reagan, on behalf of the National Trust

Kirkwood Mansion

for Historic Preservation, presented the Swayzes with the National Honor Award in recognition of their outstanding restoration. Call for a mansion tour between the hours of 9:00 A.M. and 5:00 P.M. Monday through Saturday and 1:00 to 5:00 P.M. Sunday. Admission.

Overnight visitors can make reservations at ***Oakmont Bed & Breakfast*** (205–372–2326), owned by Deborah and Scott Stone. Situated on a grassy knoll at 107 Pickens Street and framed by wisteria, azaleas, camellias, and magnolias, Oakmont stands three stories tall with a widow's walk roof railing. Deborah said she had never heard of Eutaw (population 2,000) until a few years ago. Returning home to Madison, Mississippi, after a visit to Atlanta, she exited the interstate on a whim when her mother noticed a small HISTORIC HOMES sign. After discovering a lovely columned Greek Revival home for sale, Deborah called her husband, and the couple soon became the new owners. They completed a restoration of the circa-1908 home and in January 2002 opened it for bed-and-breakfast guests.

Deborah serves as the Greene County Historic Society's president and spearheads the annual Eutaw Pilgrimage, an event that showcases the town's architectural treasures on the second weekend of October. She shares insider tips on what to see and do in Eutaw and the surrounding area. Guests can anticipate a Southern gourmet breakfast that starts with fresh fruits and juice as a prelude to bacon, cheese-topped baked tomatoes, and French toast with pecans or an equally enticing menu. Standard rates. Preview the property at www.oakmont.biz. HGTV fans may have seen Oakmont on an *If Walls Could Talk* episode.

After exploring Eutaw head west to ***Gainesville,*** a delightful piece of the past populated by 307 people. Most places like this charming town have vanished from today's landscape. Here you'll see historic cemeteries and churches like the First Presbyterian Church, which dates from 1837 and has been rescued from flames on three occasions—once with a hand-to-hand bucket brigade. Interior features include whale-oil lamps, box pews, the altar's original chairs, and a bell with a tone enhanced by 500 melted silver dollars. Because several denominations share this church (one per Sunday), attendees label themselves "Metho-bap-terians." Other sites of interest include the 1872 Methodist Church; St. Alban's Episcopal Church, founded in 1879; and the Confederate Cemetery. For more local information stop by one of the downtown stores.

Afterward continue south to nearby *Livingston.* The town was named for Edward Livingston, who served as Andrew Jackson's secretary of state.

On your way into town, stop by Sumter County's *Alamuchee Covered Bridge,* across from the Baptist Student Union on the campus of Livingston State University. Capt. W. A. C. Jones of Livingston designed and built this 1861 structure, one of the South's oldest covered bridges. Made of hand-hewn heart pine held together by large wooden pegs, the bridge originally spanned the Sucarnochee River, south of town. In 1924 the bridge was taken down and reconstructed across a creek on the old Bellamy-Livingston Road, where it remained in use until 1958. The bridge was moved to its present location and restored in 1971. You might enjoy seeing more of the campus, which also boasts two lakes.

Downtown you'll see a lovely square surrounding the impressive domed Sumter County Courthouse (circa 1900). This area remained Choctaw country until 1830, when the United States acquired it in the Treaty of Dancing Rabbit Creek.

Local businesswomen Mary Tartt, Molly Dorman, and Louise Boyd find that *The Dancing Rabbit* (205–652–6252) is a good name for their shop near the courthouse square. Located at 307 Monroe Street, the charming store features silver, crystal, antique linens, wicker items, china, Christmas ornaments, and other collectibles along with a variety of rabbits (but not the real live kind). Hours are 10:00 A.M. to 5:30 P.M. Tuesday through Friday and 10:00 A.M. to 4:00 P.M. Saturday.

Head to *York,* about 11 miles southwest of Livingston. In this small town near the Mississippi border, you'll find a wonderful art museum inside *The Coleman Center* (205–392–2005 or 205–392–2004), at 630 Avenue A. The museum, a library, genealogical room, and a cultural center occupy an early-twentieth-century general store. On an exterior wall of the building, a repainted vintage ad shows silent film star Clara Bow promoting an early brand of gasoline. You'll enter The Coleman Center through a courtyard on the opposite side.

A staff member described the four-building complex as a community effort and the only facility of its kind in Sumter County. Local citizens contributed the land, building, services, and funds for the center. In addition to its permanent collection, which includes an original etching by Renoir, prints, paintings, pottery, and other items, the museum features traveling exhibits. The facility closes each day from noon to 1:00 P.M. and also on Thursday and Saturday afternoons. Otherwise, hours are 9:00 A.M. to 4:30 P.M. or by appointment. The museum closes on Sunday. Admission is free. Visit York on the first Saturday of each month and take in some special events at local galleries.

Timberland

Timber is big business in this part of the state, and hunting and fishing are popular pastimes. If you're in the mood for a feast, head for *Ezell's Fish Camp* (205–654–2205) near *Lavaca.* This out-of-the-way restaurant is definitely worth adding some extra miles to your trip. In fact, some customers fly in, and an Ezell's staffer meets them at the airport. The restaurant also gets a lot of river traffic and often provides transportation into town for boating customers who need motel lodging.

To reach the restaurant from Lavaca, take State Route 10 east toward Nanafalia and turn left just before reaching the big bridge. Located on the west bank of the Tombigbee River, this family operation is the granddaddy of "catfish cabins" you might see while driving through the state. Following family precedent, each of the Ezells' three children went into the restaurant business.

Need Some Mama Nems Pepper Jelly?

Then hurry to the **Alabama Rural Heritage Center** (334–627–3388) in Thomaston, a Black Belt hamlet northeast of Lavaca. Here, director Gayle Etheridge reports brisk sales for the facility's logo item. Along with batches of the popular pepper jelly, you'll find a wide selection of Alabama art and handmade crafts in the gift shop. A jar of watermelon rind pickles just might make the perfect souvenir.

The once-humble facility now boasts a new facade, interior, and restaurant, thanks to the innovative efforts of two teams of fifth-year architecture students from Auburn University, who designed and worked on the project over a three-year period. The restaurant serves dinner on Friday and Saturday nights and also a Sunday buffet.

Annual events include Evening under the Stars, utilizing the new Heritage outdoor stage, on Friday and Saturday evenings during Mother's Day weekend, and an annual Rural Fun Day with storytelling, spinning, weaving, quilting, and other crafts demonstrations the fourth Saturday in August. "We are excited that we can provide some lively and wholesome family entertainment right here in Thomaston—population 387, " said Etheridge. Hours are 8:30 A.M. to 4:30 P.M. Monday through Friday or by appointment on weekends.

As you arrive, you'll see a large rustic structure with a roof of wooden shingles. The restaurant started out as a Civil War–era dogtrot cabin, and the Ezells added more rooms for their brisk business. The rambling structure now seats 400 people. Mounted deer and moose heads line the walls. (Mr. Ezell, an avid angler, hunter, and trapper, used to ship his furs to New York's garment district.)

The back porch, a favorite spot for eating, overlooks the river. Start with an appetizer of onion rings, crab claws, or fried dill pickles. In addition to catfish, the restaurant serves seafood specialties such as shrimp and oysters. Entrees come with slaw, potatoes, and hush puppies. Moderate prices. Open every day except Monday, Ezell's has flexible hours, but the typical schedule is 11:00 A.M. to 9:00 P.M. Sunday through Thursday and to 10:00 P.M. Friday and Saturday.

Traveling south from Lavaca takes you through large expanses of timberland. Forestry and related industries play major roles in the area's economy. Clarke County holds the title of Forestry Capital of Alabama, and Fulton, a small town south of Thomasville, pays tribute to this important industry by hosting a **Sawmill Days** celebration each fall.

If you head south from Jackson, you'll pass unusual geographical features known as salt domes. (A salt dome is the tip of a huge mountain of salt forced to the surface from deep within the earth.) According to a local historian, the salt domes in this area are as close as any to the earth's surface, but you probably won't recognize them as such because they're covered with foliage. After Union forces cut off supplies during the Civil War, the local salt mines became extremely important. Many people made their way here for this commodity, essential for curing and preserving meats.

At Carlton, about 12 miles south of Jackson, the **Indian Artifact Museum** beckons travelers who like to delve into Native American history. Retired Mobile police officer Tommy Hart welcomes visitors and shares his expertise along with some local lore. His fascination with Indian artifacts goes back to childhood. A giant tomahawk marks the entrance to the building he constructed in his front yard to house his extensive collection of points, spears, pottery shards, sharks' teeth, Civil War relics, and more. Hart has been known to take travelers to see the intriguing grave sculptures in the nearby Mount Nebo Church cemetery. Call (251) 246–7666 for directions and more information. No admission charge.

Take your time while discovering the treasures and pleasures of the Black Belt, a region where history still resonates in its stories—the kind best savored on front porches. Kathryn Tucker Windham, Alabama's famous First Lady of Folk Tales and Ghost Stories grew up in Thomasville, located about an hour south of Demopolis on U.S. Highway 43. Make your first stop the bank where her father once served as president and now the headquarters for ALA-TOM

Discover St. Stephens—Alabama's Territorial Capital

No Black Belt ramble is complete without a visit to **St. Stephens Historical Park.** It was here, in 1799, the first U.S. flag flew over what would become Alabama. Executive director Jim Long, sixth-generation grandson of John McGrew, who settled in St. Stephens during the 1770s, can share many anecdotes about the original site of Alabama's territorial capital, the now vanished but once-thriving Old St. Stephens.

Make your first stop the 1854 territorial courthouse, now called the Old Washington County Courthouse, on U.S. Highway 34 West to collect information. A trio of flags fronts this two-story white building, which houses a museum and serves as headquarters for the St. Stephens Historical Commission. Take the tiny grill-fronted elevator or the stairs to the second floor for a look at the exhibits, which include Indian artifacts, a dugout canoe made somewhere between 600 to 1,000 years ago, portraits of early settlers, and the Old Washington County courtroom with its original furnishings. Once a major fossil site, this area shipped fossils to museums in other parts of the country, and you'll see some interesting specimens.

Afterward, head to the 200-acre park, which offers camping, fishing, and other outdoor recreation. Exploring the park, you'll see an architectural site, old cemetery, and the unusual Indian Baths. "They've been called the Indian Baths as far back as anyone knows, but their origin remains unknown," said staffer Wanda Braun, who came across a mention about mineral springs here in 1818 and also heard speculation that this feature might have been part of an early Spanish irrigation system.

 For a modest park admission, which you pay at the camp store by the lake, you can spend a full day hiking, swimming, picnicking, and relaxing. Campers will find that the "view of the night sky is fabulous, and you can hear coyotes howling," said Long. The facility opens at sunrise and closes at sunset, and the main gate is locked at 10:00 P.M. For more information on this intriguing site, located on the west side of the Tombigbee River in Washington County near Jackson, take a look at www.oldst stephens.com or call (251) 246–6790.

If you visit on the last Saturday in October, you can view "Old St. Stephens—Through the Eyes of a Child," presented by elementary students from gifted education classes in nearby Jackson. "They dress in period costumes to retell the history of old St. Stephens, the birthplace of the state of Alabama," said Braun, "and their program is based on the writings of Mary Welsh who grew up there in the early 1800s."

At this annual festival, attendees can see artifacts from past digs at the site, enjoy catfish dinners, and munch on Indian corn, roasted peanuts, and fried pork skins. Live music, arts-and-crafts exhibits, and demonstrations of basket weaving, blacksmithing, pottery making, quilting, shingle making, and more round out the day's activities, which conclude with a fireworks display over the Tombigbee.

Just a Sample of Black Belt Hospitality

An old song goes, "If I knew you were coming, I'd have baked a cake." Well, that's exactly what St. Stephens resident Lola Grimes, fondly known as Miss Lola, did when we visited St. Stephens Historical Park. But Miss Lola did not stop with one cake. She produced a yummy pie, banana pudding, and more—all positioned in a most tempting display at the end of a long table laden with an amazing variety of salads (including congealed, leafy, and her potato salad, "which is legend"). But that's not all. The menu also featured deviled eggs, stuffed celery, homegrown butterbeans, corn, peas, and a sweet-potato casserole, plus cornbread and biscuits. As for meat dishes, Miss Lola tempted us with chicken and dumplings, pork roast, and bacon-wrapped chicken breasts. To accompany this fine fare, well, what else but gallons of sweet iced tea—the table wine of the South? The feast looked like a spread from *Southern Living* magazine or a church supper where everybody brings a favorite dish. Except for some help from staffer Wanda Braun, Miss Lola prepared the food herself. And every bite was scrumptious.

Miss Lola thinks nothing of getting up at 4:00 A.M. to start cooking. She's always first on the scene to comfort a grieving family, visit someone just home from the hospital, or greet a newcomer with not just a lone casserole but an entire menu. Just a sample of local cuisine and Black Belt hospitality.

Thanks, Miss Lola, and by the way, isn't it about time for another research trip?

Resource Conservation and Development and Regional Tourism office (334–636–0120) at 16 West Front Street. Visitors can collect information here and enjoy the art gallery on the premises. "We're not New York City, and we don't want to be," says tourism coordinator Linda Vice, who can direct you to plenty of interesting, off-the-beaten-path spots in this history-rich area. "We have developed a Black History/Heritage Trail, a Native American Trail, an overall History Heritage Trail, and a Foods Trail through this area."

On the outskirts of Thomasville stands Alabama Southern Community College (334–636–9642) located at 30755 Highway 43. The college library houses the *Kathryn Tucker Windham Museum,* which fans enjoy visiting. During the school term, hours are 7:30 A.M. to 7:30 P.M. Monday through Thursday and until 2:00 P.M. Friday. You can visit between 10:00 A.M. and 2:00 P.M. on Saturday or Sunday by appointment. Call ahead for summer hours. Free admission.

Continue to *Camden,* where you'll find the new *Black Belt Treasures Gallery* (334–682–9878) downtown at 209 Claiborne Street in a handsomely restored old car dealership. The gallery showcases arts, crafts, books, and food from this region. Hours are 9:00 A.M. to 5:00 P.M. Monday through Friday and 9:00 A.M. to 1:00 P.M. Saturday.

Before leaving town, stop by *Camden Jewelry and Gifts* (334–682–4057) on the 47 Camden Bypass. Besides jewelry, you'll find a selection of taste-tempting gourmet food items, a children's section, kitchen section, bath and body products, travel items, and more. The friendly staff will help you choose the perfect souvenir or gift for everyone on your list. Hours are 9:00 A.M. to 5:00 P.M. Monday through Friday and 9:00 A.M. to 2:00 P.M. Saturday. If you visit Camden during the Wilcox Historical Society's biennial (slated for odd-numbered years) Fall Tour of Homes, you can survey some of the area's antebellum struc-

The Quilters of Gee's Bend Create a Bridge to the World

"There's only one way in and one way out," said Ollie Pettway, a resident of Gee's Bend. Despite its remote location in a curve of the Alabama River about 30 miles southwest of Selma, some visitors manage to find the home of the famed quilters whose works have captured the imagination of gallery goers across the country. Created by four generations of African-American women whose quilts have been called bold, colorful, and unique, *The New York Times* described their designs and needlecraft as "some of the most miraculous works of modern art America has produced."

The quilters work at Boykin Nutrition Center, and a nearby building houses their current inventory of colorful quilts, which sell for prices ranging from $1,500 to $4,000. On a recent visit, we met Arlonzia, Ollie, Nancy, and Lola Pettway, who greeted us warmly and signed our book, *The Quilts of Gee's Bend.*

The Quilts of Gees Bend exhibit has intrigued gallery goers to Boston's Museum of Fine Arts, Atlanta's High Museum, and others across the country. The women have also been featured in such publications *House and Garden,* Oprah's *O* magazine, *Newsweek,* and *Country Home* and on National Public Radio and CBS's *Sunday Morning.*

The quilters struck a chord with people everywhere. Why? Anniston travel writer Mary Eloise H. Leake explains it this way: "Amid a landscape of limitations, the women were and still are strongly individualistic and gifted with artistic vision. Forging bonds across generations, each quilt reflects the personality and talent of the particular woman who stitched it together. With no access to definitive quilting patterns, these women made—and continue to make—quilts with lyrical improvisational designs, amazing asymmetrical constructions, and simple minimalist motifs. While a Gee's Bend's quilt can be a vibrant Joseph's coat of many colors, its hue can also be dull and worn like the clothes from which it has been made.

"As they have traveled the country, the quilts—and many of the quilters—have shared the message that art can be created from basic necessities. Their quilts have formed a bridge from their isolated world to the wider world, and the creators have been delighted to see the joy they have brought to others. Since the quilts have been heralded as artistic triumphs by art critics and warmly received by exhibit viewers, this unaccustomed outpouring of respect and admiration have been wonderful return gifts to these ladies."

To visit the Gee's Bend quilters, head south on Wilcox County Route 29, taking a left turn when you reach a fork at the end of the road. For general information on the area, call Rennie Miller at (334) 573-2526.

tures. The stately Wilcox Female Institute, which dates from 1850, serves as tour headquarters. Located at 301 Broad Street, the former school (open by appointment) houses a small museum of local history.

For a Southern taste treat, make reservations at the **Gaines Ridge Dinner Club** (334–682–9707), located about 2 miles east of Camden on State Route 10. Housed in Betty Gaines Kennedy's two-story circa-1830 family home, the restaurant seats about one hundred guests in five dining rooms. From shrimp bisque to spinach salad and steak or seafood, everything on the menu is well prepared and tasty. (Ask Betty about the home's ghosts.) Prices fall in the moderate range, and hours are 5:30 to 9:00 P.M. Wednesday through Saturday.

Wilcox County, which promises good fishing, attracts out-of-state deer and turkey hunters, and many make their headquarters at nearby **Roland Cooper State Park.** If you're in the area during harvest season, consider purchasing some fresh-shelled pecans from Joe C. Williams. To order the local product, write P.O. Box 640, Camden 36726; or call (334) 682–4559. For more information on Camden and the surrounding area, call the Wilcox Development Council at (334) 682–4929.

Traveling south from Camden on State Route 265 takes you by **Rikard's Mill,** just north of Beatrice. Stop by to browse through the Covered Bridge Gift Shop and watch the old-fashioned water-powered gristmill in operation. You'll also find a restored blacksmith shop and hiking trails. Modest admission. For seasonal hours, April through mid-December, call (251) 789–2781 or (251) 575–7433.

Continue south to **Monroeville** (where Alabama authors Truman Capote and Harper Lee played as children) for a stop at the **Old Monroe County Courthouse.** This 1903 three-story brick structure served as a model for the courthouse in the film *To Kill a Mockingbird,* based on Harper Lee's Pulitzer Prize–winning novel (and starring Gregory Peck in the role of Atticus Finch). During my visit, I entered the courthouse and asked to see Atticus Finch. While applauding myself on being so imaginative, I learned that "everyone wants to meet Atticus Finch."

During the last weekend in April and the first three weekends in May, visitors can watch the stage version of *To Kill a Mockingbird* in a bona fide courtroom setting. Produced by the Monroe County Heritage Museum under the direction of Kathy McCoy, who heads up the museum staff, the local stage adaptation boasts the authenticity of the story's actual location plus cultural awareness and genuine Southern accents.

As guests of the government of Israel in 1996, the talented performers (and only amateur group ever invited to participate) presented this classic drama on stage in Jerusalem at the International Cultural Festival. In September 1998 the production traveled to England and was staged at the Hull Theater. In June

Monroeville—Literary Capital of Alabama

In recognition of the exceptional literary heritage of Monroeville and Monroe County, the Alabama legislature designated this region the Literary Capital of Alabama in a 1997 joint resolution. Author of "A Christmas Memory," *In Cold Blood, Breakfast at Tiffany's,* and other classics, Truman Capote spent idyllic hours roaming the town as a youngster along with friend Harper Lee, who penned the Pulitzer Prize–winning novel, *To Kill a Mockingbird.* Other writers who have called Monroeville home include nationally syndicated columnist Cynthia Tucker and novelist Mark Childress. The small town of Monroeville, which packs a rich literary history, hosts an Alabama Writers Symposium the first weekend in May. For more information on this event, contact the Alabama Southern Community College at P.O. Box 2000, Monroeville 36461; or call (251) 575–3156, extension 223.

2000 the local production traveled to Washington, D.C., for performances at the Kennedy Center for Performing Arts. For more information visit the Web site at www.tokillamockingbird.com.

Dip into the town's rich literary heritage at the ***Old Courthouse Museum*** (251–575–7433), which also features changing exhibits related to Monroe County's past and a gift shop with works by area artists. Adjacent to the courtroom, you'll see an informative Harper Lee exhibit with archival photos, quotes, and a continuous video of local citizens sharing anecdotes from the 1930s. Museum director Jane Ellen Clark can share plenty of firsthand information on the town, its celebrated authors, and the Monroe County Heritage Museums. The museum is located at 31 North Alabama Avenue; admission is free. Hours run from 8:00 A.M. to 4:00 P.M. Monday through Friday and 10:00 A.M. to 2:00 P.M. on Saturday.

Afterward, take a walking tour around town, where several buildings feature murals illustrating scenes from *To Kill a Mockingbird.* While downtown, stop by Finishing Touches at 107 East Claiborne Street on the square's south side. You'll enjoy browsing through this shop with lovely handmade items, antiques, kitchen accessories, gifts, clothing for children and ladies, customized baskets, and books. Monroeville also offers some great outlet shopping at Vanity Fair.

Before leaving the area, you might want to visit the ***River Heritage Museum,*** housed in the old Corps of Engineers building at the Claiborne Lock & Dam. The surrounding region is a great place for camping and fishing, too. Located about 18 miles from the square in downtown Monroeville, the museum can be reached by taking State Route 41 to County Road 17 and then following the signs to the Claiborne Lock & Dam. The museum's exhibits feature fossils,

Native American artifacts, and steamboat relics. With seasonal hours, the museum is open March through October. Hours run from 9:00 A.M. to 4:00 P.M. Friday and Saturday; admission is free. For more information call (251) 575–7433.

Gulf Coast Delta

After your timberland excursion head south to Escambia County, where traveling pilgrims can spend an authentic Thanksgiving Day with the Poarch Band of Creek Indians at their annual Pow Wow. Tribal members welcome friends, relatives, and visitors to help them celebrate Thanksgiving day on the *Poarch Creek Reservation,* 8 miles northwest of Atmore at 5811 Jack Springs Road. Festivities include exhibition dancing by tribes from throughout the country, a greased pig chase, turkey shoot, and much more. You can feast on roasted corn, Indian fry bread, ham, fried chicken, or traditional turkey and dressing. Booths feature beadwork, basketry, silver work, and other Native American crafts. Take a lawn chair, camera, and your appetite. Modest admission. For more information on this event, call (251) 368–9136.

Continue southwest toward the Eastern Shore and stop by Malbis, 12 miles east of Mobile on U.S. Highway 90. On Baldwin County Road 27, you'll find the *Malbis Greek Orthodox Church.* This magnificent neo-Byzantine–style structure, built at a cost of more than $1 million, was dedicated to the memory of Jason Malbis. A former monk who emigrated from Greece in 1906, Malbis traveled through thirty-six states before selecting this Baldwin County site to establish Malbis Plantation (virtually a self-supporting colony that grew to cover 2,000 acres).

The marble in this edifice came from the same Greek quarries used to build Athens's ancient Parthenon. The majestic interior features a dark-blue 75-foot domed ceiling, stained-glass windows, mosaics, and murals. Greek artists spent eight months completing the paintings that extend from the cathedral's entrance to its altar. Except for Christmas Day, the church is open daily, and admission is free. Hours run from 10:00 A.M. to 4:00 P.M. For tour information call (251) 626–3050.

Next swing westward to Daphne, perched on Mobile Bay's Eastern Shore, where you might hear someone shout "Jubilee!" When you do, people will grab buckets and rush to the water's edge for flounder, shrimp, and crabs—theirs for the scooping. Although not unique to the area, this "shoreward migration of bottom-living organisms"—to put it in technical terms—surprises most visitors. This natural phenomenon might occur several times a summer, usually during the wee morning hours. Some natives claim they can predict an approaching jubilee by watching weather conditions and studying certain indicators in the moon, tide, and winds.

After exploring Daphne continue south to ***Fairhope,*** a charming flower-filled town founded about 1894 on the "single tax" concept of economist Henry George, who considered land the source of all wealth. The Fairhope Single Tax Colony still functions today, one of the country's few model communities operating on George's taxation theories. A percentage of the town's property is held by the Fairhope Single Tax Colony office, and a resident can lease his or her land for ninety-nine years (or perpetuity). The resident pays a single annual tax on the land only—not on improvements—and this yearly payment covers school district, city, county, and state taxes as well as community services.

Save plenty of time for strolling through the pages of this storybook town with baskets of colorful blossoms cascading from every street corner and rose gardens galore in its bayfront park. Downtown art galleries, boutiques, and eateries beckon browsers. Indulge your whims as you pass restaurants featuring coastal cuisine fresh from the Gulf and shops offering everything from antiques, toys, and custom-designed clothing to nautical gear.

Wander to the ***Eastern Shore Art Center*** (251–928–2228) at 401 Oak Street and view its current exhibits. Top that off with individual galleries that call your name. At Fairhope's monthly First Friday Artwalk, you can hop a free trol-

Strange as It Sounds

Whether or not you hear the cry of "Jubilee!" during your visit to the Eastern Shore of Mobile Bay, you can see this strange spectacle depicted in a photo display at ***Manci's Antique Club*** (251–626–9917) in downtown ***Daphne.*** Located at the corner of Daphne and Bellrose Avenues, this combination bar/museum (originally opened as a gas station in 1924 by Frank Manci, converted to its current status in 1947 by Arthur Manci, and now operated by a third-generation family member, Alex Manci) houses a rickshaw, oxen yokes, and Victrolas. You'll also see collections of antique tools, cowbells, political campaign buttons, and Native American artifacts. The club boasts the biggest assemblage of Jim Beam decanters outside the distillery's own collection. Claiming the title "Bloody Mary Capital of the Eastern Shore," the house serves its specialty garnished with a pickled string bean. A sign over the bar promises FREE BEER TOMORROW.

Those who visit the ladies' room at Manci's will see the wooden figure of a man—dressed only in a fig leaf. The observant will notice the fig leaf is hinged, and the curious might go even further. Unrestrained curiosity can soon turn to horror, however, because a blaring alarm alerts all within hearing distance that one possesses an inquisitive nature. One then must make the uncomfortable choice of exiting—red-faced—to the merriment of Manci's patrons or occupying the ladies' room till closing time. Manci's hours are 10:00 A.M. to 10:00 P.M. Monday through Thursday, and on Friday and Saturday the club stays open until—.

Eat Their Words

Want to sample Fannie Flagg's own fried green tomatoes? Or Winston Grooms's gumbo? Or Pat and Sandra Conroy's dinner party mini-crab casseroles? Then contact the Eastern Shore Literacy Council (251–990–8300) of Fairhope for a copy of *Eat Their Words: Southern Writers, Readers and Recipes*. To order this entertaining 450-page cookbook containing anecdotes and recipes contributed by Dave Barry, Rick Bragg, Barbara Bush, Laura Bush, Kathryn Tucker Windham, and other celebrities, send $20 per book (which includes shipping) to:

Eastern Shore Literacy Council
409 North Section Street, Suite A
Fairhope, AL 36532

(All proceeds benefit the Eastern Shore Literacy Council, a United Way agency.)

ley or stroll a 5-block area to visit galleries like Lyons Share and Summit. For a great local souvenir, stop by the ***Christine Linson Gallery*** (251–929–2015) at 386 Fairhope Avenue and pick up a pack of note cards depicting local scenes.

On a trip to Alabama in 1998, Christine painted the town (in watercolor) and fell in love with its charms. She promptly returned to her lifelong home in Cleveland, Ohio, packed her belongings, moved to Fairhope, and opened her gallery. In addition to her popular Fairhope and Eastern Shore prints and limited edition Christmas cards, you'll see original floral and figurative art work. Also, you might meet felines Matisse and Toulouse (not aloof—only shy). Hours run 10:00 A.M. to 5:00 P.M. Monday through Saturday. Check out www.christinelinsongallery.com for a peek at the artist's portfolio.

The ***Church Street Inn*** (866–928–8976) makes a lovely and convenient base for travelers. Located at 51 South Church Street, the white stucco-and-brick home contains five generations of family photos and antiques. Visitors can relax on the front porch and watch passersby (who often wave hello) or retreat to the back-garden courtyard. The living room's window seat makes a cozy spot for reading about local history. Guests may help themselves to ice cream when hunger pangs strike and enjoy an ample serve-yourself Continental breakfast when they choose. Moderate rates.

Hosts Becky and Bill Jones also welcome visitors to ***Bay Breeze Guest House*** on historic Mobile Bay, where they can watch the glorious sunsets, go beachcombing or fishing, and feed the resident ducks. Ask Becky, a former biology teacher, about the local jubilee phenomenon. From May through September, guests can enjoy breakfast served on Bay Breeze's pier. Moderate rates. For reservations at either property, call (866) 928–8976.

Before leaving Fairhope, you might also enjoy visiting a unique museum on Faulkner State Community College's Fairhope campus that houses memorabilia from the early days of the *Marietta L. Johnson School of Organic Education* (251–990–8601). Counselor Clarence Darrow, who summered in Fairhope, lectured at this nontraditional school, which was noted for its progressive curriculum promoting creativity. The museum occupies the west wing of the historic Bell Building at 10 South School Street. Hours are 2:00 to 4:00 P.M. Monday through Friday or by appointment. Admission is free.

South of Fairhope at Point Clear (designated "Punta Clara" on sixteenth-century maps of Spanish explorers), you'll find the *Grand Hotel Marriott Resort, Golf Club & Spa* (251–928–9201 or 800–544–9933) on scenic U.S. Highway 98. This legendary resort on Mobile Bay offers facilities spreading over 550 lovely acres studded with moss-festooned oaks more than 300 years old. The locale has long attracted generations of wealthy Southern families—the site's first resort dates from the mid-1800s. Today's guests continue to enjoy "the Grand's" traditions, such as afternoon tea.

If hotels possess survival instincts, the Grand's got an instinct second to none. By the time you read this, the Queen of Southern Resorts will be in full regal mode. On April 1, 2006, half the resort reopened after Hurricane Katrina's visit in August 2005 with late 2006 projected for all rebuilding and renovation projects to be completed. Incredibly, the new fishing pier got neatly stacked in the conference center's grand ballroom as if by a careful moving crew instead of a raging storm. No stranger to adversity, the grande dame emerged from her own tsunami in the same manner she rebounded after Civil War shelling and fire during the past century and a half.

Surviving Katrina's onslaught a life-size bronze statue of local legend, Bucky Miller (whose photographic memory permitted him to call hotel guests by name even when years had lapsed between their visits), stands tall. "Bucky," as he was fondly known, greeted everyone warmly and personified the Grand's legendary hospitality during his tenure of sixty-four years. Presiding over the Bird Cage Lounge, he delighted guests with his famous mint juleps. Though Bucky died in 2002, his spirit lives on at the Grand, and his statue was dedicated on Kentucky Derby Day in 2005.

The resort has consistently earned Four Diamond status each year since 1977 when AAA tourism editors started their awards for excellence. With so much to enjoy, from fine dining and a world-class spa to water recreation, tennis, and challenging golf courses, you'll want to check out www.marriott grand.com and check in soon after. Call for current vacation packages and reservations at this family friendly historical hotel. Deluxe.

Be sure to visit a candy shop called *Punta Clara Kitchen* (251–928–8477), located in an 1897 gingerbread house 1 mile south of the Grand Hotel. Here you can sample confections from pecan butter crunch and divinity to chocolate-covered bourbon balls and buckeyes (balls of creamy peanut-butter confections hand-dipped in chocolate). The shop also sells jellies, recipe books, pickles, and preserves. Before leaving, take a few minutes to look around this historic home, furnished as it was during the late 1800s. Hours are 9:00 A.M. to 5:00 P.M. Monday through Saturday and 12:30 to 5:00 P.M. Sunday.

Behind the Victorian home stands a weathered cedar and cypress structure that originally served as a laundry and wine cellar. It now houses *The Wash House Restaurant* (251–928–4838) at 17111 Scenic Highway 98, a great place to savor Southern coastal cuisine. The restaurant features the original working fireplace and wash pot, nowadays in the softly lit bar. Behind the building, a large deck under ancient live oaks makes a romantic setting for dinner.

Owners Wade Selsor and Robert Yarbrough learned their way around the kitchen as kids growing up in Camden, a small town south of Selma. "Wade develops the recipes, but we both play around with them," said Robert, noting they also draw from a broad spectrum of family favorites. The recipe for Sissy's crab cakes, a popular appetizer here, came from his wife's grandmother.

Entree options include savory rack of lamb, seared tuna steak, and Chateaubriand, a succulent cut from the heart of the tenderloin, served with potato casserole and blackened asparagus. Green Goddess dressing makes Wade's salads memorable, and his delicious key lime bread pudding offers a different twist. Dinner hours start at 5:00 P.M. Tuesday through Saturday; closing time depends on the crowd. Reservations are encouraged. Moderate.

Ready for an antistress kind of place? Then head for nearby *Magnolia Springs,* where you can unwind in a serene setting of dappled sunlight and live oaks. In its heyday as a resort area during the early part of the 1900s, Magnolia Springs lured visitors with twice-a-day train service from Chicago, St. Louis, and Cincinnati. "Many a consumptive, rheumatic, nervous, worn-out and over-worked person whose case was thought hopeless by the physicians has found health and a new lease on life by spending a few months at Magnolia Springs," states an early promotional pamphlet.

Once known as the Sunnyside Hotel, the *Magnolia Springs Bed and Breakfast* (251–965–7321 or 800–965–7321) at 14469 Oak Street exudes a friendly aura with its welcoming wraparound porch accented by a swing, white wicker furniture, rocking chairs, and ferns. One of the county's three remaining hotels from the resort era, the historic structure is painted a buttery yellow with white trim. Committed to providing warm hospitality, owner David Worthington welcomes guests to his 1867 home, nourishes them with a delicious breakfast, and recommends local excursions. If you go cruising down the river, you'll see mailboxes at the water's edge. Magnolia Springs's first postmaster launched a mail service by water in 1915, and many residents still get their mail delivered by boat. "It's one of only a few places in the country with a water mail route," says David.

You may have seen Magnolia Springs Bed and Breakfast featured on Bob Vila's *Restore America,* a home-and-garden TV program, in *Southern Living* magazine, or maybe on a past Alabama Public Television special. E-mail David at info@magnoliasprings.com. For a virtual tour and more information, log onto www.magnoliasprings.com. Moderate to deluxe rates.

A short stroll down tree-lined Oak Street takes you to ***Moore Brothers Village Market*** (251–965–3826), a great place to catch up on local news. The market houses a bakery, deli, butcher shop, gourmet foods, and plenty of nostalgia. You can enjoy lunch or dinner Monday through Saturday at ***Jesse's Restaurant*** (251–965–3827), also on the premises.

The original Moore Bros. Gen'l Merchandise opened in 1922 and remained a family business until it closed in 1993. Then, in 1997, Charlie Houser (who spent childhood days here) returned and purchased the neighborhood store and adjacent post office. With the help of an architect and contractor, he connected and rejuvenated the two buildings to implement his image of the perfect neighborhood gathering place.

Paintings depicting local scenes, old photos, and news articles line the walls of the restaurant and also the entryway, where an antique pie safe displays freshly made pastries. Nearby, you can check your weight on the penny scales. If you find yourself penniless, there's usually a spare coin on top of the machine. By the way, it's best to weigh *before* dining at Jesse's, where the evening special might mean prime rib, shrimp scampi, or whiskey steak. Other popular entrees include crab cakes, Cajun fettuccine, stuffed flounder, and chicken Pontalba. Moderate prices.

Across the road from Jesse's stands Magnolia Springs Park, which showcases one of the town's springs and makes an inviting shady retreat.

After basking in Magnolia Springs's serenity, head for ***Foley,*** situated around the intersection of US 98 and State Route 59. The town offers not only factory-outlet shopping but a host of attractions such as antiques malls, arts centers, and charming eateries.

Start your tour at 111 West Laurel Avenue with the ***Baldwin Museum of Art*** and the ***Holmes Medical Museum*** (251–970–1818 or 251–943–1818), housed in a building that dates to the early 1900s. After viewing the current downstairs art exhibits, climb to the second floor for a close-up look at instruments and memorabilia from medicine's earlier years. Once a hospital for Baldwin County residents, the rooms contain an operating suite complete with table, bone-breaking apparatus, Kelly pad, ether container, and attendant tubes. Also on display are X-ray equipment and medical cabinets filled with delivery forceps, tonsil guillotine and snare, and other instruments. In addition to patient quarters, you can inspect a room devoted to quackery paraphernalia—a color spectrum device for treating everything from headaches to kidney infections, barber bowl for bleeding patients, and diagrammed phrenology skull. Hours are noon to 4:00 P.M. Wednesday through Friday. Admission is free.

Continue to the **Performing Arts Center** (251–943–4381) at 119 West Laurel Avenue. Step inside the lobby of the former Foley Hotel, which dates to 1928, for a look at exhibits of juried fine art, and browse back through the dining room filled with more art and crafts by area artists. Notice the extensive pottery selection featuring a variety of techniques. The facility sponsors a sales gallery (a great place to buy unique gifts) as well as cultural events and art classes. Staffed by an all-volunteer organization, the center's hours run from 10:00 A.M. to 4:00 P.M. Monday through Friday and 11:00 A.M. to 2:00 P.M. on Saturday.

Take a break next door at **Stacey Rexall Drugs** (251–943–7191), with its "Old Tyme Soda Fountain." In this delightful pharmacy at 121 West Laurel Avenue, you can savor a banana split, slurp on an ice-cream soda, cherry Coke, or chocolate milk shake, and listen to old favorites from the jukebox or player piano while watching a toy train make its rounds above the soda fountain. A penny scale reveals your weight and fate. Hours run from 8:00 A.M. to 6:00 P.M. Monday through Friday and 9:00 A.M. to 5:00 P.M. on Saturday. Economical rates.

Continuing to the next block, you'll find **The Gift Horse** (251–943–3663 or 800–FOLEYAL), located at 209 West Laurel Avenue. Beyond the restaurant's leaded-glass doors, you'll see a grand banquet table with a buffet of salads, vegetables, meats, breads, and desserts. House specialties include fried biscuits, spinach soufflé, mystery crab-shrimp salad, and the restaurant's famous apple cheese—all prepared from owner Jackie O. McLeod's recipes. Lunch is served from 11:00 A.M. to 4:15 P.M. daily. Dinner hours run from 4:30 to 8:30 P.M. or when the crowd thins out. Monday through Saturday, and Sunday hours run from 11:00 A.M. to 8:00 P.M. Rates are moderate. Jackie's cookbook, available in the gift shop, makes a great souvenir and divulges some of her culinary secrets. While in Foley you may want to visit The Gift Horse Antique Centre, too.

Follow US 98 east to **Elberta.** During the first half of the century, this fertile area attracted families from central, northern, and southern Europe, as well as Quebec. At Elberta's **German Sausage Festivals,** staged in March and October, descendants of early settlers dress in native attire to perform Old World dances. Call (251) 986–5805 for more information.

To learn more about the ethnic diversity and lifestyles of the county's early settlers, stop by the **Baldwin County Heritage Museum** (251–986–8375), ½ mile east of Elberta on US 98. In front of the five-acre wooded setting called "Frieden Im Wald," you'll see a working windmill and several outdoor agricultural exhibits.

Displays inside the museum feature the Kee tool collection and vintage farm equipment, a printing press, and an interior section of a post office from Josephine, Alabama. Household items include an Edison phonograph, antique sewing machines, stoves, cooking utensils, and washing machines. Also on display are old-fashioned school desks, folk sculpture, and a moonshine still. You'll also find a blacksmith shop and a church that dates to 1908. The museum is staffed entirely by volunteers, many of them snowbirds from Minnesota, Wisconsin, Michigan, New York, and other northern states, as well as Canada, who contribute their time and skills to restoring artifacts and putting old machinery in running order again. Admission is free Hours are 10:00 A.M. to 4:00 P.M. Wednesday through Saturday, with a special program offered at 2:00 P.M. on the second Sunday of each month. Weekday tours can be arranged by appointment.

At 12695 County Road 95 in Elberta, you can study carnivorous plants like Venus's-flytrap, pitcher plants, and other unusual botanical specimens native to the area at *Biophilia Nature Center.* "Different kinds of wildlife can be seen in season," said Carol Lovell-Saas, who promotes environmental education and takes you on a walk through her "open book of nature" that spreads across twenty acres. Tours offer a minicourse in butterfly gardening for the South and the Midwest and include free pamphlets on each plus literature on ecogardening.

From spring through early winter, several kinds of showy native butterflies are raised indoors and outdoors, allowing visitors to observe all stages from egg to adult. You'll see forest wildflower meadows and swamps, now being restored with 300 native species, and can stop by a plant nursery and bookstore on the premises. Contact Carol at (251) 987–1200 for specific directions and hours. Check her Web site at www.Biophilia.net.

Afterward make your way back to Foley, then follow State Route 59 south to the glistening white sands of *Gulf Shores.* Although a Diners' Club publication once conferred highest honors on the stretch of shoreline along the Florida panhandle between Destin and Panama City, calling it "the world's most perfect beach," fewer people know about the other end of the Southern Riviera—Alabama's toehold on the Gulf of Mexico. In fact, the relatively new town of Gulf Shores did not appear on Alabama's official highway map until the 1960s. But a retreat offering sugar-sand beaches and a balmy climate cannot remain a secret forever, and this 32-mile crescent known as Pleasure Island (once a peninsula) now attracts vacationers from across the country.

Each year, *Southern Living* magazine gives some sixteen million readers the chance to vote for their favorite places in the Best of the South Readers' Choice Awards. In 2005 Gulf Shores ranked among the top four in the Beach Town/Resort category—representing quite a comeback since Hurricane Ivan decimated much of area in 2004. As for the following season's Hurricane Katrina, most all the damage reported by newspapers and TV has been cleaned up and cleared away. Last year's beach nourishment project plus some follow-up renourishment made the white-sand playground even wider and just as enticing as before. You can check out the new Alabama Gulf Coast for yourself at www.gulfshores.com.

Situated on the shores of the Intracoastal Waterway at *Orange Beach,* you'll want to visit a brand new 220-acre resort and entertainment complex called *The Wharf,* less than 2 miles from the area's beckoning beaches. Here, in a holiday atmosphere, you can stroll along the boardwalk and browse through boutiques, local shops, and major retail stores. You can take in an exciting concert at the amphitheater or take a spin on the Southeast's largest Ferris wheel. The complex offers restaurants, upscale accommodations, a much-acclaimed destination spa, an outfitter's center, and a marina with public and private boat slips. Condominiums at Levin's Bend stretch for half a mile. The Wharf lures locals and visitors alike with something for everyone. Visit www.thewharfal.com for a look at what's happening this season on Alabama's Gulf Coast.

Some one hundred charter boats dock at nearby Orange Beach marinas, offering outings from sunset cruises to fishing excursions. Surrounding waters feature world-class fishing throughout the year. (For information about state fishing licenses, call 334–242–3829 or 888–848–6887, or check out www.outdoor alabama.com.)

While in Orange Beach, consider signing up for a cruise aboard the **Blue Dolphin** at Alabama Point to view this stretch of the Gulf Coast's spectacular inland waterways. "Out of 1,284 cruises, we saw dolphins every time except three," said Captain Jerry. You'll view other native wildlife and pass beautiful Ono Island, where several celebrities own luxury homes. Call Captain Jerry and Admiral Gail at (251) 981–2774 for reservations on this 51-foot, sixty passenger air-conditioned pontoon boat with inside and outside seating. Passengers board at 29603 Perdido Beach Boulevard just across the road from the Flora-Bama. Check out www.bluedolphincruises.com for more information.

To see some secluded portions of the area, sign up for a barefoot cruise aboard the **Daedalus** with Capt. Barry Brothers. Based at 5749 Bay La Launch, you'll find the 50-foot sailboat at Bear Point Marina in Orange Beach. Because the big vessel performs in shallow water, passengers can visit hidden bayous and bays and even venture onto an uninhabited beach. Also, you'll enjoy watching cavorting dolphins, ospreys, blue herons, and other wildlife. To book your passage call (251) 987–1228 or click on www.sailthedaedalus.com for more information.

While exploring Orange Beach, once home to myriad orange trees, search out *Bayside Grill* (251–981–4899) at Sportsman Marina. Located at 27842 Canal Road, the eatery promises lunch, dinner, and sunsets on the deck. Owner Greg Bushmohle features Creole and Caribbean cuisine in a casual setting. Ask

Flora-Bama—Home of the Annual Mullet Toss

Jimmy Buffett used to come here and jam. John Grisham wrote about it in a novel. It's the area's hottest hangout—the Flora-Bama, boasting an identity all its own. Located ten minutes from Gulf Shores on the Alabama/Florida line, the place bills itself as "one of the nation's last great roadhouse watering holes."

"You never know what'll be going on here," says a local. The crowd is mixed, and so is the music—everything from country to rock and roll—and mostly original music. Flora-Bama offers entertainment every day of the year and attracts throngs including now-and-future-famous musicians and songwriters.

The party heats up after five, and the parking lot gets full fast. Though success often invites duplication, Flora-Bama's idiosyncratic style and haphazard floor plan make cloning a remote possibility. A No Tears in the Beer demolition and rebuilding party took place after Hurricane Ivan dealt the place a big blow. Then, in 2005, along came Katrina dumping sand. "We're still functioning, and we have music here everyday," said a staffer. And you can still take in the annual Interstate Mullet Toss, held the last weekend in April. (What's a mullet toss? An event on the beach where people vie for the dubious distinction of pitching a dead fish the greatest distance—from Florida to Alabama.)

If your April calendar is too full to fit in the Mullet Toss, there's always next January 1 and the Polar Bear Dip. After testing the Gulf of Mexico's cold waters, you can warm up with a serving of black-eyed peas—the traditional Southern dish declared to bring good luck throughout the year. (The luck intensifies if you consume collards or other greens, and adding hog jowl almost guarantees more luck than you can stand.)

Otherwise you can meander around, buy souvenirs, consume beverages, visit the Beach Oyster Bar, eat crab claws or Royal Reds (the very best of steamed shrimp), purchase lottery tickets, or converse with other patrons. The person standing next to you might have a total of five dollars in his jeans pocket or five million on his net worth statement.

Located at 17401 Perdido Key Drive, with a Pensacola zip, Flora-Bama (850–492–3048) opens daily at 9:00 A.M. and shuts down in the wee hours.

about the fresh catch of the day with several choices, grilled to perfection, and served with Cuban yellow rice and steamed fresh vegetables. (During my visit, cobia, a migratory fish that passes through the area during certain months—April and May are the best times to catch it—was on the menu.) Moderate prices. Hours are 11:00 A.M. to 8:00 P.M. Sunday through Wednesday and 11:00 A.M. to 9:00 P.M. Thursday through Saturday.

You'll find more good eating at *Gulf Bay Seafood Grill* (251–974–5090) on the corner of Canal and Gulf Bay Roads in Orange Beach. Al Sawyer, known as the King of Crustaceans and the Prince of Prawns, owns both this eatery and *King Neptune's Seafood Restaurant* (251–968–5464) at 1137 Gulf Shores

Parkway. Because Sawyer knows his seafood, visitors and locals alike flock to his places for oysters, royal red shrimp, and crab claws. The restaurateur, who has appeared on the Travel Channel's *Lonely Planet* and Bobby Flay's *Food Nation* on the Food Channel, serves only oysters from Bon Secour Fisheries and Alabama wild shrimp. Visit www.gulfbayseafood.com.

During the second weekend of October, seafood lovers flock to *Gulf Shores's National Shrimp Festival.* The 2005 Shrimp Festival broke records for attendance and proved to be a big shot in the arm, said Bebe Gauntt, former public relations manager for the Alabama Gulf Coast Convention & Visitors Bureau. "All we need is to continue getting the word out that we are open and ready for business." Speaking of shrimp, this is the place to walk into a seafood outlet, just after the fleet has docked, and buy your dinner fresh from coastal waters. Many area fish markets will ice-pack local seafood for travel.

The tiny fishing village of *Bon Secour,* located west of State Route 59 between Foley and Gulf Shores, is home to several shrimp-packing operations. At some of these, you can crunch your way through oyster shells to watch the unloading process and buy the day's freshest catch directly off the boat. Look for signs along Baldwin County Road 10 that lead to several of these markets with their colorful shrimp boats on the Bon Secour River.

During the late 1700s French settlers staked a claim here, naming the area Bon Secour for "Safe Harbour." While driving around, notice the lovely little church, Our Lady of Bon Secour, framed with Spanish moss in its tree-shaded setting.

After dipping into the Gulf of Mexico's foaming waves and basking in the sunshine, you may want to sally forth to other points of interest, such as historic *Fort Morgan* (251–540–7127). Located at the end of a scenic drive 22 miles west of Gulf Shores on State Route 180, the fort—built to guard Mobile Bay—played a major role during the Civil War. At the Battle of Mobile Bay on August 5, 1864, "torpedoes" (underwater mines) were strung across the channel to stop the Union fleet from entering. This strategy failed when Adm. David Farragut issued his famous command: "Damn the torpedoes—full speed ahead!"

Today's visitors can explore vaulted corridors and peer into dark rooms of this historic fort, named in honor of Revolutionary War hero Gen. Daniel Morgan. Designed by Simon Bernard, a French engineer and former aide-de-camp to Napoléon, the five-pointed-star structure pays tribute to the craftsmanship of men who labored from 1819 to 1834. As technology changed, the original fort continued to be modified and upgraded, said the curator. In the

alabamatrivia

Isabella de Soto planted America's first fig trees, which came over from Spain, at Fort Morgan.

Visit Historic Magee Farm, Site of "The Last Appomattox"

Civil War and history buffs will find a gem of a house museum at Historic Magee Farm, where it's always 1865. Because members of the Jacob Magee family occupied the home from 1848 to 2004, it remains in a near pristine state. "Most of the furniture is original," said curator Jim Golden, who shares a wealth of fascinating stories with visitors. A guide in period costume brings history to life with anecdotes associated with various artifacts throughout two-story house.

Here, you can touch history with no restraining velvet ropes. You can even hold two authentic swords—one Union and one Confederate. In addition to weapons you'll see a belt buckle with two bullet holes, quilts, trunks, china, silver, an 1814 infant's christening gown, and secret storage places. Large sums of Confederate currency have been found on the property at various times.

"Family forebears came over on the *Mayflower,* and among their ranks are five published authors and two Nobel Prize winners," said Golden. "The house contained so many books it took seven women eight hours to catalog them. We have a complete set of leather-bound O. Henry first editions, signed and dated—priceless." The family hosted many famous figures including such literary guests as O. Henry, Jack London, Harriet Beecher Stowe, and Augusta Jane Evans (whose novel *St. Elmo* sold an unprecedented one million copies in 1868 in days before most women authors used their own names).

On April 29, 1865, Lt. Gen. Richard Taylor of the confederacy (son of President Zachary Taylor) met with Union Maj. Gen. E. R. S. Canby to discuss a possible cease fire and surrender. The parlor where this historic meeting took place looks much as it did then.

Visitors can enjoy sitting in rocking chairs on the front porch or exploring nature trails on the grounds, where Civil War reenactments sometimes take place. Located at 6222 Highway 45 in Kushla, about ten minutes north of Mobile, the home is open to the public from 9:00 A.M. to 5:00 P.M. Friday through Sunday. For more information, visit www.historicmageefarm.com or call (251) 675–1863 or (877) 675–1864. Admission.

museum, exhibits cover military history from the fort's early days through World War II. Except for major holidays, the museum is open daily from 9:00 A.M. to 5:00 P.M., and the fort is open from 8:00 A.M. to 5:00 P.M. in winter and 7:00 P.M. during summer months. Admission.

After seeing Fort Morgan you may want to board the Mobile Bay Ferry for a visit to Fort Gaines on Dauphin Island. The ferry transports passengers and vehicles between the two forts at ninety-minute intervals. Call (251) 861–3000 for specific times and current rates.

Don't miss nearby ***Bellingrath Gardens and Home*** (251–973–2217 or 800–247–8420), located at Theodore about 20 miles southwest of Mobile. Once a simple fishing camp, the sixty-five-acre wonderland lures visitors year-round.

Because of south Alabama's climate, you can expect gorgeous displays of blossoms here, whatever the season. Upon arrival you'll receive a map illustrating the layout of the six gardens linked by bridges, walkways, streams, lakes, and lily-filled ponds. (Be sure to wear your walking shoes.)

After exploring the gardens you may want to tour the former home of Bessie and Walter Bellingrath (he was an early Coca-Cola executive). The house contains outstanding collections of Dresden china, Meissen figurines, and antique furnishings. The world's largest public exhibit of porcelain sculptures by Edward Marshall Boehm is on display in the visitors lounge. Separate admission fees for gardens and home. The gardens are open daily from 8:00 A.M. to 5:00 P.M. To tiptoe through the tulips or see what else might be in bloom via the Internet, click on www.Bellingrath.org.

Enjoy a sightseeing tour down the Fowl River or opt for a weekend dinner cruise. For more information call *Alabama Cruises* (251) 973–1244 or check out www.alabamacruises.com.

Save plenty of time for *Mobile,* a city famous for its magnificent live oaks, some reputed to be more than 400 years old. Trimmed in silvery Spanish moss, the enormous trees spread their branching canopies over city streets. Always magical, Mobile is especially so during spring, when masses of azaleas explode into vibrant pinks, reds, and magentas, making the Church Street area, DeTonti Square, Oakleigh Garden, Spring Hill, and other historic districts more beautiful than ever. March is the month to view the azaleas at their vibrant peak. During the annual *Azalea Trail Festival,* you can follow the signs along a 37-mile route that winds past lovely homes ranging in style from Greek Revival and Italianate to Southern Creole. (Mobile's own "Creole cottage," adapted for the local clime, evolved from the French Colonial form.)

Be sure to stop by the official welcome center, *Fort Condé* (251–208–7304) at 150 Royal Street, for some background on Alabama's oldest city. Mobile has been governed by France, England, Spain, the Republic of Alabama, the Confederate States of America, and the United States. Built in 1711, Fort Condé was once home base for the sprawling French Louisiana territory, and a re-created version now serves as a living-history

alabama trivia

Mobile is Alabama's oldest city.

museum. Soldiers in period French uniforms greet visitors, guiding them through the complex with its thick walls and low-slung doors.

Costumed guides set the early scene for visitors and may even fire a cannon in the courtyard. "Twice a day you can pick up a free city tour here," notes staffer Walter Calhoun. Displays and dioramas tell the city's story. You'll see military furnishings typical of the times, photography exhibits, and artifacts such as china

Make the Carnival Connection

What better way to experience the Port City's very essence than with a cruise? Consider combining a stay in the Mobile area with a seagoing voyage to the Caribbean. To cheers and resounding applause, Carnival Cruise Lines launched the *Holiday,* one of their "Fun Ships" here in late 2004. Then—well, there's that H-word again. Following a six-month charter to the federal government for hurricane relief, the newly refurbished 1,452-passenger *Holiday* once again plows the waters between Mobile and the Western Caribbean on a year-round schedule.

Passengers can opt for four-day cruises to Cozumel departing Thursdays or five-day cruises to Cozumel and Calica/Playa del Carmen or Costa Maya departing Mondays and Saturdays. These cruises leave from Mobile Landing, the easy-to-access handsome new terminal on the city's historic bayfront.

Once aboard the floating resort, you can enjoy exciting entertainment and select from a variety of onboard diversions and dining options. With shore excursions that run the gamut from dolphin encounters, snorkeling, and scuba diving to kayak adventures and Mayan ruins waiting to be explored, you have a vacation for every interest.

Carnival puts the focus on the fun, something Mobilians know plenty about. After all, they celebrated America's first Mardi Gras in 1703. Ergo the Carnival connection. While in town you can dip into the magical world of Mardi Gras at the Mobile Carnival Museum, climb aboard the legendary USS *Alabama,* and tour antebellum districts. Nearby, you'll find world-class golf courses and Bellingrath Gardens, one of the nation's top horticultural attractions. Carnival and the Mobile Convention and Visitors Bureau can make your getaway one to remember, so contact your travel agent soon. Or call (888) SHIPMOBILE (744–7662), (888) CARNIVAL (227–6482) or visit www.ship mobile.com for a unique getaway that offers the best of two worlds—at sea or in a 300-year old seaport.

and pottery shards, brass buckles, buttons, porcelain and bisque doll parts, dice, and gun barrels. Hours are 8:00 A.M. to 5:00 P.M. daily, and admission is free.

For a breakfast you won't forget, stop by ***Spot of Tea*** (251–433–9009) at 310 Dauphin Street, across from Cathedral Square. Now celebrating more than a decade of business, the restaurant offers much more than breakfast and tea. The property features an inviting sidewalk cafe, lovely gift shop, Victorian dining room, private Victorian Tea Room, New Orleans–style carriageway, and Léstradé Dinner Theatre in the rear.

Quench your thirst with the award-winning strawberry iced tea. Breakfast/ lunch, served seven days a week, offers items such as bananas Foster French toast and banana waffles, as well as the signature breakfast choice, eggs cathedral (an English muffin topped with a crab cake, eggs, and seafood sauce). Omelets, pancakes, eggs Benedict, soups, sandwiches, and salads are all included on the extensive menu. Hours are 7:00 A.M. to 2:00 P.M. Monday through Friday and 9:00 A.M. to 2:00 P.M. Saturday and Sunday. Economical to moderate.

Take a tour of the Lower Dauphin Street Area (LoDa) and follow your nose to the **A&M Peanut Shop** with its freshly roasted nuts, served warm from a ninety-year-old roaster. Then saunter into **Three Georges Southern Chocolates** (251–433–6725) at 226 Dauphin Street, a spot that has lured locals and visitors since 1917. Marble-based cases and original glass candy jars hold hand-dipped chocolates, pralines, divinity, and many varieties of fudge plus a rainbow assortment of jelly beans and rock candy. Scott Gonzales, who purchased the historic property in 1992 and later the H. M. Thames Nuthouse, now operates four sites. His dream "is to grow into a company that makes Mobilians proud while introducing some of our most treasured Southern delicacies all over the world."

Those who subscribe to the theory of eating dessert first because of life's uncertainty can savor a praline made with oven-roasted pecans while waiting for one of the weekday lunch specialties, like red beans and rice, jambalaya, or muffalettas, now available at this vintage sweet shop. Hours are 10:00 A.M. to 5:00 P.M. Monday through Friday.

When hunger pangs hit again, head for **Wintzell's Oyster House** (251–432–4605), which dates to 1938 at its historic downtown address, 605 Dauphin Street. Wintzell's also offers its fried, stewed, and nude delicacies at other area locations, including Fairhope.

"He was a bold man that first ate an oyster," wrote Jonathan Swift, the eighteenth-century satirist. If you're bold and enjoy oysters enough to attempt breaking the current consumption record—280 for women and 403 for men—declare your intentions at any of Wintzell's locations. The staff will then alert the restaurant's suppliers if you look like a serious contender. You have one hour, while seated at the bar, to consume oysters on the half shell. If you set a new record, your feast is free, and you receive a check for $25. Otherwise, well, you would have had to pay anyway.

If you prefer your oysters not nude, then order them steamed, fried, or in stew. Other delectable versions include oysters Rockefeller, Bienville, Buffalo, Monterey, Alfredo, and Parmesan. Try the yummy gumbo while reading Wintzell's signs (on life in general) as you dine. Hours at all locations are 11:00 A.M. to 10:00 P.M. Sunday through Thursday and 11:00 A.M. to 11:00 P.M. Friday and Saturday. Slither to www.wintzellsoysterhouse.com for more pearls of wisdom on these bivalves.

At the newly opened William and Emily Hearin **Mobile Carnival Museum** (251–432–3324), you can dip into the magical world of Mardi Gras. "You can't miss it," said curator Gordon Tatum. "Look for an 1870 Italianate townhouse at 355 Government Street with two colorful 10-foot-tall jesters on the front porch."

Mobilians celebrated America's first Mardi Gras in 1703, and you'll get a great overview here, surrounded by a glittering array of memorabilia. You'll encounter a fire-breathing dragon float in the den (former carriage house) and can climb aboard the rocking float to enjoy a rollicking good time.

Both Tatum and volunteer guide and self-confessed "Mardi Gras nut" Wilbur S. Pillman have been affiliated with a number of Mobile's mystic societies and share fascinating anecdotes with visitors who view ornate regalia including elaborate gowns with their flowing trains. These creations reflect intricate workmanship, and countless hours go into their construction. According to *National Geographic,* Mobile's coronations rival those of real coronations in Europe. Today's Mardi Gras festivities, which extend over a two-month period (with preparations going on around the calendar), feature many spectacular parades and magnificent balls. At last count thirty-two parading organizations and fifty-five nonparading organizations staged balls during the Mardi Gras season. Museum hours are 9:00 A.M. to 5:00 P.M. Monday, Wednesday, Friday, and Saturday. Admission.

For fine dining in an elegant atmosphere, make reservations at ***The Pillars*** (251–471–3411) in historic Midtown Mobile. Located at 1757 Government Boulevard, the home dates to 1912 and features spacious dining rooms, high ceilings, ornate columns, and Bellingrath tile floors. An honors graduate of the Culinary Institute of America, owner/chef Matt Shipp polished his art in leading restaurants in New York and New Orleans before opening his previous place downtown, Justine's Courtyard and Carriageway.

Try a delectable appetizer like crab Rangoon, tasso baked oysters, or crab and Brie quesadillas. Shipp uses only the highest quality seafood to create his signature dishes of Caribbean red snapper and whiskey-smoked shrimp. The hand-cut steak selections include Stilton-stuffed filet of beef with lump crabmeat and rich apple brandy. Lunch hours are 11:00 A.M. to 3:00 P.M. Monday through Friday, and dinner hours run 5:00 to 10:00 P.M. Monday through Saturday. Moderate to expensive.

Look for the ***Malaga Inn*** (251–438–4701 or 800–235–1586) at 359 Church Street. A charming place to make your base, this quaint hotel started out as twin townhouses in 1862—the families of sisters shared a patio between their mirror-image houses. In 1967 the historic structures were joined by a connector and converted into a hotel.

Individually decorated rooms and suites are furnished with antiques or nostalgic reproductions. You'll enjoy relaxing in the inn's garden courtyard with its flowing fountain, umbrella-topped tables, and surrounding galleries of ornamental ironwork. The inn serves a deluxe Continental breakfast, and evening cocktails are available. Rates range from standard to moderate.

Several mansions, including the ***Richards-DAR House*** (251–208–7320), open their doors to the public not only during spring tours but throughout the year. Located at 256 North Joachim Street in DeTonti Square, this 1860 Italianate antebellum home is noted for its "frozen lace" ironwork that decorates the facade in an elaborate pattern. Be sure to notice the etched ruby Bohemian glass framing the entrance. Other fine features include a suspended staircase, Carrara marble mantels, and striking brass and crystal chandeliers signed by Cornelius. In the rear wing you'll find a gift shop. Except for major holidays, the home, operated by the Daughters of the American Revolution, is open from 11:00 A.M. to 3:30 P.M. Monday through Friday, 10:00 A.M. to 4:00 P.M. Saturday, and 1:00 to 4:00 P.M. Sunday. Admission.

You may also want to tour the Oakleigh Historic Complex in its serene oak-shaded setting at 350 Oakleigh Place. The guides dress in authentic costumes of the 1830s to conduct tours through an 1833 antebellum house/museum filled with early Victorian, Empire, and Regency furnishings.

To dip into more of the city's past, make reservations at the ***The Kate Shepard House Bed and Breakfast*** (251–479–7048) in the heart of historic Dauphin Way. Located at 1552 Monterey Place, this handsome Queen Anne Victorian home is listed on the National Register of Historic Places. Built by C. M. Shepard in 1897, it was designed by well-known architect George Franklin Barber.

"Guests can pull into the driveway and park under the porte cochere," says Wendy James, who with husband Bill owns the home. "We have a dog that will bark loudly when you arrive, but will be your best friend in minutes." The couple, who lived in Hawaii for almost fifteen years, searched the southeast for the perfect historic house and setting to establish their long-planned bed-and-breakfast. Captivating Mobile and this lovely home, surrounded by century-old

Richards-DAR House

magnolia trees, won their hearts. Along with eleven fireplaces, four original stained glass windows, and beautiful woodwork, the home came with a surprise—an attic full of treasures. Wendy shares stories regarding this *lagniappe* (something extra) with her guests.

Shepard's daughters, Kate and Isabel, operated a private boarding and day school here during the early 1900s. Wendy, who continues to research the home's history, filled several glass-front cases with school memorabilia and framed several photos from that era. Moderate to deluxe rates. For more information, click on www.bbonline.com/al/kateshepard.

Mobile's Changing Skyline

Mobile's downtown renaissance continues with a skyline that looks very different —just as it did when construction on Alabama's first skyscraper started here a century ago. Looming above its neighbors, the impressive new **RSA Battle House Tower** can be seen for 30 miles—all the way up Mobile Bay. So again this city on the move boasts the state's tallest structure—a thirty-five-story tower that stretches 745 feet skyward. Companion to the historic, newly refurbished **Battle House Hotel,** the pair represents a fusion of past and present. Nearby, the former Riverview Plaza just emerged from a major rejuvenation, and all properties will fly the Renaissance flag.

On a recent visit construction crew members led a group of us on a hard-hat tour of their work in progress, the Battle House Hotel. They explained how they replicated the detailed original plasterwork and described how the vaulted arches will look in a few short months as we stared upward, our eyes popping and mouths dropping. With visual aids and artists' renderings, some of us could imagine the future splendor with curved granite walls and white marble elevators, while others found it difficult to see past the obvious obstacles and daunting challenges. Although the multimillion-dollar project suffered a setback when Hurricane Katrina paid her unwelcome call, the property is scheduled to open in late 2006, promising classic Southern hospitality, which translates to plenty of pampering. The Trellis Room will serve regional and continental specialties with lighter fare available in the Royal Street Tavern and St. Francis Café.

Once again, guests can enjoy the hospitality of this elegant hotel, which provided a backdrop for many debutante balls with its grand staircase and Crystal Ballroom (and whispering arches that heard goodness knows how many secrets). Besides presiding over the social scene in downtown Mobile for a century, the Battle House played host to a variety of American luminaries and statesmen, including Woodrow Wilson and Confederate president Jefferson Davis. The hotel's historic roots date back to 1852, when it was founded on a former battleground from the War of 1812. For more information on this historic four-star landmark hotel located at 26 North Royal Street in downtown Mobile, call (251) 438–4000 or (866) 749–6071 or visit www.rsabattle house.com.

No visit to the Port City would be complete without scaling the decks of the ***Battleship USS*** **Alabama** (800–GANGWAY), moored in Mobile Bay. This renowned vessel played the role of the USS *Missouri* in the movie *Under Siege,* starring Steven Seagal.

Now the focal point of the 155-acre park on Battleship Parkway just off the Interstate 10 causeway, the USS *Alabama* served in every major engagement in the Pacific during World War II, apparently leading a charmed life throughout her thirty-seven months of active duty. She earned not only nine battle stars but also the nickname "Lucky A" (from her crew of 2,500) because she emerged unscathed from the heat of each battle.

She also rode out hurricanes Camille, Frederick, and Ivan, but Katrina slammed in with a 12-foot storm surge and triple-digit winds, tilting the ship by eight degrees (now corrected to a two-degree list). Setting a structure of this magnitude—half the length of the Empire State Building's height—upright does not qualify as quick or easy. Waves swept over the ship's bow, 30 feet above sea level. As for the park's Aircraft Exhibit Pavilion, hurricane winds lifted and dropped military tanks and artillery exhibits, scattering parts across the grounds and severely damaging fourteen planes. After being closed more than four months, USS *Alabama* and the submarine USS *Drum* (which received no storm damage) reopened to the public early in 2006. Repairs on aircraft and displays continue, and by the time of your next visit, the pavilion should also be open again. In the meantime, you can explore below and upper decks and roam through the captain's cabin, officers' staterooms, messing and berthing spaces, and crew's galley. Authentic touches include calendar girl pinups and background music, with such singers as Bing Crosby and Frank Sinatra crooning songs popular during the 1940s.

Anchored beside the battleship, the USS *Drum* gives visitors a chance to thread their way through a submarine and marvel at how a crew of seventy-two men could live, run their ship, and fire torpedoes while confined to such tight quarters.

Open every day except Christmas, the park can be visited starting at 8:00 A.M. Admission is charged. For more information, check out www.ussalabama.com.

Places to Stay in Southwest Alabama

CAMDEN

Roland Cooper State Park
285 Deer Run Drive
(334) 682–4838

EUTAW

Oakmont Bed & Breakfast
107 Pickens Street
(205) 372–2326

FAIRHOPE

Bay Breeze Guest House
742 South Mobile Street
(866) 928–8976

Church Street Inn
51 South Church Street
(866) 928–8976

FOLEY

Hotel Magnolia
119 North McKenzie Street
(251) 943–5297

GULF SHORES/ ORANGE BEACH

The Beach Club
925 Beach Club Trail
(251) 540–2500 or
(888) 260–7263

The Beach House
9218 Dacus Lane
(251) 540–7039 or
(800) 659–6004

Island House Hotel
26650 Perdido Beach
Boulevard
(251) 981–6100 or
(800) 264–2642

**Meyer Real Estate
(for resort rentals)**
1585 Gulf Shores Parkway
(251) 968–7516 or
(800) 487–5959

Perdido Beach Resort
27200 Perdido Beach
Boulevard
(251) 981–9811 or
(800) 634–8001

MAGNOLIA SPRINGS

**Magnolia Springs
Bed and Breakfast**
14469 Oak Street
(251) 965–7321 or
(800) 965–7321

MARION

The Gateway Inn
1615 State Route 5 South
(334) 683–9166

Myrtle Hill
303 and 305 West
Lafayette Street
(334) 683–9095

MOBILE

**The Kate Shepard House
Bed and Breakfast**
1552 Monterey Place
(251) 479–7048

Lafayette Plaza Hotel
301 Government Street
(251) 694–0100 or
(800) 692–6662

Malaga Inn
359 Church Street
(251) 438–4701 or
(800) 235–1586

Mauvila Mansion
1306 Dauphin Street
(251) 432–2492 or
(866) 432–4600

**Radisson Admiral
Semmes Hotel**
251 Government Street
(251) 432–8000 or
(800) 333–3333

**Renaissance Riverview
Plaza Hotel**
64 South Water Street
(251) 438–4000 or
(866) 749–6069

MONROEVILLE

Best Western Inn
4419 South Alabama Avenue
(251) 575–9999 or
(800) WESTERN

Holiday Inn Express
120 Highway 21 South
(251) 743–3333 or
(800) HOLIDAY

POINT CLEAR

**Grand Hotel Marriott
Resort, Golf Club & Spa**
One Grand Boulevard
(251) 928–9201 or
(800) 544–9933

SELMA

Bridgetenders House
2 Lafayette Park
(334) 875–5517

Hampton Inn
2200 West Highland Avenue
(334) 876–9995 or
(800) HAMPTON

Jameson Inn
2420 North Broad Street
(334) 874–8600

St. James Hotel
1200 Water Avenue
(334) 872–3234

Places to Eat in Southwest Alabama

CAMDEN

Gaines Ridge Dinner Club
933 State Route 10 East
(334) 682–9707

CODEN

Mary's Place
5075 State Route 188
(251) 873–4514

DAPHNE

**Cousin Vinnie's/
Guido's Italian Restaurant**
1709 Main Street
(251) 626–6082

DEMOPOLIS

New Orleans Bar & Grill
Demopolis Yacht Basin
(334) 289–2668

The Red Barn
901 U.S. Highway 80 East
(334) 289–0595

EUTAW

The Cotton Patch
Union Road
Exit 45, Interstate 59
(205) 372–4235

MAINSTREAM ATTRACTIONS WORTH SEEING IN SOUTHWEST ALABAMA

The Gulf Coast Exploreum, Science Center, and IMAX Theater, 65 Government Street at exit 26B off I–10, Mobile, features fascinating exhibits from the world of science, and that's not all. Throngs of visitors found "Mummy: The Inside Story" from the British Museum in London and later a compelling exhibit on Pompeii most intriguing. To check the current schedule, call (251) 208–6873 or (877) 625–4FUN or visit www.exploreum.net.

Adjacent to The Gulf Coast Exploreum, at 111 South Royal Street, **The Museum of Mobile** offers a treasure trove in a National Historic Landmark building that dates to 1857 and occupies a portion of the Southern Market/Old City Hall. From the entry's 1936 WPA murals depicting the history of Mobile to the hands-on Discovery Room and Special Collections Gallery, this museum offers something for all ages and interests. You'll see a dugout canoe from the fourteenth-century, relive the atrocious passage on an African slave ship, hear stories of Civil War soldiers, and learn about disasters like hurricanes, yellow fever, and fires that have impacted the area. The Themes Gallery puts the spotlight on Hank Aaron, Satchel Paige, and other sports figures from this city, known as a "baseball mecca." Check out www.museumofmobile.com or call (251) 208–7569.

Don't miss the stunning new **Mobile Museum of Art.** Established in 1964, the museum moved from its former quarters on Civic Center Drive to its present setting at 4850 Museum Drive in Langan Park. The grand lobby's commanding glass entrance hall overlooks a lake and makes the outdoors seem part of a sweeping landscape. The handsome building is home to a permanent collection of more than 6,000 works of art, which span 2,000 years of cultural history, and is particularly strong in American paintings of the 1930s and 1940s plus works by Southern artists, art of the French Barbizon School, and contemporary American crafts. For more information click on www.mobilemuseumofart.com or call the museum at (251) 208–5200.

Eutaw Diner
208 Main Street
(205) 372–0209

FAIRHOPE

Gambino's
18 Laurel Avenue
(251) 928–5444

Mary Ann's Deli
7 South Church Street
(251) 928–3663

Old Bay Steamer
105 South Section Street
(251) 928–5714

FAUNSDALE

**Ca-John's Faunsdale
Bar & Grill**
35558 State Route 25
(334) 628–3240

FOLEY

The Gift Horse
209 West Laurel Avenue
(251) 943–3663 or
(800) FOLEYAL

GREENSBORO

Lou's Bakery and Deli
1224 Main Street
(334) 624–3791

Magnolia Restaurant
905 Hobson Street
(334) 624–0777

**GULF SHORES/
ORANGE BEACH**

Bayside Grill
27842 Canal Road
(251) 981–4899

**Calypso Joe's Fish Grille
& Market**
27075 Marina Road
(251) 981–1415

Gulf Bay Seafood Grill
24705 Canal Road
(251) 974–5090

**King Neptune's
Seafood Restaurant**
1137 Gulf Shores Parkway
(251) 968–5464

Lulu's at Homeport Marina
Under W.C. Holmes Bridge
Intracoastal Waterway
(251) 967–LULU

Mango's on the Island
Orange Beach Marina
27075 Marina Road
(251) 981–1416

LAVACA

Ezell's Fish Camp
166 Lotts Berry Road
(205) 654–2205

MAGNOLIA SPRINGS

Jesse's Restaurant
14770 Oak Street
(251) 965–3827

MARION

Camellias on the Square
114 Greene Street
(334) 683–5998

The Eagle's Nest Cafe
103 East Jefferson Street
(334) 683–5044

MOBILE

The Pillars
1757 Government Street
(251) 471–3411

Loretta's
19 South Conception Street
(251) 432–2200

Spot of Tea
310 Dauphin Street
(251) 433–9009

The Tiny Diny
2159 Halls Mill Road
(251) 473–9453

Wintzell's Oyster House
605 Dauphin Street
(251) 432–4605

Zea
4671 Airport Boulevard
(251) 344–7414

POINT CLEAR

**The Wash House
Restaurant**
17111 Scenic Highway 98
(251) 928–4838

SELMA

Major Grumbles
1 Grumbles Alley
(334) 872–2006

**Restaurant on Grumbles
Alley**
1300 Water Avenue
(334) 872–2006

Tally-Ho Restaurant
509 Mangum Avenue
(334) 872–1390

SPANISH FORT

Roussos Restaurant
30500 State Highway 181
Eastern Shore Centre,
Suite 800
(251) 625–3386

FOR MORE INFORMATION ABOUT SOUTHWEST ALABAMA

Alabama Gulf Coast Convention & Visitors Bureau
23685 Perdido Beach Boulevard
Orange Beach 36561 or
P.O. Drawer 457
Gulf Shores 36547
(251) 974–1510 or (800) 982–8562
www.gulfshores.com
info@gulfshores.com

Alabama Tombigbee Resource Conservation and Development Regional Tourism Office
16 West Front Street
Thomasville, 36784
(334) 636–0120
www.alabamasfrontporches.org

Demopolis Area Chamber of Commerce
102 East Washington Street
P.O. Box 667
Demopolis 36732
(334) 289–0270
www.demopolischamber.com

Eastern Shore Chamber of Commerce
327 Fairhope Avenue
Fairhope 36532
(251) 928–6387

Foley Convention & Visitors Bureau
109 West Laurel Avenue
Foley 36535
(251) 943–1200
www.foleycvb.com
foleycvb@gulftel.com

Gulf Shores Welcome Center
3150 Gulf Shores Parkway
(Alabama Highway 59 South)
Gulf Shores 36542
(251) 968–7511 or (800) 745–SAND
www.gulfshores.com

Mobile Bay Convention & Visitors Bureau
One South Water Street
P.O. Box 204
Mobile 36601-0204
(251) 208–2000 or (800) 5MOBILE
www.mobilebay.org
mbcvb@mobile.org

Monroeville Area Chamber of Commerce
64 North Mount Pleasant Street
P.O. Box 214
Monroeville 36461
(251) 743–2879
www.monroecountyal.com
info@monroecountyal.com

Orange Beach Welcome Center
23685 Perdido Beach Boulevard
Orange Beach 36561
(251) 974–1510 or (800) 982–8562
www.orangebeach.com

Selma/Dallas County
Chamber of Commerce
912 Selma Avenue
P.O. Box 467
Selma 36702
(334) 875–7241 or (800) 45–SELMA
www.SelmaAlabama.com
info@SelmaAlabama.com

Index

About the Author

Gay N. Martin, who lives in Alabama, enjoys writing about travel in the Southeast. Her articles and travel pieces have appeared in *Modern Bride*, the *Boston Herald, Kiwanis,* the *Atlanta Journal-Constitution,* the *London Free Press,* the *San Antonio Express-News,* the *Seattle Post-Intelligencer, Far East Traveler,* the *Birmingham News,* the *Times-Picayune,* the *Grand Rapids Press,* and other publications. She has won numerous writing awards for fiction and nonfiction in state, regional, and national competitions. She is also the author of Globe Pequot's *Off the Beaten Path Louisiana* and *Alabama's Historic Restaurants and Their Recipes,* published by John F. Blair.

Before embarking on her writing career, Martin taught high school for eleven years, served as resource coordinator of her school's program for gifted and talented students, and sponsored the school newspaper. She is a member of the Society of American Travel Writers and International Food, Wine, and Travel Writers Association. Visit her Web site at www.gnmartintravels.com.